DRAMAS OF SOLITUDE

SUNY Series, Literacy, Culture, and Learning:
Theory and Practice
Alan C. Purves, editor

DRAMAS OF SOLITUDE

Narratives of Retreat in American Nature Writing

Randall Roorda

STATE UNIVERSITY OF NEW YORK PRESS

Published by
State University of New York Press, Albany

© 1998 State University of New York

For information, address State University of New York Press,
State University Plaza, Albany, N.Y., 12246

Production by Cathleen Collins
Marketing by Fran Keneston

Library of Congress Cataloging in Publication Data

Roorda, Randall, 1952–
    Dramas of solitude : narratives of retreat in American nature
writing / Randall Roorda.
        p.   cm. — (SUNY series, literacy, culture, and learning)
    Includes bibliographical references and index.
    ISBN 0-7914-3677-2 (alk. paper). — ISBN 0-7914-3678-0 (pb. :
alk. paper)
    1. American literature—History and criticism. 2. Wilderness
areas in literature. 3. Solitude in literature. 4. Nature in
literature. 5. Narration (Rhetoric) 6. Self in literature.
7. Literacy. I. Title. II. Series.
PS163.R66   1998
810.9'36—dc21   97-16933
                                                   CIP

10 9 8 7 6 5 4 3 2 1

If the world is interesting only because of the
things humans do, then it is not as interesting
as it might be.

—Joseph W. Meeker

In solitude I become social and candid.
I converse quite successfully.

—Edward Lueders

To the memory of my grandparents
in boots and mackinaws
and to the places they walked

Contents

Acknowledgments

Acknowledgment is an endless task, though anything but a thankless one. My thanks go all over. I am beholden first to my teachers at the University of Michigan: above all, my dissertation co-chairs, Jay L. Robinson, who cultivated my interest in literacy, and John R. Knott, who saw a book-length work lurking in a ten-page paper; also A. L. Becker, Julie Ellison, and James McIntosh, who read the dissertation with discernment; James Boyd White and Tobin Siebers, whose work and teaching have informed this; and Anne Ruggles Gere, from whose counsel I have much benefited. To this list I add my teachers at San Francisco State University—Jo Keroes, William S. Robinson, Catharine Lucas—who made a teacher of a lapsed poet and packed him off for a doctorate. And I thank others who commented on portions of this manuscript: anonymous reviewers for SUNY Press, *College English*, and *Arizona Quarterly*; also my colleagues at the University of Missouri–Kansas City, Kristie S. Fleckenstein and Daniel Mahala.

I have been heartened by my relations with fellow students in Michigan's English and Education program, from whose ranks I will single out Deborah Minter as representative of the program's openness, intelligence, and commitment. I have been influenced by the students and staff of the New England Literature Program, circa 1993, to whom I am indebted for the image that opens chapter 5, among other lessons and recognitions; I thank especially Walter S. Clark Jr., the program's co-founder and tutelary presence.

Finally, I am grateful to my parents, Bill and Pearl Roorda, for their continuing sustenance and love, to my wife, Susan Cobin, for enabling this undertaking in so many ways, and to my son Marshall, for prospects.

I thank the following for permission to reprint the material indicated:

North Point Press, a division of Farrar, Straus & Giroux, for excerpts from Wendell Berry, *Recollected Essays 1965–1980*, copyright 1981, and *The Unforeseen Wilderness: Kentucky's Red River Gorge*, copyright 1991.

Touchstone Books of Simon and Schuster, for an excerpt from Margaret Atwood, "The Journals of Susanna Moodie," from *Selected Poems*, copyright 1976.

W. W. Norton & Company, Inc., for an excerpt from A. R. Ammons, "Negative Pluses," from *Lake Effect Country*, copyright 1983.

Portions of this study have appeared in the following journals, to whose editors I am grateful for permission to reprint:

A version of chapter 2 appeared in the *Arizona Quarterly* 53.3 (Autumn 1997) under the title "Where the Summit Bears: Narrative Logic in Thoreau's 'Ktaadn.'"

A version of chapter 3, "Sites and Senses of Writing in Nature," appeared in *College English* 59.4 (April 1997).

Several sentences in this volume also appear in my article "Nature/Writing: Literature, Ecology, and Composition," published in *JAC: A Journal of Composition Theory* 17.3 (Fall 1997).

Introduction

This study of American nature writing dwells upon what is in my view the central dynamic of the genre: the writer's movement from human society toward a state of solitude in nature. This movement and state I refer to jointly as retreat. Narratives offered from or about a position of retreat, or relating a movement of retreat, I call narratives of retreat, or more colorfully, dramas of solitude; it's these I will explore. The questions this inquiry proceeds from, put in basic terms, are these: What interest may inhere in a story without characters or conflict in the ordinary, "interpersonal" sense? In what might the drama of such a story consist, and how is such drama constituted or conjured? To whom might the story appeal, and what is the nature of that appeal? What good can it be to retreat in this way; what is the good of narrating the retreat to others? What can it mean to turn away from other people, to evade all sign of them for purposes that exclude them by design, then turn back toward them in writing, reporting upon, accounting for, even recommending to them the condition of their absence? What do stories of nature tell us about the social or ethical purposes of solitude, or conversely, what do stories of solitude reveal of the "character" of nonhuman nature?

To explore these questions and others that develop from them, I offer readings of texts—and readings of readings of those texts—variously originary or exemplary of the sorts of "drama" I have in mind. In offering these readings I speculate at intervals on the prospects and prerogatives of an ecological criticism, a critical practice motivated by an understanding of the now-perennial character of environmental concern. And believing this concern to be of import for the sorts of behavior that general education—writing pedagogy in particular—seeks to promote, I extend this study into the domain of literacy studies at large. The increased commerce between rhetoric, composition, and literary theory of recent years has invigorated the study of literate behaviors; it is eventuating, for one thing, in greater attention to literary nonfiction, that branch of literature in which direct relations between models and their imitation, both textual and extratextual, are most widely sought and found. I wish to situate the present study within this hybrid critical context, believing that connections between what is said in text and done beyond it have a special import in the case of the genre of nature writing, particularly in narratives of retreat.

That the element of retreat—movement toward and within a state of solitude–is central to this genre is implied, I think, in its very entitling as "nature writing." While the word "nature" may be, as Raymond Williams has remarked, the most complex in our language, that aspect of its meaning upon which the label "nature writing" depends is certainly its status as counterpart to "culture." However much culture may be thought to stem from, depend upon, or emulate nature, it remains the case that where culture ends, nature is thought to continue. Thus to write about nature is to explore the peripheries of culture, and nature writing is most itself when its object is least human.

Now, undertaking to report what William Stafford calls "things that happen where there aren't any people" involves, of course, losing the humans.[1] This spells retreat of some sort, even for the purposes of such observation of the nonhuman as we would term scientific. With casuistic stretching, even peering through a microscope may be styled a retreat in some cases. I don't wish to rehearse the conundrums attaching to this, only to establish that on our own culture's terms, "nature writing" necessitates a cultural about-face, and it's this back-turning I'm calling retreat.

Talk of its necessity does not explain the desirability of retreat, exactly—the valuing of solitude integral to many spiritual practices and religious traditions. Through retreat into solitude construed as a good per se, as back-turning on vanity and illusion, we come upon nature writing from a reverse direction, with the natural identified with the divine as the "substance" sought below the veneer or "stance" of culture.[2] Imagining "things that happen where there aren't any people" means absenting one's personal self; back-turning spells self-effacement, as in Margaret Atwood's image of cutting the face out of one's own picture: "where my eyes were, / every- / thing appears" (79). From either direction—with scrupulous regard of the nonhuman entailing a move to exclude the cultural, or cultivation of solitude prompting contemplation of a divine or "selfless" nonhuman creation—the genre of nature writing exists as a function of the possibility of retreat. It is a separate kind of writing just insofar as any one of us can remove ourselves from signs of the others, in some provisional sense at least.

The circling such a project assumes—for the writer in retreat or critic in pursuit—is such that, as Kenneth Burke (the great circler) in one place says, "a direct hit is unlikely." Accordingly, I will touch back variously and repeatedly upon the topics I have just evoked in the discussions that follow—first and most notably in an initial chapter of theoretical considerations relative to issues of genre and narrative in nature writing. In this chapter the narrative of retreat is posed and delineated *as* a genre, and its relations to questions of the ethical import of narrative are discussed. This theoretical chapter is loosely but not slavishly introductory to the chapters that follow; the later chapters may be read before or without the first, but I trust that they will benefit from being read after.

The second, third, and fourth chapters are comprised mostly of readings of three narratives of retreat originating at different historical junctures yet evincing significant resemblances in narrative trajectories. Chapter 2, prefaced by a gloss on a brief passage by John Muir meant to demonstrate the operation of a "narrative logic" of retreat, takes as its prime exhibit the long travel essay "Ktaadn," first chapter of *The Maine Woods* (1864) by Henry David Thoreau. I read "Ktaadn" both as a narrative itself and as an episode in narratives of Thoreau's model life and work composed by various commentators. The essay, I claim, is model in the sense of enacting a certain formal paradigm informed by a narrative logic of retreat; I cite evidence from notes and drafts of the essay to show how Thoreau constructed climactic passages to bear out this narrative logic. Thoreau's life and work, in turn, are model in the sense of being exemplary, praised and deemed imitable by others, as narrativized (thematized in narrative form) by commentators operating from various perspectives—whether literary critical, social/historical, or "participatory," that is, based on participation in the outdoor activities the work reports.

Chapter 3 concerns *The Desert* (1901) by John C. Van Dyke, a minor classic of nature writing and an important text in the canon of writing on the American desert. My discussion centers mostly on the book's first chapter, "The Approach," a narrative portal, as it were, to a mostly expository volume. Analysis of this narrative reveals tensions and discontinuities that render problematic some key terms, tropes, and tales by which Van Dyke's current reception is being shaped in the remarks of his major commentators, in particular those who have composed introductions to *The Desert* and others of his books in current reprint versions. Issues in the creation of an ecological criticism, whether formal or historical, are broached thereby—issues revolving about the ways in which certain tropes and scripts employed by writers and critics alike may prove inimical to understandings that both presumably mean to evoke. Race, class, and gender especially rear up in this discussion, out in the middle of nowhere where we might least expect to encounter them.

Chapter 4 takes up "terms of meaning and value" in the nature essays of the contemporary writer Wendell Berry. It does so through the vehicle of one essay in particular, "An Entrance to the Woods," a narrative of solitary wilderness travel central to his collection *The Unforeseen Wilderness* (1971). In Berry's work, both the paradigmatic and exemplary aspects of the retreat narrative, as I see them, are brought to fruition; his work is in some senses a culmination of trends present in the works previously explored. I view Berry as a writer who has rehearsed repeatedly the cultural script of retreat and worked through its generative narrative logic, and who is forthcoming about his intent to moralize the events he narrates—an intent that some theorists regard as inevitable to narrative forms of any sort, whether or not it is overtly pursued. Whatever else may be said about his work, it must be allowed that in Berry, solitude in nature is predicated on ethics, on a sense of community relations, both in the vocabulary of meaning and value he employs and in the narrative forms in which his value terms are "temporized" or enacted.

The fifth, sixth, and seventh chapters extend the terms of the inquiry into the area of literacy studies. Chapter 5 explores sites, scenes, and constructions of nature writing and writers, focusing on the activities and the identities of people who write in/about nature. It dwells upon such interwoven topics as these: the figure of the solitary writer in prevailing images of writing and in nature writing; the perceived split between the realms of "writing" and "living" and the ways different sites and habits of composing may be associated with one or the other; the ways in which the occupational identity of "writer" may be assumed or resisted by nature writers; the status of the written artifact as the correlate of one's presence in the nonhuman place; and the shaping role of technological intercessions in one's conduct in the outdoors—particularly those intercessions that writing itself consists in.

Chapter 6 falls into two halves, both taking up representative images or "iconic metaphors" of literate identity and practice in nature. The first concerns John Muir's writerly ambivalence and performance: it offers an account of Muir as a reluctant writer for public consumption yet an avid one for private and interpersonal purposes, and outlines the circumstances from which his resistant writerly identity emerged. One attribute of that identity was Muir's preference for and facility with spoken language; and this, with other aspects of the discussion to that point, leads to the second half, in which issues of literacy as opposed to primary orality come to inform nature writing's fixation upon indigenous peoples. Literate practices in nature are figured in two further iconic metaphors, those of the nature savant and the literate indigen, emblems of tensions that bear upon performance in writing classes as well, under our current technoliterate social dispensation. Throughout the fifth and sixth chapters, the discussion makes reference to viewpoints emphasizing the social construction of literacy—views that I do not seek to rebut as such, but that scenes and iconic figures of nature writing, to my mind, serve to complicate and in some ways correct.

Chapter 7 entertains notions of simplicity and complexity in the ways "nature" is understood and taught, as a vehicle for expounding upon the significance of retreat narratives for general education. Taking as its point of departure student essays composed in this mode, the chapter shows how generic formulae, exceptional experiential states, affirmations of a "social" solitude, and ironized masculine identity may be represented therein. The issues these essays raise are parlayed into a wider discussion of the propriety of cultivating nature experiences in education. An orientational pivot comes in the contrast between "reinvention" and "recovery" as programs for attention to "nature"—a contrast that is not a dilemma, luckily, since both critical and experiential moments are necessary to ecological literacy. The study culminates in a qualified affirmation of the narrative of retreat, its value as a cultural resource for environmental education and change.

Having provided an overview of what this study discusses, I should note one thing that it does not. While the subject of the study is "American nature writing," I have nothing particular to say about what makes this writing "American." This does not mean that there is not a lot that *could* be said in this vein, only that I do not set out to say it — or repeat it, more to the point. For besides the many works in American studies that bear in some degree upon the national character of the sorts of works I discuss,[3] there are studies that make particular claims for nature writing as a quintessentially American literary type.[4] I accept many of these claims but will not recapitulate them or settle the differences among them. My own assertions, in any event, do not turn on them.

In part, this is because my methods are not primarily historical, even though the core of my study plots out, as it were, a trajectory of works occurring over time. My methods are more comparative and rhetorical — "formalist," even, if the term may be divested of universalizing overtones. I concur with Lawrence Lerner's misgivings over "specific historical situations" being thought incomparable to current ones; I regard as fortuitous his identifying of a "nonessentialist timelessness" that is indispensable to understanding past works under present circumstances (280). My stress in any case is on present reception of nature writing texts by whoever it is that consumes them. My interest in John C. Van Dyke, for instance, stems from the fact that his best-known book has found an audience in this day as a trade paperback, enough so that others of his books are likewise being reissued. Current interest in this writer is eventuating in a body of commentary; and this commentary very often takes narrative form itself, life stories of the author by which reception of his work may be shaped.

If there is anything innovative about this study it is the focus on narrative, the application of narrative theory to texts of a type more often thought descriptive or expository, and secondarily, to commentary about those texts. This is its most distinguishing feature, but there are others. The emphasis on the current reception of the texts examined; the presumption that commentary on these texts may warrant analysis on a par with that given the texts themselves; the fact that the texts are "literary nonfiction," epitomizing the sorts of personal and informational writing that have such widespread currency in schools; the focus on narrative as a compositional act, suasive in force, inviting imitation of various orders; and the presence of students' own writing among the textual artifacts accorded attention: all mark this study as the work of a person trained and situated in the field of composition studies.[5] The study is further marked by a certain eclecticism of method also typical of the field. I am by training and temperament more a critic than scholar, a generalist more than a specialist; my research ranges widely and draws on many critical resources but exhausts none of them. And the study, as I see it, shares the character of my research: more peripatetic than methodical; speculative, not definitive; reasonably free of blunders but reproachable even so. This is no apology but an invitation. I welcome assent but will settle for drawing attention.

CHAPTER ONE

Genre and Narrative
in Nature Writing

A HOUSE WITH TWO DOORS

We might think of literature as a house with two doors, the front door abutting the "lawns and cultivated fields" of human commerce. Access to the dwelling is gained from this, the cultivated end; no one uncultivated approaches. But there's a rear door, little used, which backs onto an "impermeable and unfathomable bog," situated "so that there be no access on that side to citizens." This is the house Thoreau imagines in his essay "Walking," only Thoreau's is reversed in direction, so that it fronts on the swamp. However it's situated, no "citizen" enters this house initially from the bog side. But once in, one may wade out that way, then reenter, dropping bundles and specimens in the rear wings of the ever more sprawling manse. These back wings, less central, less inspected than the front parlors, house the genre of nature writing.

Nature writing is that branch of literature's human estate which deals particularly with what is not human. Peripheral as it may appear, the genre thus turns out to encompass much, and to infringe upon much else that it does not encompass. There are numerous disciplines, both scientific and humanistic, that it borders upon or bridges between, such that being peripheral to each, the genre is in a sense central among all. This centrality extends to nature writing's status as literary standard-bearer for the environmental movement and the allied critical-philosophical stance of biocentrism—a status embraced by many practitioners of the genre, to the point where Barry Lopez can speculate that "a reorganization of

1

American political thought" might possibly be founded on the basis of such writing (Halpern, *On Nature* 297). These features—interdisciplinary siting, political and epistemic status, transformational potential—join with nature writing's pertinence to aspects of teaching practice (journal writing, personal narrative, nonfiction modes and genres,"organization" in its root connection to "organic,"[1] etc.) to make the genre an object of interest to rhetoric and composition as well as to literary studies within English studies proper.

Yet coincident with the recent surge of interest in "nature writing" is contention over what the term entails. Though a reading public seems content with the term and publishers have dignified it with suitcase-sized anthologies, some commentators are uneasy. Their qualms extend from boundary problems of various sorts. One concerns relations to more conventional generic distinctions: whether any work at all that deals with "nature" qualifies as "nature writing," though framed as nonfiction, fiction, or poetry. Another involves the boundaries of "nature" itself: whether the term "nature writing" and works so designated serve to reinforce a nature-culture split that writers and critics should seek rather to dissolve. There are historical boundaries to patrol, as well: at what point "natural history" may have mutated into nature writing with the advent of formal science; whether nature writing in turn has given or is now giving way to other generic formations not just titularly but epistemologically more "ecological." All these problems devolve in some degree on issues of genre, and there's a question as to whether nature writing ought to be thought a genre at all. Certainly the notion of genre must flex to accommodate the range of discourses grouped under this heading. How much so can be seen in Thomas J. Lyon's taxonomy of nature writing, which dramatizes how a paper in ethology, a field guide to wildflowers, a tale of a brush with death on a Sierra cliff, a diary of a farmer's seasonal routine, and a foray into speculative cosmology can all be lumped under a single ungainly imprimatur.

My own focus is narrower, fixed on texts depicting a narrative movement that I take to be integral to the genre as a whole. In this chapter, I will discuss both genre and narrative in nature writing, separating for the sake of discussion what are closely related conceptual entities. In the terms of my analogy of the house of literature, I would offer that our inspection of the back wings themselves—their construction, the manner of their partitioning and furnishing—corresponds to our analysis of genre, in which textual artifacts repose by category. Our concern with narrative, by contrast, involves the movement in and out through the house's back door.

FIXING THE GENRE

I employ the term "genre" to refer both to "nature writing" in general and to what I am calling the narrative of retreat, which exists within nature writing as a subset of the larger set. Some confusion may inhere in this usage, since the two genres qualify as such in different ways. The larger genre of nature writing warrants the designation by virtue of being widely recognized as such, notwithstanding uncertainties in determining just what has been thus recognized. The more particular genre of retreat narrative is not recognized at all, except implicitly in ways I am describing; yet it better fits the notion of "genre" as most usefully construed.

To see why this is so, we might strike a comparison with genre fiction. As Morris Dickstein notes, "Popular reading is essentially rereading, the pursuit of a known quantity, a familiar experience" (35). Hans Robert Jauss extends this understanding, claiming that the mode of reception of genre fiction is such that it operates not so much within as between works. Its meaning depends on repetition of a particular reading experience (144). If you've read just one mystery you can't be said to have read a mystery at all. We might propose that nature writing similarly depends upon repeated reading experience—a repetition further enacted in anecdotes, advertisements, even single expressions like "to get away from it all"—from which springs a certain familiarity and set of generic expectations. In the domain of "nature writing," these expectations do *not* depend solely on a text's having nature as its subject: not every text depicting nature ranks as "nature writing" any more than every story containing mystery is a "mystery." Instead, it seems to me that readers of nature writing, like those of popular fiction genres, seek out repeated instantiations of a certain core *story*, and it's this I am concerned to delineate.

The comparison to popular fiction might remind us, too, that determinations of genre serve best to account for the actions and expectations of actual writers and readers, not to pinpoint divisions in a realm of ideal forms. As Adena Rosmarin holds, genre is a tool of explanation, the critic's equivalent to what "schemata" or "premises" or "models" are to the literary or graphic artist (21): something the critic or rhetorician must always "choose or define" and actively shape to his or her purposes (8). In the practice of what Rosmarin calls "an expressly deductive genre criticism"—"fully pragmatic and rhetorical," one that "would make its reader aware of its premises and, simultaneously, convince him of their explanatory power"—it turns out that "there are precisely as many genres as we need, genres whose conceptual shape is precisely determined by that need" (24–25). Proliferating versions of nature writing's generic makeup, then, provide an index of needs the explanations arise to address. I regard my own procedure of arguing "from purpose to premise to particular text" as "pragmatic and rhetorical" in the sense Rosmarin offers: this is my rationale for delineating a genre within the bounds of a genre.

A useful parsing of such nested generic designations—a "taxonomy of nature writing"—has been put together by Thomas J. Lyon. As Lyon maps it, nature writing at large is seen to have "three main dimensions to it: natural history information, personal responses to nature, and philosophical interpretation of nature," with works in the genre located more particularly according to how these aspects are mixed and weighted within them (3). The informational dimension is featured most exclusively in "Field Guides and Professional Papers," the leftmost in a linear "spectrum" of categories, followed by the "Natural History Essay," in which information on nature gets "fitted into a literary design" (4). Next is the category of "Rambles," in which a participant-observer's personal experience acquires emphasis on a par with that granted the information conveyed. An explicit narrative element first appears in this "classic American form" of the writer-naturalist's excursions in local woods and fields—an author who is solitary as much as by definition, in mode of attention, at least. The following three categories, gathered under the heading of "Essays on Experiences in Nature," correspond to the trend of retreat in decreasing proportion as they move further right along the spectrum. The "Solitude and Back-Country Living" cluster is the primary site for the retreat narrative: *Walden*, the genre's originary instantiation, belongs here. "Travel and Adventure" also includes narratives of retreat, but the "experiences in nature" reported there are less apt to exemplify the drama of solitude, for reasons we will explore. While the backwoods travels recounted in Thoreau's *The Maine Woods* (the subject of chapter 3) enact the retreat motif in germinal ways, many tales of "outdoor adventure" fit the genre of retreat, and sometimes the entire nature writing genre, hardly at all. The next category, "Farm Life," in its focus on "cultivated fields" falls mostly outside the range of texts I'm considering, though the issues that place it within nature writing at all ensure that within it, some writers will dramatize retreat (as Wendell Berry does, in ways discussed in chapter 4). Finally, the rightmost pole of Lyon's "spectrum," the category of "Man's Role in Nature"—in which the philosophical, the third of the genre's three dimensions holds sway—moves beyond the realm of personal experience and thus outside narrative as well.

Upon these categories, then, the narratives I'm examining exist at the larger genre's core, where observed nature borders observing self. That this core is fluid, this border far from hard and fast, with trade between information, experience, and philosophizing free and open across it, is a recognition such writing exists in large part to explore.[2] If an element of retreat from what's human does indeed thread through and tie together the genre's disparate types, such retreat might best be figured as an encounter rather than an escape, conducted at this (shifting, or imagined, or negotiable) border of observed and observer. This is where Thoreau situates his "experiment" in solitude at Walden, which he explains as his effort "to front only the essential facts of life" (*Walden* 90): it's understood that the "facts" he's after are not "essentially" social.

Thus one condition of nature writing as involving retreat is that human presence or companionship, while not ruled out, is either incidental, beside the point; or it is put at issue, figured as an element or an impediment in the narrative line. The latter approach, tracking the withdrawal from human presence, is important to *Walden*, of course, and informs the story line to Thoreau's "Ktaadn," the first section of *The Maine Woods*, as I will argue. The former approach, which as nearly as possible renders human company invisible, informs the sort of attention paid in many "rambles" (which are seldom through wilderness) and wilderness trips (which are seldom undertaken alone). Thus John Burroughs, recounting his Catskills nature walks, is not inclined to dwell upon the coachloads of Vassar schoolgirls paying him pilgrimages; and in watching Annie Dillard act as a "pilgrim at Tinker Creek," we can easily overlook that the teeming, unreinable terrain she circulates through is from time to time revealed as something quite like a neighborhood. By the same token, when Ed Abbey rafts the Colorado with his gimpy pal, who lags behind in hikes up side canyons, they're *both* there to lose the humans, and the commerce between them is transmuted into something simpler than, and preferable to, usual conversation.[3] Whether in these calculated evasions of human presence, or in the pure retreat of the rhapsode and solitaire John Muir, the "essential fact" of the retreat narrative is an essentially nonhuman world.

I have called this posture toward human company a "condition" of the retreat narrative as a genre, one that by and large rules out stories of adventure, exploration, and settlement, however outdoorsy or "natural" the "scene" they may unfold in. Calling this a "condition," I invoke the terms by which Stanley Cavell reconfigures the concept of genre in *Pursuits of Happiness* (1981), his study of the cinematic "comedy of remarriage." Posing an analogy between a narrative genre and a visual arts medium or musical form, Cavell proposes that "members of a genre share the inheritance of certain conditions, procedures and subjects and goals of composition, and that in primary art each member of such a genre represents a study of these conditions," in some measure "bearing the responsibility of the inheritance" thereby (28). This understanding, he claims, is preferable to that which holds genre to be "a form characterized by features"—a view that, among other shortcomings, depends upon a suspect calculus of presence and compensation for absence in order to explain why members of a genre do not share *all* requisite features, and further cannot account for why members that *do* share all features are not then "indistinguishable from one another" (28–29). This shift from "features" to "conditions" is an important move to construe generic resemblances, we might say, as homologous rather than analogous, evincing commonalities of development even as specific traits diverge—an approach especially apt for analyzing a genre with origins in Linnaean taxonomy. Especially helpful is the suggestion that each work in a genre discharges in some manner a responsibility their joint inheritance entails; this helps underscore an ethical aspect in that pattern of movement away in retreat then back in published language that the genre I am delineating dramatizes.

Cavell insists that a genre "has no history, only a birth and a logic (or a biology)," the "internal consequences" of which are developed in subsequent works. Often regarded as the founding text of nature writing in general, Thoreau's *Walden* marks the "birth" of the retreat narrative genre as well.[4] The birth is not *ex nihilo*, though: it has what Cavell styles a "prehistory, a setting up of the conditions it requires for viability," conditions material and technological as well as social and ideational. Following this suggestion, we may detect in the tradition of natural history writing at large aspects of a "prehistory" that this more particular genre's birth in retrospect both depends on and generates, and trace therein certain conditions of the sort Cavell describes. To tap Thoreau as the retreat narrative's progenitor is in no way to deny his relatedness to the likes of Gilbert White; but it does involve claiming that it's the Walden story, not the Selbourne one, that consumers of the genre want most to recapitulate.

An important condition of the retreat narrative is that it *not* be a story reported of another. It is tacitly first-person, though not always explicitly so, as I will show, for instance, of the scrupulously depersonalized narrative lines of John C. Van Dyke (detailed in chapter 3). Its "procedures of composition" are those of the first-hand observer in "the field," its antecedents more properly the travelogues of the naturalists Bartram and Audubon or the aesthete Gilpin than yarns about John Chapman or Daniel Boone, however wild and solitary the latter may have been. The retreat undertaken eventuates in a *testament* of the sort Sharon Cameron sees Thoreau as creating in his *Journal* as well as in *Walden*. Cameron remarks on the "singularity of vision" such a narrative asserts, upon which its effectiveness depends:

> In practical terms, this means that, whatever the subject, we do not suppose we are being told one of many possible stories the man has at his command, but rather that this is the one story the man has to deliver. Hence the prophetic mode and the urgency of discourse. For the implication of a testament is that only this man can tell this story, and, concomitantly, that it is the one story this man can tell. (30)

This sense of the integrity and exclusivity of the writer's account accords, certainly, with the retreat narrative's inheritance of the tradition of natural history, the contributions of whose practitioners, if not so urgent and prophetic, are certainly particular and induplicable. A birdwatcher's "life list" is a modest, tabular "testament" of this sort— there can be no rival versions, and no one can add a bird to your list for you. In sum, such observations (such a "life list") may possibly ascend to the prophetic status Cameron describes, as is the case with the story Darwin found to tell, as with Muir's testament of Yosemite glaciation.

But again, the genre arises where natural history per se spills over into personal report, and the notion of "testament" stems more clearly from the latter, experiential domain, which in turn shades into religious tradition. In *The Senses of Walden,* Cavell expounds on the resemblance of *Walden's* author to an Old Testament prophet, a Jeremiah or Ezekiel, and this vein of resemblance extends to other instances of the retreat genre, to other voices emanating, if not crying, from the wilderness. More applicable yet, and far from unrelated, are insights gleaned from the generic study of autobiography. I say "gleaned" because such theory cannot be offloaded in entirety. The narrative of retreat is not autobiography per se, still less memoir; it is less itself, in important ways, the more autobiographical it becomes, as personal displaces natural history and landscape in the "facts" the writer "fronts"—an equation we may highlight as another of the genre's conditions.[5] Yet there are obvious and helpful consonances to explore, one of special note in the notion of "conversion" as elaborated by Geoffrey Galt Harpham in his essay, "Conversion and the Language of Autobiography" (1988).

To Harpham, autobiography is "the conversion of experience into narrative," issuing from lives lived in expectation of such issuance, "in consciousness of their own narratability"—lives, that is, of *action* in Arendt's sense of "a mode of being" oriented toward "its own eventual conversion into narrative, its own eventual reading by others" (42). This "conversion into narrative" is manifested at a level secondary ("conversion$_2$") to the lived experience represented in the action of the text ("conversion$_1$"). Harpham, delineating these levels in autobiography's generic "birth" text, Augustine's *Confessions,* explains:

> The first conversion is marked by an epistemological certainty that heralds a sense of true self-knowledge; the second confirms or actualizes this certainty in a narrative of the self. They are not different in kind, for both lead away from what Augustine calls "old life," "habit," or "nature's appetites," and toward an arrest, a stabilization that produces a virtually new self. Formally, conversion$_1$ appears as an exemplary plot-climax, a reversal of a certain way of being and a recognition, an awakening to essential being, to one's truest self. Conversion$_1$ is a token of literary form experienced as a change in the character of life; conversion$_2$ is a literary act that takes its character from events in life. (42–43)

It takes but few alterations to recast this passage as a description of retreat narrative, even of less self-conscious, more "informational" sorts. The "epistemological certainty" that's "confirmed" in retelling; the movement away from "habit" and "appetite" (not "nature's" but "society's," though); the effects of "recognition" or "awakening" in experience reported: all these moments pertain to the texts I will examine. Only some references to self require discounting—and not because such effects are absent or negligible in dramas of retreat. It's rather a matter of attention, of the sort of action being lived toward recollection, with the action of nature writing more often concerned to elide, evade, or problematize personal history in determining what's iterable in text. To simplify, we might say that where conversion$_1$ is figured as retreat, conversion$_2$ will be other than autobiography, but otherwise the same dynamics, the same tensions of imitation and recreation will apply.

In Harpham's formulation, they come to apply very widely indeed, with the notion of "conversion" construed in expanding ripples of significance, first as "simply a strong form of reading" (44), then as the biological grounds of language acquisition, and ultimately as "the unchanging condition of our existence" (48). With this core notion spun out so spectacularly, the genre of autobiography acquires a nearly boundless generic "inheritance." While Harpham, like Cavell, rejects views of genre as a static collocation of traits, from this point their conceptions peel off on opposite tracks, with the wide "conditions" that Harpham outlines for autobiography inviting endless reiterations or "versions" of the genre, and Cavell's "comedies of remarriage," by contrast, very narrowly delineated. The difference resides in the generic "inheritance" each posits, Cavell's closely historical, Harpham's existential, even biological.

For my part, I am inclined to split the difference. I acknowledge a generic inheritance determinate enough to issue in particular conditions that retreat narratives play out—which distinguish them from the larger spectrum of nature writing Lyon describes, or from all "conversion" and thus all language as per Harpham. Yet something of Harpham's perspective will persist in my account of the genre's orientation and purposes. These are far from monolithic, but they do involve existence and biology writ large—what "fronting the essential facts" is about. And often they can be thought to involve "conversion" in the primary, commonplace sense of changing belief or allegiance, so that a critic of nature writing like Scott Slovic might without irony ask, "how can nature writers lead the way in this awakening, this 'conversion process'?" (15); and a writer like Annie Dillard, fastening upon some party-goer with urgent news of the two hundred-some muscles in a goat moth's head, can insist, "I am not making chatter; I mean to change his life" (*Pilgrim* 132).

The relation of chatter to life-changing suggests a further generic condition of retreat narrative, one that distinguishes the genre from those forms of nature writing more readily categorized as adventure or even travel. Consider how Dillard expects her entomological trivia to transform lives, how Thoreau, in "Walking," depicts his daily walk as at once a radical crusade and as the emblem of repetition and routine—such that, as A. R. Ammons has it, each day, "a new walk is a new walk." In these instances an element of conversion sought after—an element of action, quest, pursuit of the extraordinary and transformative—is lodged squarely in the routine and ordinary, in daily existence understood to be not uniquely but continuously transformed or converted through the experience of retreat. It is a condition of these narratives that, just as the "essential facts" to be fronted in retreat to nature are not social, so too they are not exceptional. Their fronting through observation and contemplation becomes the writer's daily business, and the retreat narrated is of a sort either habitual to a way of life (as with most "rambles") or continuous with or reiterated in counterpoint to routine existence (as with wilderness travel). The drama of solitude is a tale not of adventure or diversion but rather of absorption, its concern not events coming once in a lifetime but one's lifetime coming in the rhythm of events.

This amounts to saying that the nature writer (in the particular sense I am promoting) establishes in the activity of retreat a *role* proper to a certain *way of life*. If this is so, then investigating the narratives (the modes of quest) that configure this role would mean, as Alisdair MacIntyre has it, investigating at some level a social order, along with the virtues proper to it. Again, we take our cue from Thoreau, who in "Walking" playfully claims a special status for members of his fancied "Order of Walkers," a splinter segment of the larger society whose exceptional ambulatory capacities are matched by exceptional duties—even civic duties, like that of "Inspector of Snowstorms" he claims in *Walden*. In Thoreau's ironic formulation, one born to the role of walker reiterates daily the hearth-quest cycle of epic, constantly prepared to forsake all social ties for ends understood all the same to be not just personally but socially redemptive. The complexities of this formula—retreat from others as exemplary to others—spin themselves out in manifold ways in the genre. But one broad observation will indicate how stories of facing nonhuman "facts" may be taken as embodying values, as intimating a resolution to the fact-value split MacIntyre details—perhaps even offering, as Lopez hopes, "the foundation for a reorganization of American political thought." It is that dramas of solitude, while defined precisely as sited outside human presence, cannot be understood as sited outside a web of community relations—community like that which MacIntyre sees in premodern "heroic" societies, in which fact and value, character and incident are integrated alike, and every virtue is understood by its place "in a certain kind of enacted story" (125). These dramas might be regarded as a mode of "enacted story" or quest performing virtues proper to a larger-than-human community, what Aldo Leopold terms "the biotic community"—a web of relations imperceptible from within the enclave of material culture but "eventful" nonetheless. And the political reorganization Lopez projects, informed by such stories, would be one that recognizes this biotic dispensation and observes virtues proper to it.

It is true that tales of the biotic community may feature as eventful the activities of some fairly uncommunicative "characters." But this does not rule out a parallel with the sort of community MacIntyre describes. As the epic or saga captures a way of life already formed but in so doing claims an understanding denied to the characters depicted (124), so also can be seen the understanding claimed in much nature writing. Leopold coming to learn the interconnectedness that "thinking like a mountain" entails; Muir at the summit of Mt. Ritter apprehending the whole dynamic pattern of the landscape: these are success stories, successes in comprehension sought and attained in the course of exceptional (because solitary) yet *not* extraordinary actions, actions not surpassing the ordinary way of life that the writer, at least provisionally, has assumed. Of course, this way of life, because solitary, most often *is* provisional—why Dillard's self-troping as "pilgrim" is apropos; why Thoreau's "experiment" at Walden is ultimately discontinued in favor of his "other lives"; why even Muir must descend now and then to solve "the bread problem" and regale others with his tales. But I will identify as one further condition of the genre that the destination of retreat be figured *as* a community or web of relations that the writer feels implicated in and is concerned to comprehend—figured, in a word, ecologically—not as mere scene or backdrop against which a lone agent acts exclusively for and upon himself. As much or more than any I've cited, this ranks as a condition in Cavell's sense—a dynamically enacted "procedure, subject and goal of composition"—and not a static feature.

And this condition, in turn, points back to the genre's rootedness in the tradition of natural history, which investigates such ecological communities. Only in quite recent years has any "nature writer" of the sort I'm exploring not been invariably a "naturalist" as well: either a scientist drawn to letters (like Aldo Leopold) or a "humanist" turned naturalist by default (like John Burroughs or Joseph Wood Krutch). By contrast, one might understand the interest of such nature writers as Barry Lopez in the cultures of aboriginal inhabitants of wild areas as relating to the fact that no separate category of "naturalist," or for that matter of "nature," exists by and large among such "traditional" peoples, whose ways of life bear the seamless quality of the premodern societies MacIntyre prizes. (Nor do "traditional" peoples practice or contemplate "writing"—a consideration I will return to later in this study.) Thus any dissolution of the modern fact-value split that nature writing might help bring about would likewise tend to dissolve the conditions the genre enacts. Getting "back to nature" would mean pulling back from "nature writing," back from its forms of conversion and retreat: a retreat from retreat. We needn't hold our breath for this, of course: the plot of the story of these stories appears, if anything, to be thickening.

SOLITUDE AS STORY

To say a plot thickens is to identify a rise not just in intricacy but in interest. I turn now—have turned already, with this talk of roles and community—to the question of the interest to be found in the narrative genre I have been delineating. The term "interest" I invoke in its full register of senses, to stipulate not just the curiosity or concern that attends a thickening plot but further any perceived benefit or advantage to one's self, also a claim or stake held in the contractual sense. While these senses are interrelated, there is plenty of give between them, even an ambivalence that Kenneth Burke draws upon in explaining that what is *in* one's *interest* is distinct from and potentially even opposed to what one is *interested in* (*Permanence* 37–38). Burke's remark could serve as a slogan for much theorizing about narrative in recent decades, which similarly questions whether peoples' interest in stories—certain stories, or story in general—serves their own best interests.

I pose this question to broach some issues attending how interest is attributed to dramas of solitude—the essentially depopulated narratives of retreat. To this end, I will sample an exchange between Hayden White and David Carr over the "reality" of narrative form and the interests to which it answers—an exchange characteristic of recent discussion on the ethical import of narrative. Summarizing this, I will draw terms by which to place retreat narratives in relation to our commonplace notion of story: that of human characters whose conflict generates plot which thickens in specifically human interest.

In "The Value of Narrativity in the Representation of Reality" (1980), Hayden White indicts narrative on the grounds that, in representing events as having beginnings and endings, it is untrue to the character of "real events," to the world as it "really present[s] itself to perception"—a world that for all its manifest sequence is conspicuously short on endings (23). The impulse to narrativize is moralistic and authoritarian, White insists; narrative closure can hardly be reckoned as anything but "the *passage* from one moral order to another," since "real events" themselves will hardly have drawn to a close with the close of a story (22). Among the responses White's well-known essay has elicited is "Life and the Narrator's Art" (1985) by David Carr. Examining White's stance, Carr finds that it hinges upon a distinction between art (i.e., narrative) and life (i.e., "real events"), yet in attending to art, fails to take a principled look at life. Such a look, Carr claims, will confirm that narrative hews faithfully to the reality of lived experience, "an extension and confirmation of its primary features" (111).

The difference to Carr is that while White has in mind a "physical reality" of causal succession or random operation (whichever you please), narrative is not properly charged with faithfulness to a reality so "indifferent to human concern." On the contrary, "It is human reality that is portrayed in stories, plays and histories," against which narrative's fealty must be judged (111), even if, as has mostly been the case in the past, "physical reality" has been philosophically privileged. This "human-physical" pairing is a near equivalent to the "action-motion" distinction that Kenneth Burke posits. "Things move, people act," Burke's slogan goes, as he holds for adopting ultimate terms based on tropes of human (motivated, poetic) "action" rather than material (mechanistic, reductionist) "motion."[6] But where Burke derives from these terms a pair of rival orientations toward *both* people and things, Carr divides the two, seeing in story the mode of "reality" proper to what's human *in particular*. His account thus recapitulates the commonplace view of story as characters enacting plot in a setting:

> What stories portray is not physical reality as such but human
> activity, including the very activities of projecting meaning
> onto, or finding meaning in, physical events. The physical
> world does find its way into stories, of course, but always as
> backdrop and sphere of operations for human activity. . . .
> Life—not biological but human—is the reality of narrative,
> and it is of this reality that we must ask whether it is indeed so
> devoid as the standard view claims of the characters ascribed
> to it in stories. (111)

Carr suggests that the act of finding meaning in physical events is itself
eventful in narrative terms; I will return to this suggestion for what it can
offer the account of nature stories that follows. But at this point I'm
interested in noting how the nature writer's drama of solitude complicates exactly these assumptions of Carr's: that "physical reality" is distinct from "human activity" and is necessarily its passive object or
"scene" in story; that "biological" and "human" life are distinct, with
only the latter authorized in "the reality of narrative." In sorting things
out in this way, Carr as much as reinscribes the "standard view" he attributes to White, only shifting the status of "reality" from one side of a
dichotomy to the other—rendering the dumb, aimless, unsignifying
realm of "physical reality" somehow unreal (since unstoried) for
humans, as unreal as White finds narrative closure to be.

It's not hard to find stories in which scene takes on agency, in
which something physical "acts" or "biological life" undergoes
escapades. If a claim that the "reality of narrative" is human amounts to
saying that the things and creatures "acting" don't themselves hear and
repeat the stories they act in, then the claim is mostly unexceptionable
(except as compromised, on one hand, by the invocations of hunting
peoples, and on another, by accounts like Vicki Hearne's of horses and
dogs going sane by learning fit "stories"). But the claim amounts to more
than this, no doubt, to a version of the "social constructionism" that
loosely encompasses this entire exchange. Then the question arises as to
whether nonhuman actors, *as* actors, are construed by definition as
human, for the purposes of story, at least. If so, any narrative account
that did *not* cast the actions of animals, for instance, into behaviorist
terms of sheer physical response or "motion" (as sheerly "scenic," as
Burke would further say) would be considered *ipso facto* an instance of
"personification." Stories are about humans; thus any story not explicitly

about humans can only be understood as though it *were* about humans. Here is how Tobin Siebers puts it:

> To be a successful story, a narrative must tell about human beings (or about characters endowed with human qualities), their actions, and their problems. If any of these elements is missing, the reading or hearing of the story draws upon the interests of those who are reading or listening to provide what is missing. No interest. No story. (7)

Thus if the fox acts cunning, if the sunset waxes tranquil, if the tempest gets tempestuous, we necessarily understand these "characters" as human and their attributes as something "endowed." Or if not, then by default they draw upon our "interests," and since Siebers is preparing to say that the test of a story is in its retelling, these "interests" work in a circular way as both explaining why and asserting *that* a story has been retold. Since passing on stories is the human estate, though, these "interests" must themselves eventuate from narratives, in the retelling of which the interests are themselves constituted, and these narratives in turn must presumably exhibit or stand in for the "human qualities" that make a story a story, and so on—a circle drawn close around "humankind" in a loose sense, one which might seem to blunt from the outset any project of nonhuman "fronting."

This circling is not a problem in itself, to my mind: I see it as a further, necessary manifestation of the orbiting we call hermeneutical. What I want to express instead is a preference, not a set of verities, as to just what the circle might be thought to encompass in swinging from "story" to "qualities" to "actions" to "interests," all within the orbit of the "human." It's a preference as well as to where in this circling we might opt to come to rest—which is to say, to start out. I take it as given that things "as they are" will not rear up to sanction or contest any stipulating of human qualities and interests as *exclusively* human—not in any ultimate way, beyond consequences issuing from actions we undertake with purposes informed by such an understanding and such terms. This is Burke's more-or-less pragmatist point in espousing an orientation based upon poetic "action" rather than physical "motion": that we might prefer some terms over others for what we believe may ensue from their use. This is nothing like saying that wishing makes it so; the world makes it so, which is a way to say that we must try to say what's true (what Noel Perrin calls "the first and essential requirement" of writing about nature—and of a testament, too, I'd add). But the wishing is integral. I want to suggest that the truths and terms of ecology may bear upon this understanding of story as peopled with people, or at any rate, that it's the possibility of such that informs the narrative of retreat.

Language itself must be the prime example and issue here; and there may be some question as to whether asserting that nonhuman actors are understood as "endowed with human qualities" amounts to saying anything more than that the stories they act in are made of (converted into) language. If some such presumption underlies this understanding, it in turn rests on a view of language as discontinuous with the nonhuman. The conventional truth of this view is clear enough. Yet without elaborating much, I want to suggest that this view may be compromised and realigned, even from a "scientific" viewpoint concerned not with casuistry but with (to adapt Thoreau) slicing things at the joint. Just as mechanistic, "non-anthropomorphic" conceptions of instinct-driven, ineducable, uncommunicative creatures have given way to richer pictures of animal learning, teaching, and self-awareness, so might notions of symbol use as exclusively human give way to more inclusive understandings. Thus Frederick Turner, citing a neurologist's assertion that all vertebrates have brain regions devoted to symbolic activity, locates in myth an ancient legacy of organic adaptation, such that "myths are not decorative and outmoded fictions but the instinctual and sure responses of the organism to Life" (*Beyond* 10). Nothing in this expanded "true story" about the truth of stories dismantles what Siebers says about narrative's recourse to human interests. Rather, it extends the sense of those interests, in something of the way that Leopold widens the boundaries of "community."

In determining what it is that "interests" people in a story without human characters, we can do no better than nature writing as a phenomenon has, and go back and forth on the question of qualities identified or endowed. "Nothing is more controversial in nature writing," remarks Frank Bergon, "than the comparisons naturalists make between human beings and other animals" (525–26); "pathetic" comparisons with non-animal or inorganic entities are less controversial only because more universally deemed untrue. On one hand, it may be that interest created or found in a drama of solitude hinges exactly upon finding analogues to human character and action among the narrative's nonhuman elements. Yet on the other hand, a prime impulse in relating such narratives is to resist or complicate or sidestep this correspondance, however feasible, suspect, or misbegotten the project may appear, depending upon whether one honors a "physical reality," a "human reality," or something less categorical. This bears upon whether and how one credits White's assertion that a narrative effects a passage from one moral order to another. For it raises the portentous question of what interest any such order might hold in narrative that does not (overtly) depict nonhuman creation as a simulacrum of a social dispensation. We all know how the animals and landscapes of fables are stand-ins for human types, funhouse facsimiles of household, market, and court; might such "characters" and "settings" be fabled in ways that conduce to the transformation of human estates they are held *not* to resemble?

Such a prospect is best left posed as a question, I think, to be not solved but reenacted. It *is* being reenacted, certainly, through what Lawrence Buell is calling the "ecocentric repossession of pastoral" in recent nature writing, heralding a "shift from representation of nature as a theater for human events to representation in the sense of advocacy of nature as a presence for its own sake" (52). Nature's "own sake" is never purified of ours, the designs of retreat notwithstanding; the distinction between "sakes" may even be independent of formal designs, with "pastoral as ideological *form* tend[ing] to remain more or less constant even as ideological content changes," as Buell notes (51). The same designs can bear different valences: "The 'retreat' to nature *can* be a form of willed amnesia . . . but it means something different when held up self-consciously . . . to appeal to an alternative set of values over and against the dominant one" (49–50). Yet alternative values are still human ones, whether any human character holds sway. In retreat this categorical vacillation gets structured, not settled, in ways that eventually (following Harpham) I will come to call "ascetic."

In any event, there's always *one* character in a story of retreat, whose actions are an obvious source of interest and drama. As Lyon notes, the nature experience essay, in departing at once from straight observation and from an emphasis on human contact, increasingly features the writer's own personality, such that "we are placed behind the writer's eyes . . . , moving through [the landscape] with the protagonist" (6). We can spin out some implications, some sources of interest, from this. One concerns metaphor and sensibility, the drama behind those eyes as to how the nonhuman becomes figured as human or inhuman, action or motion, insensible to or integral to our actions and concerns— the drama of the "human activity" Carr identifies in the finding or enforcing of meaning. This drama of the writer's understanding becomes our own as we deem these figurations interesting and apt, or mechanistic, pathetic, sentimental, or enfeebled, as the case may be. This implication leads to another, which is that, in recognizing the writer *as* a protagonist, we are posed in dramatic contradistinction to the writer; we both "move through with" and come up against that writer. This is especially true with the radical, extravagantly standoffish personae of writers like Thoreau and Edward Abbey; but it holds true as well for other writers, who however self-effacing still exhibit bents of style, action, and attention that have the effect if not the purpose of self-characterization. Thus we enthuse with a writer like Muir, through his eyes; but part of us gapes at him, too, as at a spectacle; and there is drama in this encounter.

Finally, the notion of "moving through" a terrain in this way suggests modes of formal patterning, story forms, based upon the writer's physical movement—especially *walking*—and analogical extensions of such movement. We have encountered such formal modes already in Lyon's subgenre of "rambles" and Thoreau's conceit of a walk as a quest. And the analogical extensions are commonplace in discourse that figures experience or text as terrain and thought as movement through it. Thus in the action of walking we recognize a principle of plotting by which stories of retreat may be particularly configured, and in terms of which other formal principles might be derived and "stories of attention" recognized and explored. Being "placed within the writer's eyes" and "moving through" a world from this position, as Lyon describes it, will mean attending to different sorts of sites and sensations in different sequences, for various sorts of purposes bearing various sorts of interest. Much of what follows will substantiate this suggestion and characterize such movement.

For the narrative of retreat, the primary movement or quest is the movement outward from the human to the nonhuman—the retreat to solitude in nature—then back again in the retellings of text. I began this preliminary textual excursion by evoking this movement, and I'd like to bring it back around by remarking further on the trajectory of solitude posed in writing that depicts such a movement. In some sense of the terms, it seems as if *leaving* humanly inhabited space must mean *entering* "the wilderness," however understood; and this double character of departure and approach informs the plot of retreat narratives. By the logic of these terms—a narrative logic, I will maintain—if one's "self" is figured as an inhabited space, then retreat, to be successful, would involve its being vacated. The very impulse to retreat might be read as a species of what Richard Poirier calls "writing off the self," the ancient and ongoing entertaining of "proposals to do away with the self"—one further answer to the question, "How would you like to disappear?" (182). Whether the self's dissolution is experienced as alienation or (more often) reintegration, the effect characteristically is as Muir describes it: "You cannot feel yourself out of doors. . . . You lose consciousness of your own separate existence" (*A Thousand-Mile Walk* 212).

Accordingly, it might seem that nature writers seek out what in MacIntyre's view would be most unthinkable to the heroic character, one whose role and virtues are enmeshed in a way of life. For the heroic character to withdraw from his place in society would mean "trying to make himself disappear" (126), yet this seems to be precisely what these writers are up to, the mingled impulse and peril of self-effacement an active element in their stories. Yet if the stories are vehicles of conversion, to be taken as exemplary, then a different order of quest and thus heroism is suggested, one that would steer toward "a shore without house or anchorage" not to fetch Philoctetes but for its own sake, whatever that may be. Such a quest is an exercise in self-effacement converted in the text's self-assertion, the reiteration of experience provisionally stripped of the biographical, perhaps of any vantage beyond the moving posture of the eyes we're placed behind.

There may even be a heroism to a sort of willed purposelessness, one reflecting on the "human reality," the purpose or telos Carr describes to our selection and recapitulation of events in narrative. Carr cites so-called "action theory" to indicate that every "action," broken down, nets not components of an action but further, more local actions, similarly inseparable into parts. The very "action" through which this recognition is derived suggests the existence of varying rhythms or tempos of attention, constituting different temporal dispensations, so that in attention to actions at a certain level or setting, purpose is effaced on purpose, one's historical self is a nonentity, and "time is the stream I go a-fishing in" as Thoreau says; a day, as Muir has it, is neither short nor long. If the eyes move but the "self" they funnel into is somehow subordinated or effaced, then writer and reconfigured reader are the heroic vehicles of a truth not essentially historical—a truth in which human identity, if not the "self" as such, is productively reconstituted. This would be, as Poirier stipulates, "evidence that human beings can exercise a capacity to wish themselves radically other than what they are"

(196)—"what they are" being the products of a social dispensation largely inimical to the greater biotic community. Or so the story goes. The degree to which all this is authentic emission or aesthetic posturing, exemplary behavior or irresponsible escapism, and the reasons for preferring one description to another, and the sorts of rhythms and actions such writing might in any event depict, and the ways in which we might want or believe ourselves to be interested or changed thereby—all this remains to be explored, though hardly settled, as we proceed.

CHAPTER TWO

Going Out, Going In

Narrative Logic in Thoreau's "Ktaadn"

FIRST THERE WAS NO STORY

> Not like my taking the veil—no solemn abjuration
> of the world. I only went out for a walk, and finally
> concluded to stay out till sundown, for going out, I
> found, was really going in.
>
> —John Muir

There's an old story about stories, E. M. Forster's, that goes: The king died, then the queen died—of grief. First there was no narrative, just chronology, this story goes—until those last two words. Then plot succeeds sequence, time is redeemed in meaning, and a chapter in narrative theory (and Intro to Lit) is inaugurated.[1]

It may kill a fable to take it apart; one hopes that something of the fabulous is resuscitated in the act of dramatizing what is tacit. What I'm out to dramatize is not Forster's model tale, at any rate, but the testament or parable I've quoted above from John Muir. I want to claim that Muir's little story can be read as a paradigm in something of the way that Forster's can. Only it delineates a different sort of story, one that depends on relations not between human characters but between a single human subject and a nonhuman landscape that the subject moves into or within: a narrative of retreat.

Though the import of the Forster story is manifest enough, I'd still like to tease it out a bit, so as to say by cross-reference what it is that Muir's statement does that makes it likewise a story and not just a log or quip. Most evident in the Forster passage is that through the added two words, a connection is established between two events: it's because the king died that the queen died. The connection may be causal, as it is here, or otherwise;[2] in any event, where two "points" existed before, a trajectory is established, a "middle" that makes over those points into a "beginning" and an "end."

Further, the narrativized version of the two royal deaths evinces transformation or reversal of various sorts, at various levels.[3] There are the obvious reversals of condition or status—from live to dead, sad to sick, mighty to humbled—implied in the relations of parts; these we will not belabor. A couple more subtle sorts of transformation merit attention, though. One is that the shift, the sensation of reversal in this little tale depends for its effect on its "delivery." I mean that the order in which "events" are presented is not the same as their presumptive order in time—the former (the *syuzhet*, roughly, in Russian formalist terms) reverses the parts of the latter (the *fabula*), placing the implied "middle" in the position of the "end."[4] The effectiveness of the pared-down narrative depends upon this transformation in manner of delivery: if the second, narrativized version of the two royal deaths were to read, "The king died, and then because of grief, the queen died," the results would still be a story, but not as successful a one.[5] That Forster's version is so widely repeated attests to *its* success as a story, for what's the test of a story if not repetition?

Except that in this case, what's so often repeated is not simply the second, "storied" version of the moribund royals, with its narrative reversals riding on the final two words. What is repeated, rather, is that version coming on the heels of and repeating the preceding, nonnarrative version. The two versions comprise, in effect, a *single* story: a story of becoming a story. Transforming (and reversing) an old pop song/Zen parable, we could say this story goes: first there is no story, then there is a story, then there IS—and what there is, at last, is the difference, the transformation. In *this* story, what's crucial is that those last two words are something that *happens*, just when it might seem, in the repetition that precedes them, that nothing is going to. Though the whole bit is an exercise in definition by exemplification, its upshot as definition is storied itself, by dint of how it is arrayed and deployed—of what might be called style. This might alert us to look for modes not only of "style as argument" (to echo Chris Anderson) but of style as story, even in putatively nonnarrative texts—especially in the realm of reception, of how readers may be led to experience features of a text as events in a span of time or terrain traversed.

Forster's story is a setpiece: a quasitechnical demonstration in how narrative is constituted. It is true that Muir's passage does not proclaim its status as exemplary and paradigmatic as Forster's does. Yet the passage enacts such a status, in its substance and manner of delivery and, further, in light of the contexts in which it is read.

The Muir passage, like Forster's, is widely repeated. I've seen it used in several places as a tone-setting quotation at the start of a chapter, as I have used it here. Instances of its use are likely to draw upon some prior notion of Muir as writer and figure, such that readers will harbor some idea of how far "out" this speaker has gone, what "in" he's been to, what sort of self, in its public manifestations, the passage gently deprecates: "I *only* went out for a walk." We read this disclaimer in light of our understanding of Muir's accomplishment, to which the modesty of his proclamation serves as reverse index. We read it, that is, in light of the fact that we are reading *him*. Muir's writerly ethos, his vast prestige among those likely to read him, combines with the broad terms in which he depicts what seems the very image of his life endeavor, to render the passage exemplary. Even archetypal, in a sense: for as Forster's demonstration works in part through the surplus of meaning[6] generated in the figures of king and queen (especially in conjunction with "grief"), so Muir's assertions work through the figures he evokes and the cultural scripts they figure in.

Muir's figure is that of seer and wanderer in wilderness, a type with entitlements he evokes in his protested aimlessness and spontaneity; and this figure, in turn, is defined in contradistinction to the type that "takes the veil." This is the type of the ascetic mystic—nun, monk, hermit—to whom "going in" is an intended, not incidental, outcome, and to whom "going out" into a world "solemnly abjured" is a sure way to frustrate, not to invite, that outcome. The ascetic retreats to "wilderness" not for its features but for its putative featurelessness, the ways in which it is not "the world"; on his walk, Muir does no such thing. Still, Muir protests too much: there's more than a touch of the ascetic to the ethos he evokes. He denies the motive of "abjuration," after all, because the outcome at stake—transcendence of some order—is the same for him as for monastics. It is the basis of his claim upon readers, which though vested in his own story is ultimately not personal but ethical. There is much of the mystic, further, in Muir's abjuration not of "the world" but rather of any particular transformative intent—any expectation, that is, of story. It's a commonplace in meditative traditions that what you would find, you prepare for but do not seek. As the watched pot does not boil, so the willful, self-conscious meditator finds no satori, no closure in story. What's "found" in the course of one's habitual practice—one's walk-taking—cannot be sought, can only happen; and this, in part, is what Muir's passage schematizes.

But this schema turns not upon just any practice but upon a particular sort, for which it serves as parable. It's the schema, as I've said, of retreat. To represent the passage as a paradigm of retreat, comparable to Forster's exhibit both in what it does and where it departs, let me recast Muir's parable after the model of the Forster setpiece, to expose the structure of the action—the transformation, the accomplishment—that it formalizes. It might read like this:

I went out, then I stayed out—because I found out.

Distilling Muir's pronouncement this way exposes the "transformed" beginning-end-middle structure that highlights—one might say drama-tizes—its character as narrative. In its mode of delivery, it emphasizes how the causal *logic* of the sequence is something that *happens*. What joins the beginning to the end is a finding out, a recognition—and when the subject, in "going out," *finds* "out," this recognition has the character of an event. It is eventful; and as such, it is transformative. "Out" is re-versed to "in"; and the end of such a story is to *stay* in, to dwell in that recognition, which is also a *place*—to "in-habit" it. In broadest terms, this is what differentiates the narrative of retreat from travel or adventure stories: the story's "proper" end is not reemergence but inhabitation, at some level or other. The historical Muir may emerge to write his books; but in his parable of retreat, he stays "out"—he dwells in a recognition.

Crucial to this paradigm is that the place entered is figured as a scene of instruction. This could be said of any narrative to the extent that "reversal" constitutes "recognition" and thus learning of something or other. But these implications seem all the more pronounced in nature writing, not just because it is ordinarily so informational a genre but precisely because nonhuman "scene" is figured *as* teacher. It is not just scene but agent of the subject's reversal. The nature writer's ethos is expressly that of one who has learned, been "in-formed" by what he or she "in-habits." Even quite informational nature writing implicitly assumes, is predicated upon, a narrative of retreat to such a scene, though the manner of narration, or the character of the predication, can vary widely. A common field guide might be construed in this manner, for instance, as the artifact of innumerable past "in-formings" and as the instrument and portent of recognitions yet to be enacted.

The reader who understands all this—who seeks out this sort of writing, who follows its informing scripts—harbors consonant expectations. They are generic expectations, in a sense constituting the genre. The expectations may be very particular in the realm of information, dictating that what the writer has learned in the unpeopled place will be transmitted back out as facts: names, descriptions, reports. In narrative terms, the expectations are less determinate. One expectation, in fact, concerns a certain suspension of expectation, as exemplified in Muir's protest that he "only went out for a walk." It's the expectation of the bear that went over the mountain, which Annie Dillard takes as her own: "to see what he could see." What you're likely to see, as Dillard knows, is "more of same": same mountains, same trees (*Pilgrim* 11). But with expectation suspended, sameness gets punctuated with the unprecedented; that is, with moments of recognition. What has never happened to you may happen, and be recognized as that which perennially happens. Or sameness may be found consequential; there may be singular instances of repetition, events in which the perennial is exposed in the episodic—when what "happens" is manifest in what "happened."

What is it that differentiates a "walk" from a story, after all? As with Forster's unplotted version of the royal deaths, losing the human may entail "going out" into a domain of unconnected though sequential events, of "this, then this"—or so it may seem. (I think of the *New Yorker* cartoon captioned, "He didn't know how to appreciate nature": a necktied man in an easy chair weirdly situated outdoors is thinking, "There's no plot.") But to one who comes to "in-habit" that domain— who walks it, then walks it again—recognition ensues, doubling back to inform what was taken as mere sequence. Story is "delivered"—most often a story about recognition become habitual. "First there is no story, then there is a story, then there IS." And this "IS" may be some mystical, ineffable "presence," or simply the perennial presence (and present tense) of natural fact, what "is so" about birds or trees or terrain. Nature writing ordinarily will intimate both, the factual and mystical, in varying proportions, variously conventional modes.

"I care to live only to entice people to look at Nature's loveliness," wrote Muir. The passage I've been expounding upon maps a mode of enticement. The roles of both mystic and adventurer—seekers of unprecedented states and sights, respectively—are enticing, yet in his aphoristic passage, Muir as much as disclaims them both. He would prefer to entice to the habitual, the ordinary: "going in" as going home. But his enticement is enacted in his writing, it's the reason he says he writes; and his writerly role or ethos is more complicated.[7] What he disclaims is what he enacts, though he's not being disingenuous: it's just that *this* sort of normalcy *is* mystical and adventurous, precisely because of its reversal, its "conversion" into written narrative.[8] The adventurer comes back; the mystic reports: their roles consist in this. If they don't, they disappear. Muir may dwell in recognition, in story, but as a writer, he turns around, comes back, and entices well enough to invite another order of repetition: that of reputation (of being "considered again"). Thus the passage I've been glossing can be read further as an exercise in the maintenance of reputation: Muir's attempt to slip or to finesse the cultural scripts in terms of which his narrative is becoming "reputed." He does not want his story plotted as heroism or hagiography in any conventional sense; he means to stress not anomaly and difficulty but normalcy, the ease and inevitability of recognition in wild nature. Such an emphasis is not only more enticing; it better fits Muir's own sense of the import of his story, which in the many repetitions it had already undergone may have threatened to escape him. This passage correcting the terms of his reputation comes from the late journal of a famous man;[9] it suggests that under some circumstances, the writer's own enticement or conversion is the first he must "consider again."

No nature writer—perhaps no American writer of any sort—has been more "considered again," more contended over in terms of reputation, than has Thoreau. Even more than the much-storied Muir, Thoreau has been the topic of considerations and reconsiderations that have come to constitute the "generic reputation" that nature writers inherit and enact. No book more than *Walden* depicts "going out" as "going in," the ordinary as heroic, the natural fact as transformative. But there's a work of Thoreau's that more nearly follows the core paradigm of retreat narrative I see distilled in Muir's statement, the movement "out" to lose the human and "in" to whatever recognition or instruction eventuates or is "found" thereby. I'm speaking of "Ktaadn," the first of three wilderness travel stories in *The Maine Woods* (1864). I propose to examine how "Ktaadn" instantiates a certain structure, or better, a narrative logic of retreat. I am further interested in this text as an exhibit or event in tales of Thoreau's reputation—which is to say, stories told of a Thoreau that spans his discrete texts, which his reader-commentators construct for considerations of their own. These stories of a biographical Thoreau depend heavily upon a narrativizing of his textual effects; in large part, upon stories of his composing. And these stories of reputation and composing, in turn, bear more generally on how narratives of a subject in wild nature may be taken, with Thoreau's own narrative an emblem of what they may consist in.

EXEMPLAR AND PARADIGM

On the terms I have argued so far, Thoreau is originary of nature writing *because* he is progenitor of the narrative of retreat. He is progenitor of retreat because he is reputed to be—not as the first to compose a report of his hermitage but as first to be so widely "considered again" in just this light. He is originary of the genre not only in the character of the literary responses he devised to conditions in which the genre arises, but also in the ways his literary effects have been narrativized and popularized in a life story, the basis for what Buell describes as the "Thoreauvian pilgrimage" in all its manifestations. "Thoreau" refers to a model text and a model experience, in both of which nature writing is generically constituted.

The text and the experience are both called "Walden," of course. Yet the two were not coeval. The text *Walden* did not emerge until years and drafts after the Walden experience was concluded. The book that Thoreau did produce during his stay at the pond (*A Week on the Concord and Merrimac Rivers*) reported an excursion from years before his arrival there and drew heavily upon journal entries from the earlier period. Just one fully realized text was both undertaken and completed by Thoreau during his Walden years: this is "Ktaadn." Quite apart from the fact that it neglects the experience of the pond proper, "Ktaadn" is in some ways an anomaly, potentially even an embarrassment to the tale of Thoreau as popularly scripted: an apparent threat to the *Walden* author's model status.

To see how this is so, let me return to some terms I broached in discussing Muir's "going out, going in" passage: the adjectives "exemplary" and "paradigmatic." In essence I suggested that the narrative of retreat presents a model in two senses of the word: as behavioral exemplar and formal paradigm. While these senses are interrelated, in some ways mutually implicating, I would still like to tap a wedge between them, by way of characterizing Thoreau's text more particularly. "Ktaadn," I would say, splits the difference between the terms: it is more paradigmatic than exemplary of the narrative of retreat. The distinction follows from some ways "model" may be taken. "Paradigmatic" suggests a systematic or patterned resemblance, consonant with the structural, schematic sense of "model" in such usages as "model airplane" or "economic model." "Exemplary" lacks this formal dimension and bears instead an ethical sense, the sense of an imitable character, as in "model citizen" or "model cities." "Ktaadn," then, is paradigmatic in the trajectory of retreat it describes—a narrative progression describable *as* a trajectory, with a logic that it follows, a sort of formula that, like calculus, it "plots." But as a story of the character of retreat, "Ktaadn" is not exemplary, really, since its upshot is so unusual, its climax and findings so exceptional, both for the genre of nature writing and (what may amount to the same thing) for Thoreau himself. The upshot, to all appearances, is not nature writing's exemplary one, which Joyce Carol Oates lampoons as "MYSTICAL ONENESS,"[10] but something more nearly the reverse. That this model of retreat may not be model in its outcomes makes it all the more interesting, I think, as an exhibit of how a story of retreat can be made and what can be made of it.

WHAT "KTAADN" IS ABOUT

"Ktaadn" recounts the first of three trips Thoreau made to Maine, the subjects of the three narratives comprising *The Maine Woods*. This 1846 trip, undertaken near the middle of Thoreau's stay at Walden Pond, had as its centerpiece an ascent to the summit of Mount Katahdin (a variant spelling of which Thoreau adopts, without explanation). This mile-high mountain, New England's second-highest, was known to have been climbed only a few times previously. Thoreau himself takes pains to point this out and to remark on the particulars of previous ascents. It is much to his purpose that his trip is not much precedented, for that purpose consists in seeking out utter wilderness, unpeopled terrain: in short, losing the human. The story, in a nutshell, is that he succeeds.

Here are some lineaments of Thoreau's account. In the company of a relative of his (unnamed and undescribed), he proceeds by wagon up the Penobscot River from Bangor, remarking on features enroute: lumber mills, a boat factory, Indian villages, and especially, the habitations and outposts the two pass, increasingly scattered and crude. They attempt to retain an Indian guide (wonderfully named Louis Neptune, and closely described) who subsequently stands them up. They go to the end of the road, meet up with two more companions (unnamed and so utterly undescribed that it's easy to miss the point where they enter the story); the four continue upriver on foot, past houses, huts, logging camps notable for their infrequency and yet (or so) warranting more extended attention than the details of the dense surrounding woods. They reach the backwoods farm of "Uncle George" McCauslin. Louis Neptune having failed to show, they convince McCauslin to accompany them as guide in the trip upriver by batteau (a long, narrow-beamed river boat). A bit further on, they take on another guide, a settler and boatman named Tom Fowler, and a chronicle of lakes, dams, rapids, portages, and camps ensues, with continued close attention to signs of prior human presence, especially of loggers and logging. They pass the last house. They make camp at a spot with incredible fishing, due south of Ktaadn, and the next day, after gorging on trout, begin their ascent. Through trackless, moose-nipped woods they struggle, finally camping in a windswept gorge below the summit. Thoreau continues upward alone that evening, mounting a high ridge through a ravine of preternatural ruggedness until halted above treeline by low clouds. Next day, Thoreau outstrips the party on their final ascent and attains the fogbound, wind-driven, rock-strewn summit by himself. He turns back, meets up with the group, and they descend through creek, forest, and an open area called the Burnt Lands, back to camp and boat. Their rations exhausted, they make haste downriver, riding heedlessly through rapids and falls, till they've made it to food, shelter, and a final encounter with Neptune. A postscript appends some morals of sorts. Whether they are ones the story warrants is a matter of some dispute.

What moral might fit the story depends on what one thinks the story is about. I read "Ktaadn" as "about" losing the human; I will pursue this reading further before surveying other sorts of accounts, other dramas of reception in which it figures as an exhibit.

In my retelling, I have featured the status of Thoreau's co-travellers—whether they are named and described or not, whether they occupy space or are given weight in the account. Three of the six men in his party, I've suggested, are ciphers, unnamed, undifferentiated. Interchangable, too: when Thoreau rejoins them after his evening climb up the gorge he finds that "one was on the sick list, rolled in a blanket" (62)—never mind which one. Whoever it was, it could not have been McCauslin or Fowler, for they have names in this story. The ones who are named (this holds throughout the book) are the denizens of the place, the woodsmen and Indians. In effect, they are features of the landscape—something you may find if you go there, as Thoreau and these other nameless interlopers did.[11]

Another way to view the distinction might be to say that only those characters warrant names who could get through this country alone. The guides, whether Indians or backcountry settlers, can manage this; the anonymous downriver visitors cannot. Thoreau himself is in a middle position. He's a visitor, certainly, a transient like his townspeople peers. But it's clear from his account that he distinguishes himself from the others by the level of his participation in activities by which the group makes its way, his role, for instance, in helping "warp up" the batteau through rapids and falls while his less capable companions carry the bags on shore. More telling yet is how Thoreau claims to have contemplated undertaking the expedition alone. His pronouncement to this effect is one of the opening gestures in his narrative. He intended, he says, "to accompany a relative of mine engaged in the lumber trade in Bangor, as far as a dam of the west branch of the Penobscot, in which property he was interested," and from there, "to make excursions to mount Ktaadn . . . and to some of the lakes of the Penobscot, *either alone* or with such company as I might pick up there" (3, emphasis added). Thoreau's later recognition of "the importance of a pilot on these waters," upon which "a stranger is, for the time at least, lost" (37), does not lead him to disavow that original resolution in any straightforward way; indeed, his evident determination to lose sight of his fellows at the journey's culmination on the summit serves to reinforce it. Nor is the decision of his "relative" (it's his cousin) to accompany him beyond the dam ever remarked upon. The story Thoreau wants to tell just isn't about his cousin or the likes of him;[12] it's about seeing what it might be like if the likes of him weren't around.

This is as much as to say it's a story about wilderness *as* wilderness. What Thoreau is rehearsing is neither typical of his time nor exemplary of what we've since come to think of when we think about wilderness travel. Rather, "Ktaadn" is sounding out what a story of wilderness retreat may consist in; it is offering tentative scripts of response to readers who can be presumed to have little firm notion of such experience, of what it might be, that is, for citizens like them to undergo such travel undertaken with such motives. These motives are not yet typical, as Thoreau's statement of solitary intent implies and his narrative confirms. While his relative is travelling to further his business interests in logging, Thoreau is out to climb a mountain, something loggers or settlers (or Indians, for that matter) are hardly wont to do.[13] There for the view, he's a sort of Petrarch among practical men, the signs of whose transgressive activities are (except on the mountain itself) pervasive.

They pervade, at any rate, in the attention of the narrator. The level of attention this narrator gives to signs of human presence—to dwellings, logging scars, established camps, and finally stray and peculiar single artifacts—seems inversely proportional to the space these signs take up in the landscape. Indeed, a drama develops in the attention devoted to such artifacts as the expedition proceeds and the party moves further beyond civilization's pale. This is a drama enacted somehow in any movement of retreat to unpeopled nature. In essence, it's what this chapter is about: how the "artifactual" may exist in tension with the "natural" in a manner figured and emplotted in retreat.

This constituting of human signs as narrative events is a phenomenon variously remarked upon or passed over in other readings of "Ktaadn." To see what these other readings consist in—what they opt to be "about"—I will venture a rough analysis of the ways "Ktaadn" and *The Maine Woods* get read. I do so not only to broach terms and issues important to the analysis of "Ktaadn's" composition, but also to suggest something of the ethical, critical, and political motives for reading retreat narratives and nature writing in general.

THREE WAYS OF READING

There are at least three ways or reasons or situations in which this story is read, overlapping and interrelated. First, "Ktaadn" may be read as a

straightforward tale of wilderness travel, by those who engage in or contemplate such travel (campers, hikers, canoeists, outdoor enthusiasts in
general), for the purpose of emulating, comparing notes with, vicari-
ously participating in the journey narrated. The book may end up in a
pack to Katahdin or a canoe on the Penobscot, or on a lap in a laziboy
with an atlas alongside. This is what I'll call a participatory reading.
There are ample signs of Thoreau's anticipating such reading, anticipating practical uses, in fact, for which the book is now obsolete. He lists
locations of and distances between the scattered dwellings on his route
for the use, he says, of those who may go that way later; and he appends
to his book, besides plant and animal lists, an "Outfit for an Excursion"
checklist with items and expenses, including nineteen dollars for twelve
days hire of an Indian and his canoe (318–20). Thoreau is conscious of
providing an orientation to a mode of existence his contemporary readers may find unfamiliar, taking pains, for instance, "to convey some idea
of a night in the woods" to readers presumed to be unacquainted with
such (41). Information conveyed for the benefit of subsequent travellers
presumes their ability to replicate the experience upon some terms or
others, and many of the book's readers are out to do just that.

"Ktaadn's" currency with participatory readers is unquestionably
enhanced, even largely constituted by its having been written by the
author of *Walden*. Much the more popular knapsack read and model for
reader emulation, *Walden* is also far more an object of literary study, sustained engagement with which is deemed rewarding and attended with
prestige. Thus the second readership for "Ktaadn" I want to identify is
that of literary scholarship and criticism. In this realm "Ktaadn" is read
primarily as an episode in the life and career of the author of *Walden*.[14]
It turns out to be a key episode in the Thoreau narratives some scholars
offer. Describing what makes it key, however, will involve my owning up
to a significant omission in the selective recap of "Ktaadn" I've offered
above. Those familiar with the story may have wondered when I'd get
around to this, since it has everything to do with the claim I've
advanced, that this story, while paradigmatic in shape, is not exemplary
of narratives of retreat in its upshot.

What I've omitted is the fact that at certain key junctures in the
narrative—in his evening scramble to a ridgetop, his ascent to the
summit, and especially, the passage through the "Burnt Lands" on the
way down—Thoreau seems shook up, disconcerted. He seems prey to
sensations and notions the antithesis of the exaltation, mystic merger,

peace, and bliss one might, on the face of it, expect from *Walden's* author—sensations the more puzzling for their having been expressed in the middle of the author's Walden sojourn. This Thoreau does not "imbibe delight in every pore" or "go and come with a strange liberty in Nature, a part of herself," as he does in *Walden* (129). He does not imbibe but appears to lose vitality; he feels not liberty but constriction, a sense of having intruded without warrant. Of the windswept, clouded-in summit ridge, Thoreau says:

> It was vast, Titanic, and such as man never inhabits. Some part of the beholder, even some vital part, seems to escape through the loose grating of his ribs as he ascends. He is more lone than you can imagine. There is less of substantial thought and fair understanding in him, than in the plains where men inhabit. His reason is dispersed and shadowy, more thin and subtile like the air. Vast, Titanic, inhuman Nature has got him at a disadvantage, caught him alone, and pilfers him of some of his divine faculty. (64)

If we take the present-tense "he" Thoreau speaks of as a version of himself in his own recollected experience, it would appear Thoreau found his ascent of Katahdin to be dissipating and chastening in the extreme, enough so to lead him rhetorically to distance himself (or some part of himself) from it in this manner.

This impression is furthered—culminates, in fact—in one of the most remarkable passages in the Thoreauvian corpus: one of the most remarked-upon passages, indeed, outside *Walden*. This is the paragraph in which Thoreau describes the descent through an open area he calls the "Burnt Lands," in the process expressing sentiments of estrangement that rise to a hyperbolic pitch. Trimmed nearly by half, the paragraph reads as follows:

> Perhaps I most fully realized that this was the primeval, untamed, and forever untamable *Nature*, or whatever else men call it, while coming down this part of the mountain. . . . It is difficult to conceive of a region uninhabited by man. We habitually presume his presence and influence everywhere. And yet we have not seen pure Nature, unless we have seen her thus vast, and drear, and inhuman, though in the midst of cities. Nature was here something savage and awful, though

beautiful. I looked with awe at the ground I trod on, to see
what the Powers had made there, the form and fashion and
material of their work. This was that Earth of which we have
heard, made out of Chaos and Old Night. Here was no man's
garden, but the unhandselled globe. . . . There was there felt
the presence of a force not bound to be kind to man. . . . [I]t
was a specimen of what God saw fit to make this world. What
is it to be admitted to a museum, to see a myriad of particular
things, compared with being shown some star's surface, some
hard matter in its home! I stand in awe of my body, this matter
to which I am bound has become so strange to me. I fear not
spirits, ghosts, of which I am one, —*that* my body might, —but
I fear bodies, I tremble to meet them. What is this Titan that
has possession of me? Talk of mysteries! —Think of our life in
nature, —daily to be shown matter, to come in contact with
it, —rocks, trees, wind on our cheeks! the *solid* earth! the
actual world! the *common sense! Contact! Contact! Who* are
we? *where* are we? (69–71 —emphases in original)

This is the story's culminating passage, a crescendo—the summit of
"Ktaadn," as it were. Prior to doubling back upon this moment, I was
suggesting that in the perspective of literary scholars, "Ktaadn" warrants
attention as a key incident in the life story of its creator, who in turn warrants attention primarily as the author of *Walden*. If the Burnt Lands
passage, with its tenor of alienation and alarm, is Point A, and if Point B
is *Walden* with its delight in every pore, then the task at hand becomes
to connect the points, to narrate a Thoreau continuous with both. In all
such accounts, the constant purpose is to accommodate the seeming
anomaly of Thoreau's outburst into a narrative of writerly development
that might otherwise tend to reject it.

A typical literary reading is often considered to broaden or enrich
participatory reading, even to supplant it. Less often considered is how a
participatory reading may inform or correct the literary. A case in point
comes in James McIntosh's account of "Ktaadn." Though complemen-
tary to my own in most regards, McIntosh's reading, emphasizing
Thoreau's "shifting stance toward nature" throughout the author's work,
does not mention the attention to human artifacts and habitations that
marks the first section of this narrative. The sole exception comes with a
human dwelling that McIntosh remarks upon in detail: a logging camp

hut that Thoreau depicts as typical of several such camps his party came across. The description, to McIntosh, is telling as "an image for the life of natural men" in the woods (193)—men like his guides McCauslin and Fowler. Here is a passage of Thoreau's that McIntosh glosses:

> [The camps] are very proper forest houses, the stems of the trees collected together and piled up around a man to keep out wind and rain: made of living green logs, hanging with moss and lichen, and with the curls and fringes of the yellow-birch bark, and dripping with resin, fresh and moist, and redolent of swampy odors, with that sort of vigor and perennialness even about them that toad-stools suggest. (*The Maine Woods* 20)

This is lush description, certainly, loaded with images of "rich, dense," even "erotic" nature, as McIntosh has it. It is even likely that "fungi, toadstools, and swamps are . . . sexual symbols" to Thoreau, as McIntosh, following Raymond Gozzi, maintains. This line of interpretation parts company, though, with what I'm calling a "participatory" reading, in proceeding to this further assertion: "it seems that [Thoreau] lights on such imagery here *because* he is on a masculine adventure in Maine" (194, emphasis added). It is true that he uses such imagery and that he is on such an adventure, a gendered one; but to one who has participated not only in reading this text but in moving through a landscape of this sort, the attribution of cause here seems out of kilter. It appears to neglect the existence of the forest itself, the boreal forest of mosses and fungus and sappy logs, which has just the character Thoreau attributes to it. It is a fact of the boreal forest that it's fungus-ridden; there's not a worm in the place, and fungus fills their function. It is hard to see what other "imagery" this writer could "light on" and still remain faithful to that forest. He lights on what's below him.

I do not mean to suggest that "literary" and "participatory" orientations, while sometimes divergent, are mutually exclusive. The two orientations may stress one side or the other of an apparent opposition: fungus as phallus, fungus as irrefrangible fungus. But neither facticity nor allusiveness can be relinquished when reading so tangible an "adventure" as Thoreau's. This is a way of intimating what Barry Lopez ✓ puts in terms of relations between two "landscapes": that the function of story is that it "draws on relationships in the exterior landscape and projects them onto the interior landscape" in order to "reorder a state of psychological confusion through contact with the pervasive truth of those relationships we call 'the land' " (68). If Lopez is right, it follows that a certain familiarity with and faithfulness to the relationships that constitute "the land" have a place in our critical practice, if we see that practice as conducing to the alleviation of "confusion," personal or societal. It is a tenet of ecological criticism as practiced by Buell, among others, that the participatory sense of the land itself must inform and correct the exuberances of literary reading.

Not all readings of "Ktaadn" as an event in a life story of Thoreau remain within the compass of literary biography. There is a third way or situation in which the narrative may be read, one that takes "Ktaadn" as an episode in Thoreau, but takes Thoreau as an episode in a larger story of ideas, attitudes, and habits. Readings in social and intellectual history — the more prevalent sort of readings given to nature writing in general, if not to Thoreau in particular[15] — consider how a story of Thoreau has developed over time to inform the responses of "participants" who read and reenact aspects of that story. Such readings are further a way of taking part in that development, as can be seen in two social-historical readings of "Ktaadn" originating roughly a generation apart: those by Roderick Nash, in *Wilderness and the American Mind* (1967), and by Max Oelschlaeger, in *The Idea of Wilderness* (1991). Their accounts of "Ktaadn" concur in deeming the summit experience the pivotal event in the story, the story a pivotal event in a Thoreau life story, and the life story crucial to the development of cultural scripts with ethical dimensions. Beyond this, their readings diverge widely, along lines consonant with a split within environmentalist ranks, between mainstream "managerial" environmentalists, so to speak, and advocates of "deep ecology" — a split that exemplifies points of stress critical practice faces as it seeks to assess the social import of nature writing.

The divergence between Nash and Oelschlaeger turns upon whether "Ktaadn" can or should be read as exemplary, or whether it is better construed as something like a cautionary tale. Nash, the mainstream environmentalist, takes the latter view in his story of Thoreau. This story starts with a Thoreau enthusiastic over but unfamiliar with trackless wilderness. His first trip to Maine effectually chastens him, dealing a "rude awakening" that pushes him back from the extreme position he had espoused, into advocacy of "a middling position" between "the wild and the refined" (92). "Ktaadn," in this view, offers counsel of a sheerly negative sort, meant to frighten the intemperate into positions of negotiation and managed change. Oelschlaeger, for his part, agrees that Thoreau was unsuspecting, drastically ignorant of what awaited him in Maine. But to Oelschlaeger, the "new and radical" challenge of the excursion instead deals a death blow to inadequate Emersonian notions and quite a few others as well:

> As an Emersonian transcendentalist armed with conventional categories and comfortable conclusions, Thoreau had died on Ktaadn's ridge, and he verged on achieving a primordial, if threatening, relation to the universe. . . . All the Homeric odes and poetry of Virgil, the transcendental principles of Emerson, and even the romanticizing of nature's beauty were suddenly meaningless. (147–48)

This negative pole in Thoreau's explorations of nature is redeemed by these positive repercussions: first, that it kills off his vapid transcendentalism, and second, that it "sharpens [his] understanding of interrelations between humankind and nature," catalyzing the growth of "a profound evolutionary perspective on nature" that is eventually instantiated in *Walden* (149). Oelschlaeger's story is one of breakthrough, not repulsion, of categorical change and transformation, not negotiated settlement. It rates "Ktaadn" as exemplary indeed: the vehicle of its author's rebirth as authentic being.

Most literary readings of "Ktaadn" extend from a consensus: they agree on what "prior texts" (Romantic ones, mostly) Thoreau drew upon and transformed, and they set out to comprehend this one writer's development, no other. These social-historical readings express a consensus, too, with both narrating Thoreau as an exemplary figure in a larger cultural story that informs what we make of our circumstances to this day. Oelschlaeger would agree with Nash that Thoreau "cut the channels in which a large portion of thought about wilderness subsequently flowed" (84). But they map those channels in very different ways. These readings, while treating his prior texts, are more concerned with how Thoreau's texts have become prior for us now. On this there is no consensus, and the stakes are different: a rhetoric of balance or transformation, a politics of management or confrontation.

But I'll go further and say what I think is common to *all* these readings. In the stories they construct that include and retell "Ktaadn," all tend *not* to read "Ktaadn" itself as a narrative construct. Attending to the "constructed" character of the narrative would mean identifying some logic or grammar in terms of which its "events" are rendered coherent.

Further, it would mean acknowledging how the time in which the narrative is made is not the time that it represents. I want to discuss the latter criterion, exhibiting the habit of reading I mean to question, by way of returning to the former, the question of "narrative logic" with which I began.

SELF WRITING AND SELF WRITTEN

The habit I'm referring to is that of recapping or glossing events in the text as though they represented a faithful, accurate, essentially transparent tracking of what was happening from moment to moment in Thoreau's trip — in effect, as though it were all "taken down" *at that time* by a preternaturally sensitive reporter. This tendency to read the story as transparent report is present despite the fact that literary commentators universally acknowledge how resourceful or (to twist McIntosh's "shifting stance" thesis) "shifty" this writer is. Frederick Garber, for instance, while finding the narrative "accomplished" and "dramatic" (75), is prone to treat aspects of tone and motif in the narrative as if they were themselves events or attributes of the trip. "Near the beginning of the trip," Garber says, "while they were still close to the coast, [Thoreau] was confident enough to be mildly sardonic" about the relative dearth of human signs in the landscape (77): this as though a quip in Thoreau's post facto report constituted a record of his mood *in situ*. The tendency holds even in critics who attend in detail to the evident *process* of composition of this and other Thoreau texts. Adams and Ross, whose book constitutes a study of Thoreau's composing, maintain that in this story Thoreau is "experimenting" with "the role myth can play in shaping narrative" (66). But thinking about narrative "shaping" does not prevent them from asserting that "On the trip up the river he emphasized the clearings and evidence of human activity; back in Massachusetts he remembers most the 'continuousness of the forest' " (75) — as if the *whole story* were not "remembered" and shaped "back in Massachusetts." Finally, the historian Nash verges on perfervid in the liberty he takes, depicting a "near-hysterical" Thoreau "clinging to the bare rocks of Katahdin's summit" (91). This is not to say that Thoreau necessarily was not or did not do what Nash says; only that, on the basis of this story, we really can't tell.

Part of what's happening in these passages may be chalked up as a sort of ellipsis, the eliding of an understood qualifier, "Thoreau depicts himself . . . ," before each action or notion. These readings are stories themselves, after all, and deserve what drama they can responsibly muster. But in a sense, it's exactly the fact that Thoreau is depicting himself that gets lost here. The presumption of reportorial transparency promotes a slippage between the "character" Thoreau and the writer identified with him. The excerpts from Adams and Ross above exemplify this handily. It's certainly accurate to say of the "character" narrating the story that he "emphasized" one thing or another "on the trip up the river"; this much might be reported of any character in a story. Huck Finn emphasized things on his river, too. But Huck Finn is not "experimenting" with ways of "shaping narrative," either, the way this putatively self-same "Thoreau" is.[16] Yet the one name does duty for the two. What character Thoreau did on the mountain gets muddled with what writer Thoreau does in the text. But does "Contact! Contact!" take place on Katahdin or in Concord? Does it report an event or create one? Is there a difference?

This slippage between self writing and self written may appear less problematic in the event that the one writing is writing in the event: sitting in the midst of what happens, scribbling away. What is taken down will be ipso facto an attribute of the situation and have the character of an event; it will be no more mediated than any other aspect of what's happening there and then. This may indeed be a condition sought after: Sharon Cameron, for one, finds "Thoreau's unmediated relation to nature" to be the constant subject of his journal and *Walden*'s "best subject" as well, however thwarted it may have been in the latter by contrary needs of making it public (29). Scott Slovic even claims that, because of the way on-site journals and notes enable naturalists "to entrench themselves in the specific moment of experience," Thoreau's *Journal* provides "an example of nature writing at its purest, with no conscious attempt having been made to obscure and mystify" the writer's relation to "natural surroundings" (4–5). Thoreau fantasizes somewhere about having a machine that will transcribe unspoken thoughts directly, and the text created *in situ* may be thought to approach this character — as if the flight recorder from a downed plane were picked up on a summit and, played back, piped up, "Contact! Contact!"

Yet however desirable or chimerical the prospect, for "Ktaadn" this scenario of unmediated, on-the-spot reporting and hence constituting of events appears moot. This is the case in part because no "first-level" on-site field notes or entries are extant, but even more because crucial climactic sections of the text seem clearly not of this order. Notes and drafts of "Ktaadn"[17] show three further levels or stages of composition beyond missing *in situ* inscriptions. The first is a sort of outline for the narrative, plotted day by day, not in tabular form but as a running list of words and short phrases of an evidently mnemonic cast, cues to events in chronological order. This much, it's speculated, was sketched out on the basis of field notes.[18] Second is a series of passages or set pieces a couple or few paragraphs long, apparently set forth not in any deliberate order, though the order they *are* set forth in seems suggestive in ways I'll discuss later. Among these is a much-worked early version of the climactic "Burnt Lands" passage. Then finally follows the draft, the whole story, composed to all appearances in one fell swoop over the course of a couple months. What most bears remarking is that in this first draft, which in most respects closely resembles the finished essay, the crucial Burnt Lands episode is *entirely missing*. Likewise, the episode is represented in the story's initial, mnemonic "outline" version only in the phrase "Burnt lands" — a cue only to a place traversed, not to any panic or portent there experienced. Evidently, as a sensation or response or *theme*, the story's climax is present in some form nearly from the outset; yet as an *event*, a "historical" episode, this climax initially finds no place.

Thus the time in which this "climax" is composed cannot readily be identified with whatever time it is taken to "represent," and in this sense the story has the character of something constructed. Examining the record of the story's composition in this manner reinforces impressions that a reading of the final, published version alone may occasion. For this evidence of a narrative climax not initially "fixed" in time correlates with a narrative logic discernable in the finished text. I'd like to expand on the reading I began above in this light, drawing further upon attributes of the story's composition to elaborate this narrative logic.

LOSING THE HUMAN

The logic of retreat, as earlier suggested, might be broached in the form of a proposition. If the premise of a trip to wilderness *qua* wilderness is that the artifactual will diminish and vanish, giving way to a nonhuman realm, then a major feature of such a trip as narrativized will be the recognition that this state has been reached and "wilderness" attained.

Events of observation—things noticed and described—have a definitional character within this scheme: what's seen may be remarked, or plotted, as either consonant with or foreign to a wilderness condition. There is nothing exceptional in this: it's a stock feature of response to nature variously wild or "tamed." Any hiker will know the sensation of spotting the odd gum-wrapper at trailside, so disparate in character from what surrounds it, and like Thoreau will find it "startling to discover so plain a trail of civilized man" in that locale (42). "Take nothing but pictures, leave nothing but footprints," the Park Service says—or used to say, until footprints too were redefined as impure and disruptive. (Perhaps the most "startling" sign of the artifactual that Thoreau and his party happen upon is one of their own footprints, encountered on their way back down.) By contrast, other features will further the sense of wilderness approached and attained—signs or sightings of wild animals, especially, like the fresh moosetracks Thoreau remarks upon just before the Burnt Lands passage. Mapped out in this fashion, the wilderness trip becomes a drama of recognition, with the artifactual contending with the natural for possession of the traveller's experiential domain. Then the wilderness condition is attained to the degree that the artifactual is left behind—or framed out, or otherwise reconciled to the wild. And this condition, once attained, is recognized as the scene and agent of instruction in the "essential" character of the place, its "nature."

When Thoreau, early in "Ktaadn," states his intention of travelling to a spot some thirty-five miles "beyond the last log hut," going "alone or with such company" as he runs into en route (3), he is plainly, if not that dramatically, stating what he is after. The course of events he relates follows the logic of that intention. The movement to wilderness renders every relic a milestone: last road, last house, last trail and camp, last brick and scrap of printed matter run across are all constituted as portents in the tacit drama of the artifactual. They show that Thoreau is not "there" yet—and/or by their gum-wrapper exceptionality how close he is to arriving. When with his party he outstrips the artifactual altogether in the move to the summit, Thoreau takes the further, "logical" step of outstripping the others and climbing alone. What he happens upon confirms the narrative logic that leads him there. If his intention is figured as "losing the human," then Thoreau's narrative virtually perfects itself: its key moments at the summit and the Burnt Lands depict a Thoreau to whom the human is lost indeed—just how lost, we shall see.

From this perspective, in these formal terms, "Ktaadn" is a success story. However unnerving his summit experience is taken to be, in refiguring his trip Thoreau depicts himself as having found what he came for. The evident shift between the climax passages and what transpires thereafter, through the added-on "moral," is intelligible in these terms as well. Adams and Ross remark on this shift from emphasis on "evidence of civilization in the wilderness" to a reverse emphasis on the wildness, expansiveness, and aboriginal past of the landscape (67). Similarly, McIntosh identifies a polarity between the sense of estrangement from wild nature at the climax and the sense of reintegration with its wildness in the conclusion. Noting that both the climax passage and the concluding afterword were add-ons to the first draft, he infers that Thoreau meant this polarity to act as a structural element within the narrative, a way of balancing off "extreme statements to express both sides of a mixed truth" (210). I concur with these readings and want further to figure the shift or polarity as an aspect of a narrative predication. This polarity expresses not just two "sides of a mixed truth" like a pair of thematic bookends but rather two necessary elements of a master plot. The story is premised on losing the human; the human is lost; thus the writer dwells thereafter on a world less exclusively human. He dwells in a recognition.

This is the logic of retreat in broadly paradigmatic form—paradigmatic in that it makes sense of narrative units or stages with reference to a higher-level, overarching logic or set of correlations. It does not assume or require that aspects of a text be otherwise reconciled, as indeed, in "Ktaadn," they are not—only that each stage be represented. The key late additions to the first draft, in fact, enforce a nondialectical dualism[19] so extreme it verges on the schizoid; read in biographical terms, it conjures a picture of a Thoreau who has fallen apart then been miraculously (or disingenuously) restored. But the status of these passages as add-ons correlates with this other reading I am giving: the passages fill functions that the narrative logic mandates. If they do not cohere, nevertheless, they fit.

It appears that, at least upon reviewing his first draft of the story, Thoreau at some level recognized and moved to fulfill this narrative logic. The evidence for such a recognition goes back even further in his composing than that, back to the initial passages drafted for the story, those that come after the mnemonic outline and precede the continuous, chronological first draft. A look at these passages suggests that Thoreau thematized or harbored a "logic" for his narrative at the very outset of composing. It suggests that Thoreau labored over a notion of what the narrative was to "come to," what climax might be proper to it, quite early on. Yet the fact that this climax is omitted altogether in the first draft raises a further possibility: that this climax, while proper, had no necessary connection with any *particular* event in the narrative, but rather, in revision, came to be attached to one. Thus a "double logic"[20] of narrative conversion appears to be at work: the upshot of the Katahdin experience as Thoreau came away with it becomes thematized in a manner that helps determine how the experience itself is represented.

BEFORE THE BEGINNING

These first passages show a writer casting about for a way of opening, a way of shaping a "whole," as yet unformulated narrative for public reception. Though the essay that eventuates will ultimately follow a thoroughly chronological plotting, there's no question yet of beginning at the beginning. Instead, Thoreau seems to light upon whatever resonant scene comes to mind, as a way of warming up, of sounding out tone and intentions. Here is how he begins:

> It was with pleasant sensations that we rowed over the North Twin lake by moonlight—now fairly beyond the last vestige of civilized, perhaps of human life—in the midst of such environment and such civility there as nature allows[.] For still I could think of nothing but vaster cities there concealed on the distant shore and ports and navies—and the orient and occident—the levant and the Pacific of trade— (277)

Thoreau homes in immediately on the crux of the narrative paradigm I've described. From the outset, he moves to identify the scene as beyond any "vestige" of the artifactual. Yet full recognition of the non-human is pending, not yet achieved: by stipulating that he is "still" embroiled in thoughts of the civilized world, Thoreau implies that he will not long continue to be. This sense of impending recognition is furthered in the contrast Thoreau proceeds to evoke between the "enthusiasm" of the party singing its "boat songs" and their sense, when they'd stopped to listen, that wolf, deer, or moose might be "even then gazing at us," while the boatmen "heard only the hooting of owls." This scene of arrival is staged in an open, inviting, "yet uninhabited" terrain presided over by mountains that periodically rear up into view, particularly Ktaadn. In a sense, everything pertinent is represented in this sampling: both the intention and the realization of the move to nonhuman wilderness, the mingled excitement and uneasy anticipation, the sense that a more thorough recognition awaits beyond the night circle of the boating party's song.

This first passage, three paragraphs long, is followed by a continuation of the account of North Twin Lake by moonlight, with the party steering for an island in the dark and amusing itself with the fantasy of inhabiting a lighthouse thereupon. The party pulls up, makes camp—and the passage shifts:

> At length we drew up our batteau . . . and proceeded to make our camp—
>
> It is difficult to conceive of an country [sic] uninhabited by man we naturally suppose them on the horizon everywhere— And yet we have not seen nature unless we have once seen her thus vast and grim and drear—whether in the wilderness or in the midst of cities—for to be Vast is how near to being waste. (277)

The disquisition that follows the landing and camping will be recognized as part of what became the climactic Burnt Lands passage. In fact, the first version of that passage follows. By the associational logic at work here, though, the notions this passage puts into play are derived from the moonlit lake episode; they give rise to, rather than follow from, the depiction of the Burnt Lands. Such a logic is indicated, for one thing, in that the terms used to characterize uninhabited nature—"vast and grim and drear"—are consonant with the setting of the wild lake at night: both are stock properties in the discourse of the Romantic sublime. The Burnt Lands setting offers no such store of associations; on the contrary, as we shall see. Further, this order of derivation helps explain the aside about an "uninhabited" nature being seen "in the midst of cities," which persists in the finished version. In the moonlight boating passage, this remark gives a further twist to the irony of Thoreau's musing upon exotic distant cities (also a fixture of the Romantic sublime) while having arrived in the midst of uninhabited nature. In the Burnt Lands passage as it ultimately evolves, the reference to cities seems to come out of nowhere; here, it is clear where it comes from.

As positioned in this early draft, the passage shows Thoreau moving to thematize his as yet unformed narrative at a level so general, any number of particular instances might be derived from it or bear it out.

The lake scene follows from the statement just as surely as the Burnt Lands one does, and the Burnt Lands is clearly just one episode that may epitomize it: *"perhaps* I most fully realized" nonhuman nature at this point, Thoreau proceeds to say (278, emphasis added)—perhaps, not certainly; most fully, not exclusively. An entire narrative trajectory is implicit within the passage: the initial difficulty of conceiving (reaching) the nonhuman; the moment of full recognition of nonhuman nature; and the subsequent realization of a "horizon" not presupposed to be exclusively human, not even "in the midst of cities."

The first version of the Burnt Lands episode itself consists mostly of a section I left out when quoting it above. I was able to omit it readily enough while preserving and even promoting the tone of the passage as it ultimately develops. Much of the section is descriptive not of an agitated mental state but of the terrain itself, a low-key, even inviting terrain, open enough to traverse easily, stocked plentifully with blueberries as burnt areas in the boreal forest tend to be: a scene conducing more to the familiarity of the picturesque than to the terror and drama of the sublime. The import of the passage hinges upon Thoreau's second-guessing his own initial presumption of familiarity, his recognizing that this terrain was no "pasture run to waste" but rather an utterly "unhanselled" landscape. The irony is that, in an area so generally difficult to traverse as the Maine woods and the mountain's summit, this easy stretch should be the site of his realization. In the final version, this irony persists but is quickly overridden by the intensity of what's added on. There, the debunking of familiarity is *followed* by the passage that, in this first version, *precedes* it ("It is difficult to conceive of a region uninhabited"), then lifts into the crescendo of estrangement that figures so heavily in our various Thoreau stories. But in the first version, just the merest hint of estrangement appears: "I expected the proprietor [of the landscape] to dispute my passage." The hint is not developed; instead, the passage trails off into an evocation of those animals that *do* frequent and feed at this terrain—bear, moose, and partridge—and eventuates in a quite explicit critique of anthropocentrism: "The main astonishment is that man has brought so little change— And yet man so overtops nature in his estimation" (278). In a sense, the entire *last* section of the narrative is distilled in this early draft of the climax: the tacked-on postscript that affirms the unlimited and nonhuman character of the woods. This early version of the Burnt Lands anecdote brings into proximity and relation exactly those features that seem most polarized in the final version: the "fully realized" strangeness of the Burnt Lands, on one hand, and the conclusion's integrative vision of a landscape "so little changed" for all man's presumption, on the other. This further ratifies the narrative trajectory plotted in fine in the passage just before, from difficulty through recognition to an aftermath of comprehension.

For all this, though, Thoreau is not yet ready to begin at the beginning. A further episode, most wondrous and resonant, comes to his mind, one not yet entered into this narrative calculus: a first version of the account of the incredible trout fishing at the campsite below the mountain. Once again, an associational logic links it with what precedes. The trout are figured by Thoreau as a mediating element between human emotional or aesthetic response and the essential integrity of a nature not anthropocentrized—a tacit solution to the antinomies of ease and difficulty, familiarity and strangeness, in the early Burnt Lands version. Thus the fish are figured in terms of dream, which similarly mediates or translates between inaccessible and familiar domains. The trout, exclaims Thoreau, "made beautiful the lord only knows why, to swim there, leaped from the stream to our frying pan by some orphic process"—a phenomenon "so like a vision" that he "rose by moonlight" "in that wholly visionary dream land" to test the truth of "the fable" by catching more fish (278). As incredible as the profusion of this "orphic" offering, this piscene transubstantiation, is the beauty of these creatures so patently "made beautiful" for other than human ends—a further rebuke to man's misestimation of his stature. In the story's final version, Thoreau will call them "painted fish." Again, as in the first of these early passages, Ktaadn looms in the moonlight over the scene.

The moral, the recognition Thoreau draws from this, concerns "the truth of mythology"—of "history" put to a "celestial" use (279). Arriving at this, it may have seemed to Thoreau that he had a purchase on his subject, thematically speaking, for the passage he drafts next has all the earmarks of an opening line, a first, false start to the story: "One memorable evening and moon lighted dawn I first caught the trout in the Maine wilderness. . . . And the fable of the trout was realized to me." The line reiterates the just-worked material in a "once-upon-a-time" tone, couching it in the form of a presiding realization, and further, as the culmination to a quest, his search for "a larger specimen" of a type of fish familiar to him. "I had come so far to catch my fish," the passage concludes, presumably gearing up to tell just *how* far.

But Thoreau wisely abandons this awkward attempt to plunge *in medias res*, attempting next to begin at the beginning—or *a* beginning, since the one he ventures is an earlier beginning than the one he ultimately adopts. In its final version, "Ktaadn" essentially begins with the trip out of Bangor and addresses the traveller's conveyances thereto in perfunctory fashion. This earlier beginning instead dwells at length on the voyage out of Boston by steamboat. But in casting about for a way to start here, Thoreau is still toying with the plunge into a dreamlike realm his fishing episode had evoked, depicting his steamboat travel as "a transient and dream like experience," one of those "singular reminiscences in the life of every man—of seasons when he was leading a wholly unsubstantial and as it were impossible life" (279). The passage proceeds to relate a shipboard incident wherein Thoreau and a group of travelers have awakened and come on deck at a time they believe to be just before dawn, only to find it's just eleven o'clock. Oddly and interestingly, a version of this false start, which in its evocation of a disoriented state vaguely heralds what the Burnt Lands passage was to become, does end up in *The Maine Woods*—only it prefaces "Chesuncook," the account of a trip taken nine years later! So much for the transparency of *that* first-person account.

In its draft version, "Ktaadn" proper begins thereafter, on the buggy from Bangor. Its narrative movement thenceforth in both draft and final version is so rapid and evidently straightforward in sequence and style that it is little wonder commentators so readily assume its transparency. But as I have been demonstrating, a nascent narrative logic is evident early on, the logic a retreat scenario effectively demands. This logic may be expected to influence selection of events, helping to determine what for the story's purposes should be taken as eventful. In fact, a glance at events reported in both outline and draft forms yet ultimately *excised* from the published "Ktaadn" reinforces this impression of active shaping in accord with a narrative "double logic."

THE CUTTING-ROOM FLOOR

Events that don't make the author's cut appear to fit a few loose criteria. It may be inferred that similar criteria helped determine what escaped notice or got sorted out before even the earliest transcription, going altogether unremarked. Predictably, some criteria involve the presence (or absence) of Thoreau's cohorts. Most conversation between them goes unrecorded; of what little talk does get taken down, a lengthy, light-hearted account of how Thoreau "discoursed philosophy" with the woodsman Tom Fowler in the boat's bow gets cut (346–47), as does the banter about lighthouse-keeping on North Twin Lake mentioned in the earliest passages. Other personal touches that don't promote the imper-sonal scene likewise get excised. Thus while sightings of single artifacts may further the narrative logic, and the sight of one companion rolled up sick in a blanket may promote the edgy spectacle of camping near the summit, one event that combines these motifs is dropped: when one of Thoreau's companions, having lost a tooth on a piece of hard bread that subsequently got stuck in his windpipe, bends over the river to get a drink and spots a rusty kettle at the bottom (326). This convoluted little scene evidently is recognized as a sort of protuberance on the narrative trajectory, too personally particular and faintly absurd to retain.

Similar criteria apply to the author's inclusion of events depicting himself. For instance, not everything that reflects on his expertise is nar-ratively admissible. Thoreau, as noted earlier, is ready to depict himself as fairly skilled in the wild, as in the passage where he assists the boat-men in "warping up" a waterfall. But a passage evincing skill of another sort is deleted, one in which the narrator fixes a long-defunct clock on an inn wall (288–89): this mechanical acumen does not fit the woodsy ethos he is developing. More significant yet is that the writer's activities *as* writer are likewise deemed not pertinent. Any depiction of the act of writing in itself that has entered the draft is excised in revision. The first version of the "warping up" scene, for instance, alludes to the boatmen's having observed Thoreau's taking notes, the implication being that they were spurred to their risky maneuver by the presence of this evident reporter, rather as if they were showing off for a camera (322). The final version, with this reference cut, makes their feat seem like simple high spirits, not a bid for attention. Also cut is a mention of Thoreau's staying up by firelight to count fin rays and scales on one of the "painted fish" they'd caught (331)—neither woodsy nor "fabulous" enough an event, it may be.

Most telling, to my mind, is the mention of some fish that are not figuratively but literally "painted." A conspicuous oddity in the journal "outline" for "Ktaadn" is found in the midst of these notes for the account of the evening below the summit and Thoreau's first solo climb up the near ridge:

> torrent—camping ground leave party go up torrent fir trees lakes rocks—clouds—sick and weary camp green fish fire at night—wind up ravine (275)

Everything we read in these spare phrases has its analogue in the finished story—except "green fish." There are no "green fish" in "Ktaadn." It requires a look at the story's first draft to decipher this cryptic inscription. It turns out that the party, running short on provisions, had bundled up into a blanket a bunch of the fish they'd caught, to pack along with them to the summit. This much *is* reported in the finished story, which further includes a wry sketch of the men at a lunch stop roasting the fish on sticks, crowding each other for position over the fire. What the first draft adds is that the blanket was green. And so:

> We went supperless to bed tonight for our remaining fish had contracted a green hue from the green blanket in which they had been rolled and so were condemned and other food was scarce. (338)

Why is this vivid episode removed? The writer's decision may have turned on the faint absurdity of the image or the lapse in judgment and competence it appears to evince (resembling the broken tooth-sunk kettle scene in these regards). But there's more to it, for not just the tinted fish but the fact the party went hungry that night goes unreported, finally—hungry after an all-day bushwhack straight up an unblazed mountain slope in the midst of the dank, rocky, tree-strewn boreal forest. The jotted note "sick and weary" may refer to the one rolled up in the blanket on a rock shelf, but it might as easily refer to the status of the entire party at that point—even, it may be, Thoreau, as he clambers up the torrent alone.

What this suggests is a further criterion of selection, in accord with which the worst signs of privation are excised. Thoreau is simply not out to relate in detail the physical hardships of the trip, though indications of these are clear enough in the finished story. There are no cold hands or cold feet, no eyes watering in a stiff wind above treeline. Yet upon a speculative and "participatory" reading, some of the story's "metaphysical" crises might be construed as having physical analogues. When

Thoreau stands off in third person, as it were, to describe the ridgetop experience—"Some part of the beholder, even some vital part, seems to escape through the loose grating of his ribs as he ascends" (64)—one acquainted with such a situation may be excused for wondering if he does not allude to first signs of hypothermia.

This tendency to elide or thematically "convert" particulars of physical hardship bears directly on a mostly unremarked problem in reading "Ktaadn's" crucial climax passage. Readings of all three types I have surveyed are mostly uniform in agreeing that the outcry, "*Contact! Contact!*" is indicative of some crisis or upheaval in the writer's development. But while the tenor of panic in the passage is clear, much less clear is what actually *happens* to Thoreau at this juncture in the story; or more precisely, what *happened* to Thoreau at the juncture in time putatively reported. There seems no *tangible* indication whatsoever as to what may have transpired there—no quickened pulse, shortness of breath, panicked movement, wild animals rearing up from haunts to "dispute his passage"—nothing but a (false) sense of familiarity suddenly reversed into a sense of awe and estrangement. This climax, if an "event" at all, seems an event of a sheerly attitudinal order, the fear expressed ("I fear bodies, I tremble to meet them") a sheerly metaphysical fear. And as noted above, the first draft of the passage hints at no such fear, while the first draft of the story omits the passage altogether. Under the circumstances, what are we to make of this crisis?

"WHERE AWAY DOES THE SUMMIT BEAR?"

Some readings of "Ktaadn" construe its climactic passage as a sort of delayed reaction or culmination to the accumulated stress of coping with a hostile terrain. Literary readings find this a stress particularly upon the self's imaginative capacities, consonant with the work's Romantic pedigree. The reading I am offering suggests stress of another order, one that does not displace but informs these other readings, as the participatory informs the literary perspective, or the external the internal "landscape." I think it likely that, at a minimum, Thoreau and his party were exhausted and hungry as they descended to the Burnt Lands, that they plucked the blueberries in that place with more than usual relish. But there is more. To dramatize this, I'd like to quote the "*Contact!*" passage again, slicing it this time in a way it never is—through the bones and not the joint, so to speak:

> rocks, trees, wind on our cheeks! the *solid* earth! the *actual* world! the common sense! *Contact! Contact! Who* are we? *where* are we?
>
> Ere long we recognized some rocks and other features in the landscape which we had purposely impressed on our memories, and quickening our pace, by two o'clock we reached the batteau. (71)

The "joint" in question occurs between the two paragraphs. There are reasons enough to think them separate units. Most notable is how the tone Nash reads as "hysterical" drops off at once into the matter-of-fact reportorial voice of the narrative at large. If as Adams and Ross assume, the climax passage represents something Thoreau had to "recover" from (65), this shift in tone suggests he must have recovered at once. The tonal shift corresponds with a shift in discursive function, from dramatic evocation of an attitudinal state back to chronology of concrete events— from tour de force to report. The paragraphs further belong to different stages of composing, with "Contact!" a late addition, and "Ere long . . ." a feature of the original draft. The seam that shows between them is a common enough feature of a worked-over, spliced-together text; though infrequent in "Ktaadn," it's the sort of thing that led Margaret Fuller to complain about hearing the tools at work in the "mosaics" Thoreau created.

Yet if this is indeed a joint and not simply a collision between parts, how is it articulated? The hinge point—or the grout between tiles— extends from the fact that the second of Thoreau's rhetorical questions is effectually *answered* in the most tangible of terms. "*Where* are we?" is a question of more than figurative import, it appears, for in addition to being tired and hungry, this party of campers is not sure where they are. They are literally disoriented. They're *lost*. Once they figure out where they are, they don't amble around the blueberries; they "quicken their pace" and rush back to the boat.

It is possible to discern that this is their situation earlier in the narrative. Shortly before, the party, "being in doubt about [their] course," had sent Fowler up a tree to look for landmarks, pressing upon him from below the questions, "where away does the summit bear? where the

burnt lands?" (69). Evidently, their purpose for traversing the Burnt
Lands in the first place has been to seek out those landmarks they'd
memorized. In the story's first draft, this is more evident yet, for in the
absence of the lengthy added-on climax, the accounts of the tree-
climbing and the reorientation come in quick succession, some dozen
or so lines apart. There is no trace of panic or even consternation
throughout.

What is happening, then? It is possible that Thoreau experienced a
moment of panic at that location more pronounced than the ongoing,
undifferentiated discomfort and concern the situation must have occasioned. But except for the histrionic "Contact!" addendum, there seems
no reason to suspect this, as his equanimity is otherwise unbroken. Nor
does the climactic passage itself, in its cadences, its reversals, its word
play, promote this impression except in its sheerly textual effects. It is
panic-inducing itself, as a rhetorical performance; but it cannot be said
to record a panic, only to evoke or rather to enact one.

More likely is that in scripting the passage, Thoreau identified an
opportunity to fulfill a narrative imperative. As I have argued, this writer
had thematized, had plotted a logic for his narrative from the earliest
moments of its composition. With the aid of transcribed field notes, he
could command a thorough chronology of concrete events. Early on, he
had identified that narrative logic loosely though not exclusively with
one episode in that chronology, the passage through the Burnt Lands,
where evidently *something* had occurred to him, some train of thought
and sensation, some recognition. Whatever it was, though, may well
have been ineffable—enough so, at least, that it was not to figure in a
draft that hews quite faithfully to the previously outlined chronology.
Upon those terms, it did not yet have the stature of an event. Perhaps the
recognition, the sensation of concern or disorientation, had developed
in recollection "back in Massachusetts," becoming more definitively
"eventful" as the writer retrospectively crisscrossed the textual Burnt
Lands. It's not possible to say. What can be said with confidence is that
the story in its first version *needs* something. The frustration of the
cloud-bound summit had failed to produce a workable culmination, a
clear epitome of the theme and scheme of retreat. So Thoreau manufac-
tures a climax, heaping up a rhetorical divide for a narrative trajectory
that had lacked one.

The climax he devises so overwhelms the concrete scene it's
dropped into, it nearly obliterates it. Just as it is difficult to locate the

point where the two anonymous companions creep onto the scene, so it is hard to keep in mind what Thoreau is tangibly *up to* in his movement over the Burnt Lands. But this is no big problem for the story; indeed, as a narrative of retreat, the story benefits from this, as it does from Thoreau's other decisions. For the story is not really *about* being lost, breaking teeth, eschewing green fish, though it *is* about orientation, privation, and sustenance at some level, as camping stories will be. As a retreat into wilderness, it's about recognizing and relating the character of wilderness as experienced, and Thoreau constructs a climax that does this.

The fact remains that the recognition he dramatizes, while fulfilling a paradigm, seems far from exemplary upon terms we're now accustomed to. Why does Thoreau, apostle of wildness, picture himself as so badly rattled? Accounting for this, most stories of Thoreau's development capitalize upon the fact that "Ktaadn" is a fairly early work. It may be that the climax passage represents a rearing up of anxieties otherwise kept in check, which later were sublimated or reconciled. Or as a developing writer anxious for recognition, perhaps Thoreau went overboard, crafting a passage more "extra-vagant" and "shifty" than necessary, playing to a public's appetite for the dramatic.[21] However understood, it's obvious that Thoreau was to grow more "exemplary" in his works and life to come, with results that rank as historical.

The reading I prefer accords with Oelschlaeger's: it finds the attitudinal rift between estrangement and familiarity in this early text to be in part a problem of precedent. Just as Thoreau depicts a Mother Nature mouthing the proto-evolutionary sentiment, "This ground is not prepared for you" (64), so Thoreau projects himself into a situation, a paradigm, for which prior texts have not prepared him, at least not adequately. He works with those he has, with Milton, Virgil, Aeschylus, Emerson, Lyell's geology, conventions of travel literature, above all the rhetoric of the Romantic sublime; but what he is after—a tradition, a "fable" of seeking and recognizing the nonhuman in itself, not as a foil for human prowess—he has to devise, to intuit or bang together, himself.[22]

Other, later writers are better prepared. John Hay, for instance, below the same mountain's summit, can declare with full affirmation, "The Katahdin spirit is full of incorruptible danger," then proceed to detail the harsh character of the terrain and the features of the alpine plants that flourish there (46–47). Hay, like Thoreau, recognizes that this terrain is such that "we could not live there." Yet familiarity with, habituation to not only the mountain itself but texts the likes of Thoreau's equips Hay to believe that Katahdin "invites you out on a wing of the universe . . . to experience how limitations may lead to the unlimited" (48). This is not so different from what Thoreau rehearses in his story, only not riven with the ambivalences that Thoreau inherits and in some measure reenacts.

Such an interpretation bears upon a literary reading as well, one focused on the author's individual development. For one thing, it reinforces Buell's account of a Thoreau whose "transitional struggles of a lifetime are . . . fully reflected" in *Walden*, including the struggle "to overcome an intense preoccupation with himself" (118). "Ktaadn," you will recall, recounts a voyage undertaken in the middle of Thoreau's Walden Pond residency, with *Walden* itself composed mainly in the years following his departure. Just as *Walden* is a retrospective meditation on the pond experience, so the climax and conclusion of "Ktaadn" may be seen as retrospective meditations on the experience of Maine, not a report thereof. "Contact! Contact!" is composed at the pond and has as much to do with the drama of self-assertion and self-dissolution enacted there as with any particular episode in Maine. Its composition is itself an event from the Walden residency, the scene it depicts reminiscent of the "pastures run to waste" characterizing that Massachusetts landscape; it is expressive of the author's concerns in composing at that scene, the anxieties held in check and vented there, including those of an author desirious of reception.[23] That residency, in turn, changes character in retrospect, with both the succession of drafts and the final version of *Walden* evincing, as Buell notes, a "changing ratio of homocentrism to ecocentrism" as the proportion of material on nature's facticity increased (121). The project of cobbling together a "fable" for nonhuman encounter that does not aggrandize the self precedes, succeeds, and surpasses the Maine experience. "Ktaadn" takes its place as an episode in a process of composing that culminates (but does not conclude) with *Walden*.

Buell finds "two forms of relinquishment" prevailing in American environmental writing: one the "relinquishment of goods," the other, "more radical relinquishment" that of "individual automony itself." *Walden* is a core instance of the former, the "epic of voluntary simplicity"; "Ktaadn," upon my reading, turns out to concern the latter, a loosening of what Buell calls "the authority of the superintending consciousness," an experience which may give pleasure yet "can also be unsettling" (144–45). They're treated separately by Buell, yet viewing the "Ktaadn" climax as an episode in the Walden experience helps us see these two relinquishments as continuous, subsumed alike under the logic and imprimatur of retreat. As Thoreau's own reformulations of Walden (and *Walden*) tend increasingly to the ecocentric, so an element of self-relinquishment (rather than self-sufficiency) figures more heavily therein, manifested in attention more to natural processes than to the human works that preoccupy both *Walden*'s first chapter, "Economy," and the earlier episodes of the "Ktaadn" narrative. "Ktaadn" enacts a formal logic more broadly discernable in *Walden*, its manufactured climax rehearsing the most "unsettling" dimensions of an ascetic trajectory described in both.

Yet that climax is not uniformly unsettling after all. Though the summit "crisis" is generally discussed as unrelievedly negative in its effects, we should not overlook how thrilling is the experience of nature's extremity as Thoreau depicts it, with what manifest enthusiasm he deploys a rhetoric of threat. Even as he asserts that the "grating of his ribs" is set to relinquish a vital essence, he insists that when he descends he is "compelled to" (65), not eager to. Perhaps this is bravado; certainly it derives from a rhetoric of the sublime that, in Burkean form, is ever a function of terror and thrill. Even more, I think, it reflects an ascetic impulse, of a sort that Geoffrey Galt Harpham regards as containing and surpassing the category of the sublime—an impulse to self-sacrifice, in terms of which dissolution of personal identity is an attraction, consonant with recognition of the nonhuman. In *Walden* Thoreau figures a fact as something that, fully recognized, will cut you in two and kill you; yet it's "facts" he is after. Similarly, in the climax of "Ktaadn," his evocation of identity's loss out on a "wing of the universe" bears traces of longing even as it speaks of fear. Again, this drama of the self's dissolution and reconstitution has much to do with the paradigm of retreat, by which identity itself may be figured in or among the artifacts systematically relinquished.

I will conclude with one further gloss on the subject of Thoreau's Katahdin "crisis." However disturbing his summit experience may appear, the fact remains: Thoreau goes back. The upshot of the "Ktaadn" trip includes its repetition in the other two narratives of *The Maine Woods*; the crisis of "Ktaadn," whatever its bifurcations and ambivalences, cannot help but be read in light of these returns. In this respect, and on the account of the story's composition I have given, the true center of "Ktaadn" might be found not in the loss of "contact" but in the dream of painted fish—a bounty and beauty from nowhere human, encountered in a visionary landscape over which the mountain presides. Fish with definable fin rays; mountain of hard matter. And by now, a common dream.

CHAPTER THREE

The Subject of *The Desert*

Of no account you who lie out there watching. . . .
　　　　Mary Austin, *The Land of Little Rain*

[W]hen you begin to consider the situations
behind the tactics of expression, you will find
tactics that organize a work technically *because*
they organize it emotionally. . . . Hence, if you
look for a man's *burden*, you will find the principle
that reveals the structure of his unburdening.
　　　　Kenneth Burke, *The Philosophy of Literary Form*

The love of nature is after all an acquired taste.
　　　　John C. Van Dyke, *The Desert*

Books of nature writing from *Walden* to the present often take a place name for a title or incorporate some place name therein, some "Sand County" to be an almanac for, a "Tinker Creek" for pilgrimage. This holds for John C. Van Dyke's *The Desert* (1901) as well, only the "place" entitling the book is broader, more generic than these others, seeming to refer less to a particular destination than to a general subject. On my shelves, the titles most resembling it belong to field guides and tourbooks—*Grasslands*, *Eastern Forests*, *Desert Southwest*—the names of whose authors are present but not prominent on their spines. They are informational, expository—not all that literary.

　　In some measure, the impression its title imparts is borne out by a look between its covers.[1] *The Desert* is not a story or memoir, essentially, but a book of information on the subject of "the desert." As exposition, it seeks to "expose" this subject with an exhaustiveness evident not just in

the wide-ranging categories of its chapter headings but in subheadings
spaced along wide outside margins, two or three to a page, and gathered
in the table of contents, in something of the manner of textbooks. It
seems a book to be referenced, not reverenced—an unlikely candidate
for a literary reading.

Yet *The Desert* is no textbook, no generic square peg forced into a
round hole of reader response. Its appeal in literary terms has in fact been
established from the start. Here, for example, is the response of the original reviewer for *The Spectator* of London: "The reader who once submits
to its spell will hardly lay it aside until the last page is turned." Such a
rhetoric of enthrallment is associated more with "novelistic" than informational writing. Spell-casting is a literary entailment.

The stock claim of compulsive page-turning may help to sell
books—and in this case, was intended to do just that, for the endorse-
ment cited is drawn from blurbs for *The Desert* listed in an ad at the
back of a later Van Dyke book (*The Money God*, 1908). But it does not
get us far toward explaining the "spell" of a book of fact which is, as I've
said, essentially not a story. More particular leads occur in the ad's other
blurbs. For instance, the reviewer for *The Athenaeum* of London, calling
the book "strong wine" compared to "the tepid rose-water" of garden
nature books, observes: "Mr. Van Dyke unquestionably knows his desert;
he has the true wanderer's eye for its essential fascination." We find this
reviewer at once touting the author's factual command of his subject,
associating this grasp of facts with something "essential," and suggesting
(or presupposing) that grasp of both fact and essence is proper to the role
of a "true wanderer." An untrue or ersatz wanderer, presumably, would
lack this grasp, either through not having truly seen (lacking that "eye")
or not having really wandered. On these terms it follows that the very
success of the book—its "fascination"—must be testament to a personal
history of an exemplary sort, a history "true" in its particularity (since
this is "his desert," not just anyone's) yet recognized and valued as a
type. If the book is not itself a story, still it must be underwritten by a
story, if its "essential fascination" is to be properly accounted for.

Another laudatory blurb, this from the *Atlantic Monthly*, fixes more
particularly this sense of a covert personal history. Remarks the reviewer:
"The writer's personality is carefully subordinated, but one cannot help
feeling it strongly; that of a man more sensitive to color than to form,
enthusiastic, but with a stern hand on his own pulse." The sense of a
personal presence held in check—a presence somehow more impressive

for having been thus disciplined and meted out—is seconded by Van Dyke's modern commentators. Two are most notable. First is Richard Shelton, whose Introduction to the 1980 reprint edition of *The Desert* still offers the first word on Van Dyke for most current readers.[2] The book, says Shelton, is

> about the desert, not about the man. Van Dyke never intrudes upon his subject. He is merely an observer, although a passionate one, who records, explains, and sometimes comments. The reader who wants an account of the author's adventures . . . will have to look elsewhere. (xvii)

Yet this very reluctance to "intrude," coupled with the sense of "passion" subordinated, seems only to fan desire for word of "the author's adventures" among such readers as Shelton, who proceeds to attempt to satisfy this desire by constructing his own narrative of the author's wanderings. A second commentator, Peter Wild, has even more than Shelton sought to fill in what Van Dyke elides, in articles, forewords to Van Dyke reprints, a monograph on the author, and a detailed editing of Van Dyke's own previously unpublished autobiography. Like Shelton, Wild at once praises the author's literary self-abnegation, which he regards as "noble," yet regards it as a deficiency to be remedied through literary biography.[3] It would seem these commentators flout Van Dyke's example of refusing to "intrude upon his subject"—except their subject is not the desert but Van Dyke himself.

That is, their subject is Van Dyke *as* a subject, a directing, spectatorial presence felt as pervading or lapping into the texts that bear his name. With this talk of "subjects," we focus in upon grounds for the "literary attention" accorded this essentially informational book. In his collection of essays claiming such attention for works of "literary nonfiction" in general, Chris Anderson offers a definition of literature as not an elitist body of texts but "a way of looking at the world, a way of knowing, a form of inquiry—concrete, dramatic, *grounded in a self*" (*Literary* xix, emphasis added). There is a multiple valence to this definition, which maps onto the several senses, commonplace and specialized, of "subject." Literature may be taken as residing in any text that evinces such a grounding in a self or self-aware "subject." Or literature may represent "a way of looking" at any text at all, so that poem, field guide, or phone book alike may be "subject to" acts of literary reading. Or it may be thought that groundedness in a self is manifested precisely by virtue of "concrete" and/or "dramatic" treatment, such that any "subject," any content area or category, may be given a "literary" treatment by dint of detail and drama. All these senses may be superimposed on the *Athenaeum* blurb cited above: "Mr. Van Dyke unquestionably knows his desert [his subject]; he has the true wanderer's [that subject's] eye for its essential fascination [to which he's subject]." In his "noble" but not total self-effacement, our subject is subjected to his subject.

We may pull together these stray senses of "subject" by attending to what composition scholar Susan Miller remarks about "the subject of composition." There is "a twofold prospect" to this "subject," says Miller. First is its sense as "academic subject": the "sense of subject as content" proper to any disciplinary "field." But this claim entails a second sense:

> Content, the body of knowledge within a field, also implies a human subjectivity of a particular sort, a characterization of those who learn and profess its methods, solve its problems, and take seriously its most prominent issues. And this subjectivity works to create a field's content, often in covert ways. A "subject" is thus not a static body of knowledge, but an affective space. . . . The "content" of any field is realized only in relation to those who participate in it. (84)

Subject as content and subject as self are not separate but reciprocally implicated, defining each other. And this "twofold prospect" further involves our third sense, for a "subjectivity" thus "characterized" is in a sense "subject to," even "subjected" to the methods, problems, and issues of the field.

In this formulation, then, the sense of a "field" as a "static body" is replaced by "affective space." Like "field," "body" and "space" are both spatial metaphors, but the latter is filled in or occupied *in time* through an activity of "characterization." It is a space no longer "static" but *narrativized*. This view of a "subject" is different in that it moves to recover the reiterated *actions*—especially pedagogical actions—by which the configuration of a discipline is continually being reestablished.[4]

I want to draw a general implication from all this en route to particular observations on the multifold "subject" of Van Dyke's desert. This positing of two opposing senses of "subject"—one a dynamic, temporalized "affective space," the other a "static body of knowledge" —

rather neatly recapitulates the paired dimensions of personal experience and scientific information by which nature writing is characterized. Historically, a narrative element to the domain of nature writing emerges as the experiential dimension begins to rival the informational in visibility. Such narrative, I am arguing, is prone to be figured as a retreat from the human, whether it follows a logic of scientific exclusivity of attention — framing out features incidental to the "subject" at hand — or one of experiential or spiritual "fronting" of "essential facts" unattainable within cultural precincts.

Yet it should be clear that these paired dimensions are not simply complements or alternatives but in some measure, rivals — just as to Miller, subject as "affective space" stands opposed to subject as "static body." The atemporal configuration or "single thought" of a work of nature writing, then, is represented in the place name that entitles it: a "static" or persisting place where the writer has been and the reader, in principle, can come to be too. But the narrative of retreat that frames or informs the work will be marked by negotiations between the experiential and informational — between the affective space figured in an individual "subject's" movement through the place, and the impersonal understanding of the place abstracted from this. This understanding of place as "subject" is in principle endlessly replicable (any reader employing similar methods could come into it there) and hence "timeless."

These abstract considerations translate to particular writing choices for the likes of John C. Van Dyke. The notion of subject (static content *and* temporal characterization) as affective space is useful in considering a writer whose "literary" effects bespeak a certain personality or "character" yet whose (generic, disciplinary) methods, problems, and issues call for and center upon impersonality. Effects of personality may be discussed, of course, in terms of (atemporal) "style" or "voice." But the efforts of Shelton and Wild at biographical restoration of this reluctant authorial subject should put us in mind of narrative possibilities: the choices made by a writer mindful of having a particular story or stories to tell but intent on his (nonnarrativized, nonhuman) subject and thus guarded, parsimonious with tokens of a narrativized, human self.

Thus *my* subject here is the author's subjectivity, or ethos, as obliquely enacted in narrative strategies. For this subjectivity, as it happens, *is* enacted at intervals in stretches of straight narration, especially in *The Desert*'s opening and closing, though in ways that betray constraints the author locates himself as subject to. There is, first, the "impersonal" character of informational writing to be observed, consistent with the book's claims to factual validity. This imperative is amplified by the logic of retreat, of entry to or contact with the nonhuman, mandating a focus away from personal, social particulars, if not (impossibly) from "self" altogether. This logic, in turn, contrasts with and entails the need to establish a certain ethos, the character of the "true wanderer" qualified to pronounce upon, to offer a testament to, the character of a place. The literary interest of *The Desert* resides largely, I think, in the ways that its author manages these demands of his "subject," employing true story that is not specifically *his* story to produce a work with the effect the *Atlantic* reviewer describes, of a subordinated personality strongly felt.

My procedure will be first to examine Van Dyke's storytelling in the narrative that comprises his opening chapter, through which he "positions" himself as a speaker, at once intimating and withholding personal history in ways that conduce to readerly participation in the nonhuman place he takes as his subject. This chapter, "The Approach," draws my attention for the ways it follows and enacts, while in certain ways reversing, the terms of the narrative of retreat I elaborated in my analysis of "Ktaadn." To say that the terms are reversed is to say that the same terms remain at work, and with regard especially to the drama of the "natural" and the "artifactual," I want to show how this is the case. Then I will counterpose my analysis of this narrative to the biographical creations, the Van Dyke stories, of Shelton and Wild, whose efforts to frame *The Desert* might from its own author's perspective be taken (to echo Thoreau) not as pertinent but rather as impertinent, in the sense that they reinsert what the author is at pains to crop or filter out. More crucially, they tend also to filter out some less savory sentiments the author had no qualms about expressing, and in so doing render less complex and problematical the destination of retreat as Van Dyke figures it, not to mention his (and our) construction of what he is retreating from.

Since the presence and propriety of the biographical "subject" is part of what's at issue, I will discuss the retreat narrative with which the book opens—the "going out" narrated in "The Approach"—*without* first recapping biographical particulars of the little-known John C. Van Dyke—in this way departing both from habitual expository practice and from the manner of reading that his books, in their reissued, "introduced" versions, are in this day likely to receive.[5]

NEGOTIATING "THE APPROACH"

Who is approaching what, and from where? The who and what seem clear enough initially, manifest on the title page: the writer, Van Dyke, approaches the place, "the desert." This generic place turns out to have a portal, though, a more particular feature by which entrance will be effected, evoked as the chapter opens:

> It is the last considerable group of mountains between the divide and the low basin of the Colorado desert. For days I have been watching them change color at sunset. . . . They are lonesome looking mountains lying off there by themselves on the plain, so still, so barren, so blazing hot under the sun. For-saken of their kind, one might not inappropriately call them the "Lost Mountains"—the surviving remnant no doubt of some noble range that long centuries ago was beaten by wind and rain into desert sand. (1)

It is clear that this writer is more dramatizing than reporting his approach. The present tense of re-creation, the placement *in medias res* some "days" beyond the start of the journey: these are conventional narrative attributes, readily registered and absorbed. And it is manifest that, in heading for a place so "lonesome" and "forsaken," this writer is approaching a "lost" condition, as well. All in all, it's a Romantic scene, with the range itself standing in for a picturesque ruin.

It is suspenseful, too. If there is "no doubt" about the mountains' past status, still there is no telling what the range will hold for the one approaching. Worn though they are, the mountains "may prove quite formidable heights" from up close, but neither "those with whom I am stopping" nor the native Papagoes can say, since they never go there themselves and don't even have a name for them (1). "Evidently they are considered unimportant hills, nobody's hills, *no man's* range; but *nevertheless* I am off for them in the morning at daylight" (2; my empha-ses). "Nevertheless" in this statement is a gesture of nonchalance: the sense grows that the relation is causal, that *"therefore* I am off for them" would be a truer way to put this. The destination of retreat construed as nonhuman could hardly be more purified.

In this dramatizing of the nonhuman destination, of "no-man's range," the question of from what cultural precincts this approach might originate gets even more lost than the mountains. The unnamed range gets dubbed the "Lost Mountains" quickly enough, but the names of human departure points are submerged in the earlier, unnarrated stages of the writer's journey, on the prior side of the "divide" he has crossed. This "approach" starts where the names end, evidently. Those people with whom the writer is "stopping" certainly go unnamed and unremarked; they rate mention only in terms of what they lack, namely, any knowledge of the object of the writer's fixation. Mention of this stopping, in fact, unsettles any fixed sense of from what vantage the writer has "for days" been watching the mountains at sunset. Has he been travelling for days with the mountains coming progressively into view? Has he been stopped for days partaking of an anonymous hospitality while regarding the faraway hills? There is no way to say, and in the terms of this recounting, no need to. The story begins in the fixation.[6]

This account of a nonhuman destination ratifies the sentiments of what might be called the approach to "The Approach": the book's preface-dedication. A larger cultural script underwriting the pending story of approach is evoked from the opening:

> After the making of Eden came a serpent, and after the gorgeous furnishing of the world, a human being. Why the existence of the destroyers? What monstrous folly, think you, ever led Nature to create her one great enemy—man! Before his coming security may have been; but how soon she learned the meaning of fear when this new Oedipus of her brood was brought forth! And how instinctively she taught the fear of him to the rest of her children! (v)

The Eden story is offered as analogy, of course, to a contemporary tale of a paradisiacal Nature ruined by human encroachment. But the analogy is no sooner offered than compromised, as this Nature is depicted as both creator and garden, both agent and object of humanity's malign emergence. Then in a further step, Nature's agency is itself whisked away: the human "Oedipus" is only passively "brought forth," more an unpleasant, unsought surprise than an intentional creation. Female, maternal Nature, it turns out, far from being free to choose even in folly, operates "instinctively" even in her teaching. What she teaches is "the meaning of fear," which in the terms of this myth is nonexistent prior to the late arrival of "man." The acquisition of this lesson of fear is manifested in current natural fact, for "after centuries of association" with "man," wild animals all "fly from his approach" (v).

Just as female "Nature" undergoes a series of implicit transformations in this myth, so too does the male "enemy." This analog to the "serpent," the original source of fear, is cast first as "a human being," then as "man," then as "his civilization," before which Nature's other "children" all flee. Finally, predictably, this narrowing of the human adversary from humans in general to paternal civilization in particular comes to this: "Even the grizzly . . . flinches as he crosses the white man's trail. The boot mark in the dust smells of blood and iron" (v–vi). The full sequence thus enacts an equivalence between "human being" and "white man," with the rest of creation tacitly identified with a female Nature that is at once perfect victim, thrall to the automatism of instinct, yet somehow, in her "folly," responsible for her own subjugation.

Two details of the historical Van Dyke are so expressive of the stresses this myth stretches to accommodate or repress that I will break my resolution and include them here. First, the wanderer Van Dyke himself reportedly wore moccasins, not a "white man's" boots, along his own trails—ones he claimed to have made himself from a Sioux pattern learned in boyhood. Second, the writer Van Dyke was an intimate of iron-maker (and sometime blood-spiller) Andrew Carnegie, whose autobiography he edited. This "preface-dedication," in fact, is inscribed "to A.M.C.," and the text proceeds to address a "you" that seems closely identified with the bearer of those initials, a particular individual with a representative standing: "you, and the nature-loving public you represent" (ix).[7] The functions and transformations of second-person address will occupy us further as we proceed along Van Dyke's "approach." I mention these particulars to emphasize how equivocal must be this writer's own position in the orienting scheme, the patchwork of dichotomies and commonplaces, he sets forth here at the outset.

The writer acknowledges that the myth he recites is commonplace, though not that it is a myth. " 'Familiar facts,' you will say": this is the response he anticipates, as he proceeds through a litany of equally factual, equally familiar devastations upon the land. Last of the abuses he lists is the effect of the smoke and dust of civilization upon the clarity of air and light. With this, further attributes of this writer and the readers he presupposes come into view. Centuries of civilization, he insists, have literally obscured the light of the Old World, from Europe through Mesopotamia to the Ganges, rendering the air thick and colors artificial. In comparison, the air of the Sierra Madre or Montana, where "one can still ride . . . for days without seeing a trace of humanity," is untainted, transparent (vii). This writer is an aesthete, one to whom the quality of light matters supremely, and a well-travelled aesthete at that, who can pronounce with authority on atmospheric conditions across Eurasia and North America. And he appears to presume a reader with similar entitlements and experience, one he can instruct, "When you are in Rome again. . . look out and notice how dense is the atmosphere between you and St. Peter's dome" (vii): a reader who's done the Grand Tour and is likely to go again—A.M.C., evidently, and the leisure-loving public he represents.

Key remarks follow on the writer's motives and project, the motives essentially Romantic, the project a narrative of retreat:

> You will not be surprised then if, in speaking of desert, mesa and mountain I once more take you far beyond the wire fence of civilization to those places (unhappily few now) where the trail is unbroken and the mountain peak unblazed. I was never over-fond of park and garden nature study. If we would know the great truths we must seek them at the source. (viii)

This project of "transport" to the nonhuman sublime[8] follows directly from the comparison of Old and New World light, the sunsets of Rome versus those of Arizona. Not only is "the source" construed as (female) nonhuman Nature, then, but "the great truths" sought there are visual, spectatorial. And the writer, the aesthete, having been to that source, must stand in possession of those truths. They are not self-evident, though, no more than are the virtues of desert landscapes that habitually have been neglected, considered "profitless places for pilgrimages." Nor is the writer confident that the truths he has recognized there are transmittable: "The love of Nature is after all an acquired taste," a passion developed over time and not readily analyzed (viii). He cannot convey the full glory, only an "impression" of this source, "something of what I have seen in these two years of wandering" (ix). The desert deserves "a sacred poet" but has in the writer "only a lover" (ix).

Amid these apologies and disclaimers, what is there to serve as vehicle of the promised transport to the "source"? Disclaiming poetic prowess, the writer claims instead to offer a "record" that he hopes will be taken "as at least truthful. Given the facts," he continues, "perhaps the poet with his fancies will come hereafter" (ix). On its face, this all seems prudent and reasonable; but if these "facts" at all resemble the familiar facts" the writer opens with, we might take pause. For again, unheralded transformations are at work. Are the "facts" the writer would give of the sort called scientific or do they extend from personal "impression," matters of "taste" and its acquisition? Do they consist in particular events or in a general informational residue from the writer's "two years of wandering"? How is it that "facts" and a "truthful record" are construed as fit tribute or testament from "a lover"? What makes these "facts" a condition or ground for the poet's subsequent production of "fancies"? Equivalences are assumed between these prestigious terms and functions, but the manner of their sliding each into the next makes a sort of story in itself.

The story authorizing the story of "the approach" runs something like this, then. It begins with a fall of (aggressive, white, male, recent but already Old) human culture or "civilization" from (passive, native, female, original but always New) nonhuman Nature. The rift between culture and nature is manifested as "fact" not just in history but throughout the natural order. Sustained visual regard of that order in its pure form at its nonhuman "source" will net for the viewer a yield of fact. And within this fact, or from a "record" thereof, "great truths" may be sought and found. To arrive at the source, privy to fact, is to stand in proximity to these truths. The source is accessible only through solitary, near-invisible "wandering"; the collective "tramp of human feet" sullies the air, obscures the source, and dissipates great truths. But while fact is manifest in nature, the source is not necessarily: "The love of Nature is after all an acquired taste." Taste may be mysterious. But isn't it educable? The function of transport to the source must be to provide an uncertain, necessarily indirect education in taste, through the vehicle of "impression," which here means roughly the "fact" of "taste." If the transport of fact/impression can remain "truthful" while appearing to have occurred by a sort of flight, leaving no "human tracks," then so much the better.

It's within these parameters that "The Approach" proceeds, as we have begun to see. By a sort of transport, we readers have been lifted tracklessly off from civilization to a point within eyeshot of the first spot definitively marked as nonhuman: the "Lost Mountains." And from there the story proceeds.

But what story? We might suppose this is an account of the writer's own first "approach," a chronological starting point for the "two years of wandering" alluded to in the preface. But this assumption is not borne out in details of the narration that ensues. The present-tense account describes the early-morning ride through a desert still cool but soon to grow impressively hot, toward a mountain range apparently near in the clear air but perhaps much farther away than it looks. In his detailed grasp of how the day will unfold and of the vagaries of mirage and illusion, this writer, we can tell, is already well acquainted with the place he is approaching. "Who of the desert has not spent his day riding at a mountain and never even reaching its base?" he rhetorically asks (2), and the answer is clear: not him! He is already "of the desert," familiar with its ways, adventurous yet knowledgeable and prudent enough to turn back if, by noon, "the foot hills are not reached" (3).

So it turns out this is not a story of the writer's first approach; the episode narrated represents no fixed point within his term of wandering but just one of a series of embarkings to which this wanderer has long been habituated. It turns out rather that this is *your* first approach to "the desert," not your expert guide's. The story is your means of transport "beyond the wire fence," functioning to exhibit to you paradigmatic features of the desert milieu even as it purports to enact a particular espisode the writer is undergoing.

Shifts of subject from first to second person confirm that this approach is specifically meant as "yours." It is a measure of his submission to the "fact" of his subject that Van Dyke is, as a rule, sparing in his use of personal pronouns, and in those few he does use, is more likely to attribute subjectivity to a "you" than to his own "I." There are complications to the sorts of identification this practice may promote, given the several ways the second person can be used and taken, all of which this writer exploits. As we have seen in the preface, by "you" some particular addressee, like "A.M.C.," may be meant; or some more generalized addressee whose reactions the writer anticipates and responds to: "Familiar facts, you will say." Beyond these, the "you" may serve as a syntactic marker or cipher, equivalent to "one" or the French *on*, indicating habitual action or response, things that are the case for anyone. Van Dyke's first use of "you" in the narrative is an instance of this: having described the desert sunrise and remarked on how most creatures take cover then, he reports, "there is animal and bird life here though it is not always apprarent unless you look for it" (4). This is strictly informational; no "I" could reasonably stand in for this "you." But this use is not stable in what remains a narrative account; instead, the "you" turns into a character of sorts, a marker for an unspecified participant in specific events. A first-person subject *would* make sense replacing the "you" in this sequence:

There are plenty of reptiles, rabbits and ground squirrels quietly slipping out of your way; and now that the sun is up you can see a long sun-burned slant-of-hair trotting up yonder divide and casting an apprehensive head from side to side as he moves off. It is not often that the old gray wolf shows himself to the traveller. (5)

If this rare sighting is not enough, "you" proceed to spot the seldom-seen desert antelope, too. The topic of the passage remains informational—what animals are found in the desert—except what "you" are seeing now is not typical but exceptional. The animals you *might* see in the desert you *get to* see in this your vicarious approach. It's as if your expert guide can trot them out for you, while marking "your" experience as separate from the particulars of his own approach toward the mountain range, the account of which soon resumes in first person. "Fact" and "impression" are conjoined in this mode of address; what "you" are now "seeing" seems less and less necessarily what this writer actually saw at the place and time he is ostensibly reporting. He is reporting his own approach but making yours up.

It may be that these fortuitous sightings of "yours" are not fictionalized, exactly: perhaps both wolf and antelope actually did materialize before the writer at just the juncture noted in the narrated sequence of events. In this case, the "you" might serve yet another of its functions, as a stylized form of self-reference or self-address. But it does not seem likely that Van Dyke so employs it here. Not only do the events related seem too "staged"; such a usage would leave open the question as to why the second person alternates with the first person at all. Elsewhere, Van Dyke does use such a stratagem: in the narrative sequence that concludes this book, for instance, his "you" seems a species of "I".[9] With a writer so much more absorbed in his subject than self, though, even quite specific events may be rendered more perennial than personal when recounted in the second person—which of course is the point.

The situation, then, is this. In a book pronouncing its commitment to "fact," we're inclined to presume the truth value of the events reported in this opening narrative: all this, we suppose, must have actually happened. The first-person voice is expressive of this sense of personal testament. But the narrative, we learn, is no straightforward chronicle of the writer's wanderings. Its dramatized suspension in time and space joins with pronomial shifts to suggest that the account is paradigmatic, bearing a cumulative, generalized "impression." Use of the second-person evokes the perennial, participatory character of events. What happens at this destination must be telling, then, since indicative of this writer's entire "approach" to his "subject." It must constitute what Kenneth Burke calls a "representative anecdote" that is selected to convey, or that inadvertently betrays, central recognitions about the destination, the place and condition sought. Destination may even spell destiny, to the extent that the anecdote "perfects," as Burke says, the logic of the cycle of terms on which it's predicated, enacting in what happens certain transformations inhering in the relations among those terms.[10]

So what *does* happen? In an account resumed in first person, the writer reaches the base of the range, finds there an inaccessible wall, locates a point of access in a cleft in the wall, and begins a difficult ascent. As he proceeds he finds himself moving along the faint traces of what is evidently a game trail. Initially rough, the trail grows smoother and more regular, evincing signs of improvement that finally reveal it as the product of human hands. At the summit, the writer is astounded to discover a long-abandoned fortification, the remains of a human habitation. From this vantage on the summit, he speculates on the condition and fate of its vanished native inhabitants as he describes the sweeping prospect they would have commanded from that height. Finally, he rides back down the range's further side, musing on matters we will return to.

Thus it happens that this portal to a nonhuman realm becomes notable for its signs of human presence. This makes a good story, certainly, with elements of mystery and romance and a grand reversal of expectations. But how does it fulfill the paradigmatic expectations it creates, or "perfect" the logic of a cycle of terms? That is, what makes it a narrative of retreat? I indicated earlier that "The Approach" in a way reverses while keeping in play the general terms of retreat found in Thoreau's "Ktaadn." Thoreau details the diminishing signs of human intrusion that his party encounters until, alone near Katahdin's summit, he proclaims his recognition that the place is indeed "unhanselled," unmarked by human presence. Van Dyke does the reverse: he begins in a place and with a destination already marked as pure "nature" and by increments reveals it as a full-blown culture site. It's as if the writer set out as Muir for the Sierra and arrived as Schliemann at Troy. Yet if the terms of retreat are inverted here, still, they remain in play. The narrative trajectory is still shaped by a nature-culture opposition, with the natural and artifactual contending in the attention of the narrating subject, in what we might call a trial by artifact.

Two interrelated features further mark the writer's presence here as a condition of retreat. First, the writer remains *alone*, all the more so for having strayed across a place so manifestly deserted, one bearing "not the slightest evidence . . . that any living thing has passed . . . for many years" (8). Second, the place itself is depicted as only lightly marked by habitation and as well on its way toward being "reclaimed" by Nature. It contains "not a trace of pottery or arrow-heads," and other seemingly human traces cannot be clearly differentiated from the nonhuman: signs of fire may be volcanic or domestic; a rock by a pothole may or may not be a pestle (9). What looks to be a burial mound is topped by a blossoming yucca and a saguaro cactus whose shape has "the look of the cross," as if Nature's claim had already been staked (10).

Yet if what seems most pertinent about the vanished inhabitants at first is their absence, the writer's attention shortly turns to their presence, the circumstances of their survival in a place so barely habitable. As in "Ktaadn," the movement toward the nonhuman involves the issue of a place's habitability, of whether the "ground is prepared" there for humans or not. Habitability is not only a practical concern of the sort that Muir called "the bread problem" or for Van Dyke would be the water problem. Habitability is central in a logic of retreat generated from a nature-culture opposition. Absolute nature, by this logic, must be absolutely unpeopled. But it is liable to be unlivable, as well, since practically speaking, no humanly habitable place remains wholly uninhabited. If a natural place *does* accommodate humans, either its nature is not pure or its human denizens must be natural, that is, nonhuman, too.

It follows that if a human, in particular the writer, *is* in such a place, that person must be at some peril (or else the place itself must be). The question of one's persistence there—at all, or as "oneself"— generates drama.[11] Physical danger and privation are staples of outdoor adventures, of course, such as the mountaineering stories that Van Dyke himself poo-poohed for their thrills and hairbreadth escapes.[12] Yet in a narrative of retreat, the purpose of which is not to pass *through* or overcome but rather to dwell *within* nature, the issue of habitability is apt to take other forms. As in "Ktaadn," it may be displaced in psychic or metaphysical tensions that dramatize the core problem of passing from human to nonhuman realms: namely, the persistence of one's own human self, one's identity as a culture-bearer, presumably at odds with the nonhuman destination. In perfected form, the logic of retreat dicates an impossible double-bind, such that with regard to nonhuman Nature, you can't live with it and can't live without it.

But what Van Dyke stumbles across in this opening narrative turns out to be a perspective from which this bind can in some measure be circumvented. In speculating on the conditions under which the vanished inhabitants may have existed in a place so "lost" and barely habitable, the writer can span both poles of a dichotomy. Those whose traces he finds are people both wholly *belonging* to and wholly *missing* from the place marked as pure Nature. Imagining their situation, the writer can project in detail a human presence existing over time in a timeless, nonhuman place—a presence which, importantly, is not his own. The conundrum of retreat that Thoreau works out through self-dissolution, Van Dyke resolves by self-displacement— though it is the nature of the problem that neither can entirely succeed.

Projecting the point-of-view of the vanished denizens of this mountaintop, the writer commands all sorts of prospects, straddles all sorts of divides. He can dramatize points of identity with or difference from what he infers to have been the condition of these others, all while remaining alone and unseen within the nonhuman realm he occupies. In dwelling upon *their* trials and compensations he expresses his *own* manner of dwelling within the place. He details his own observations under the heading of what these others "surely . . . must have noticed" notwithstanding their points of imperception (14), projecting upon the vanished people his own regard for the qualities of silence and solitude "with which every desert wanderer eventually falls in love" (19). But following this expression of identity, difference is swiftly reestablished. The aesthete writer is moved to note that "the sun-tanned [i.e., nonwhite] people who lived on this mountain top never gave thought to" such rarefied visual effects as he himself can discern (19). "Content" in their incomprehension, they loved the desert but never even "knew why they loved it" (19–20).

One way this writer has of establishing his own subjectivity, then, is by dramatizing the subjectivity of imagined others. Unable to reflect upon their own condition, these natives are construed as an evolutionary intermediary, a point of traffic between the human and the (nonhuman) "natural." We cannot fail to remark profound and troubling ideological overtones to this approach, which we will proceed to shortly. It remains to summarize how the narrative of retreat we're tracing functions as an "approach" to the book as a whole.

Through the narrative action of this opening, the writer has contrived to cross a nonhuman portal and conduct "you" as reader into the perennial realm of fact from which the book that follows is taken to emanate. You are led to a position from which factual information is understood as "in-formed," issuing from a personal history of lived experience. Participating in that history, you can appreciate the justice of the assertion with which the writer opens the next chapter: "The first going-down into the desert is always something of a surprise" (23). *Yours* has been, surely, as conducted through the person of this writer. Yet at the same time your sense of the writer's history *as* personal is subordinated, made diffuse. Better yet, it is refracted: passing from temporal to perennial it breaks off, gets displaced, while remaining sharply delineated. It is important that the writer's "in-forming" experience be understood as lived, narratable action: the writer's ethos as expert inhabitant and "your" sense of participating or "dwelling" therein depend on this. But it is also important that lived action *not* be represented *as such* in all its novelty and particularity, not if this distracts from or displaces the impersonal "subject" at hand—for it is the very character of *this* sort of lived action, the action of retreat, to resist such distraction or displacement.

This situation instantiates what Harpham notes about "conversion" in autobiography: how it is at once necessary and impossible to imitate the actions of others. "Through conversion one is called simultaneously to imitation and to an original condition," asserts Harpham. "The 'theme' of conversion is the oscillating interplay between original and imitation, event and repetition" (*Ascetic* 42)—an interplay dramatized in Van Dyke's opening narrative. It follows that the effects Van Dyke's reviewers both past and current remark on, the simultaneous passion and self-subordination, issue from a form of *asceticism* as Harpham describes it: as "essentially a meditation on, even an enactment of, desire" (45), but one in which "the personal is the trivial . . . which must be sacrificed in the interests of form" (25). Desire, far from being some unreined, disordered personal emanation, is "inconceivable without *resistance*," for a desire satisfied is one that ceases to exist. Resistance is desire's intrinsic structuring element: the ascetic project "recognizes and manages . . . desire, by harnessing and directing resistance" (61—my emphasis). Through resistance, asceticism maintains a "capacity to structure oppositions without collapsing them, to raise issues without settling them" (xii). This capacity to structure and sustain ambivalence holds particularly with regard to *culture* at large, to which asceticism is universal:

> But this apparent anticulturalism [that of "the retreat of the early monastic heroes to isolated caves in the desert"] should not eclipse the fact that the Desert Fathers brought the Book to the Desert, and served as apostles of a textual culture in the domain of the natural. Asceticism neither condemns culture nor simply endorses it; it does both. Asceticism, we could say, *raises the issue* of culture by structuring an opposition between culture and its opposite. . . . [A]sceticism is always marked by ambivalence, by a compromised binarism. To contemplate the ascetical basis of culture, for example, is to recognize that an integral part of cultural experience is a disquiet, an ambivalent yearning for the precultural, postcultural, anticultural, or extracultural. (xii)

The concept of resistance is crucial in configuring this ambivalence, since it provides a way of sustaining "both opposition and relation" between "two apparently antagonistic terms—one fixed," like *soul* or *text*, "the other mobile," like *body* or *reader*.

Both this expanded notion of asceticism—as integral to those culturally imposed forms of self-denial we call ethics—and the specific historical phenomena the term designates, pertain to our consideration of the "desert wanderer" Van Dyke. The expanded sense is clearly *so* expanded that it encompasses narrative form in general, as Harpham freely claims. Its many points of consonance with the narrative of retreat need not be catalogued; they confront us at every turn. The notion of resistance is especially helpful to an understanding of how the "compromised binarism" of nature-culture—the former "fixed," the latter "mobile"—can be suspended without resolution in narrative forms of retreat. But there are more particular resonances between the monastic asceticism of the "Desert Fathers" Harpham refers to and the ways Van Dyke enacts his own "disquiet" before culture. Considering these, we may better account for the formal tactics the writer deploys in concluding his opening chapter, reading therein his resistance to temptations he has earlier half-wittingly sneaked in. Such a reading will bring us back foursquare upon the ideological tangle we shelved above, which stems from the implication that native peoples may be less human to the extent that they are more natural than "civilized" ones.

CACTUS AS CROSS

The conclusion of "The Approach" must surely be found distressing to postcolonial sensibilities, as just the sort of baldly imposed, ideologically freighted closure that gives narrative a bad name in some theoretical circles—a forced march between "moral orders," as Hayden White might have it. Recall that we've left our writer's imagined natives in a state of contentment they themselves are unable to account for. Speculating finally on the manner in which they perished—it does not occur to him that they may have just left—the writer himself takes his leave, heading back down the trail. As he does he muses:

> the fancy keeps harping on the countless times the bare feet must have rubbed those blocks of syenite and porphyry to wear them so smooth. Have there been no others to clamber up these stairs of stone? What of the Padres—were they not here? As I ride off across the plain to the east the thought is of the heroism, the self-abnegation, the undying faith of those followers of Loyola and Xavier who came into this waste many years ago. (20)

With this barest of segues, and to the exclusion of any detail of the descent (though descents, it must be said, are apt to be slighted this way), the writer launches a paean to the Jesuit missionaries, beside whose exploits even "the accomplishments of Columbus, of Cortez, of Coronado" must pale, so to speak (20). And as luck would have it, while the writer is enthusing on how "the sign of the cross" has "cast more men in heroic mould than ever the glitter of the crown or the flash of the sword," he turns "to take a final view of the mountain" where "something rears itself against the sky like the cross-hilt of a sword"—the saguaro cactus he had earlier likened to a cross, with the blooming yucca next to it "like a lamp illuminating it." The upshot is, though the Padres are gone, "the light of the cross still shines" for "the peon and the Indian" of the desert borders, as it no longer does for "the inhabitants of the fertile plains" (21–22):

> They [the Indians] and their forefathers have never known
> civilization, and never suffered from the blight of doubt. Of a
> simple nature, they have lived in a simple way, close to their
> mother earth, beside the desert they loved, and (let us believe
> it!) nearer to the God they worshipped. (22)

The "us" evoked in parentheses in this, its last line, is the chapter's sole
instance of the first-person plural, the sole conjoining of "I" and "you,"
posed in opposition to a native "they."

Incoherences small and large are evident in this closing section,
from the way the cross is first contrasted with then promptly likened to a
sword, to the manner in which missionaries are figured as defending the
indigens rather than enmeshing them in the snares of "civilization" and
"doubt." Most striking in a writer noted for accuracy with passion is the
anthropomorphizing, the blatant symbolic overlay of the cactus-yucca
"lit cross." It is a moral that, on its face, seems wildly incommensurate
with the story it tops off. Only acute tensions, one might suspect, could
lead Van Dyke to narrativize so crudely, to insist so resolutely on seeing
what isn't there.

To delineate these tensions, let us return to the polarities and transformations enacted in the preface, the "familiar facts" of the book's
quasi-Edenic initiatory myth. There, pure, beautiful, passive, feminine,
nonhuman nature is depicted as ravaged, made ugly and fearful by
humans, with the most "human" humans implied to be white males, the
bearers of "civilization" par excellence. To this catalog of polarities, we
can add that suggested above between the "simple" and the complex,
represented by "civilization." Plainly, passage into the "Lost Mountains"
constitutes a crossing of the divide these polarities describe. The boundaries the writer traverses through his archaeological speculations cannot
be those between peoples' degrees of "closeness" to nature—not with
people the opposite and enemy of nature. Instead, there is passage
between degrees of humanity. In some respects, against this tacit yard-
stick of "human being," the vanished people are projected as quite
human indeed. Notably, they are as fierce and bellicose as any imperial-
ist of the time: the writer envisions the band fleeing to the summit to
gain defensive position, to "yell back defiance" and loose "a shower of
arrows, spears, and bowlders" upon a more numerous enemy below
(10). But though indispensible, this "defiance" is to Van Dyke's in-
flamed Darwinian sensibility not peculiarly human but rather a com-

mon denominator of desert life: one could claim as much of a cactus.[13] Similarly, the repose which is the reverse of bellicosity, in which the writer locates an identity between all desert "wanderers" and "lovers," cannot be an exclusively human state: its "simplicity" is allied to nonhuman purity and developmental priorness, and its achievement, while desirable, is regressive, assimilable to instinct, divorced from self-knowledge.

That degrees of humanity are at issue here is clearest in the writer's remarks on the poorly refined aesthetic sensibility of native peoples. It is here that these others are exposed as deficient, less highly developed or evolved, incapable of seeing anything but "the same dull mesquite" though the white man "exhaust ingenuity" in his efforts to point out more rarefied visual effects (13). Recalling that Van Dyke in his preface has come near to equating aesthetic "impression" with "truth," we would expect this to be a serious shortcoming indeed. Yet the writer shows little confidence in the distinction; indeed, there is anxious doubt of the sort he fancies his primitives have been spared. He takes as granted that perceptual differences mean different levels of evolutionary development, but in this case "higher" does not mean better:

> A sensitive feeling for sound, or form, or color, an impressionable nervous organization, do not belong to the man with the hoe, much less to the man with the bow. It is to be feared that they are indicative of some physical degeneration, some decline in bone and muscle, some abnormal development of the emotional nature. They travel side by side with high civilization and are the premonitory symptoms of racial decay. (13)

This is race and class anxiety of pronounced cast, ambivalent in the extreme, with human difference constructed on a pair of scales, the "physical" and "emotional" in inverse proportion, and the type of the writer himself epitomizing civilized degeneracy. Still, the writer does not reject but cultivates, revels in, this "impressionable" aesthetic character, regarding himself, evidently, as a type both exalted and doomed.

His uneven notions of evolutionary process further complicate matters, as he vacillates over the import of such terms as "fit," "progress," and "survival." Upon first discerning the trail up the mountain, for instance, the writer spots what appears to be the print of a deer hoof, sharply defined as if fresh, but turning out to be petrified, ancient. His response is to contrast the print with the "carefully guarded" yet vanished tracks of past human conquerors, a contrast he reads as an irony:

"With what contempt Nature sometimes plans the survival of the least fit, and breaks the conqueror on his shield!" (7). The drama of this outburst obscures any sense of what it might mean to be "fit" yet fail to survive, what manner of "survival" may be read in a petrified print, or what Nature's "contempt" might have to do with the perverse yet predestined survival of lesser entities. But as a statement of the anxiety of a white male aristocracy at a particular historical juncture, the sentiment is precise.

Anxiety and contempt are further mingled in another of the writer's asides about evolutionary mechanism:

> The man of the Stone Age exists today with civilized man. Possibly he always did. And it may be that someday Science will conclude that historic periods do not invariably happen, that there is not always sequential evolution, and that the white race does not necessarily require a flat-headed mass of stupidity for an ancestor. (12)

While some critique of linear human development seems intuited here, Van Dyke takes this rather as a warrant to separate developmental lines altogether between stupid Stone Age "them" and intelligent white "us." Coupled with the dread of his own racial "degeneration" expressed on the very next page, this conjecture betrays a profoundly riven attitude. Anxiety over present racial potency infects both past and future: fear that the race was not always smart; fear it will not always be strong. For all his contempt of the "flat-headed" others, the writer seems if anything more confident finally of their status than his own, taking pains to assert the probable likeness in what these others "surely . . . must have noticed" notwithstanding their perceptual shortcomings (14). He claims for whites a "higher" perceptual apparatus grounded in physiological difference ("nervous organization"), yet sees this apparatus, his own most distinguishing feature, as degenerate and doomed. In salvaging *some* formal sensibility, some love of beauty among the projected native inhabitants, he moves to redeem his own character and viewpoint, which he has just assailed. If these others "must have noticed" what *he* so manifestly notices, perhaps he too can inhabit this uninhabitable domain.

By this long way about, we return to the problem of the chapter's ending. What does the writer accomplish by his late appeal to the Padres and the trumped-up cactus cross? Let us acknowledge first that the

ambivalences I've been describing make up a system of desire and temptation. Consider that all this occurs within a narrative of retreat, with the
developments at hand occuring mainly in the musings of the solitary
writer as he passes at last beyond all sign of the artifactual, his encounter
with which has "raised the issue of culture" where he might least have
expected it to arise. His passage turns out to have been a trial of sorts, in
which temptation is configured in resistance. Through his displacement
into the viewpoint of the imagined others, the writer enacts the temptation to sacrifice his own degenerate self and become all that those vanished past inhabitants are: namely, vanished (into the landscape), past
(developmentally prior, not fully "human," juvenilized), and an inhabitant, persisting by instinct, content in unconscious love of place. But
descent from the summit from which this prospect is comprehended signals a shift. The temptation to identify wholly with these others is
"resisted": held out, then turned upon, not rejected but poised in a relation that's not resolved. One version of self-sacrifice is swapped for
another, the conventional notion of heroism. The impulse to submit as
child to a desert Mother is not countered but overlaid by the reimposed
offices of the Fathers. An "official" asceticism is reasserted by fiat, in the
face of other, potentially contrary signs and logics, other incipient
sacrifices.

This shift of focus, abrupt as it is, comes in the nick of time to salvage key features of social identity for the writer and his likely readers.
The Jesuits are emissaries of "civilization" who (like iron) are "cast" in
the "mould" of heroism and likened to such conquerors as Cortez.[14] As
such, they would seem to be allied with the original evil, the "blood and
iron" deplored in the book's opening myth. But here, these heroes are
represented as *preserving*, not annihilating, primal virtue within the
desert realm. The Christian faith they bear, figured in the lit-cactus
cross, has innoculated the natives against "the blight of doubt" associated with a "civilization" they've supposedly "never known." If this tale
seems contradictory, think what absolution it might constitute to white
male "lovers of Nature" who are also financiers, industrialists, and art
collectors, or middle-class aspirants to such status. Among its guilt-
assuaging effects: it as much as asserts that the vanished indigens the
writer has been dwelling upon are not really gone at all but instead persist, essentially untouched, bearing not despite but *through* the ministrations of the Fathers all the entitlements of a passive, innocent, feminized
nature. They are ("let us believe it!") put in their place.

And their place is the desert fringes, the margins. "The light of the cross still shines along the borders of this desert land" (21), and it's the borders to which the people are relegated. Henceforth, after the passage through the "Lost Hills" that even the Papagoes don't enter, there's scarcely a word about another human, not until another summit ascent narrated at the book's end—a climb back out of the desert to a height from which are espied the distant habitations of Southern California. Until this reemergence, the condition of retreat is preternaturally pure: the desert "subject" at last has the place to itself.

VERSIONS OF VAN DYKE

A movement of retreat is necessarily a flight from human history, one which as "natural history" is narrativized and reentered in historical scripts. The relation is an ascetic one of resistance, of structured opposites and counterparts, with retreat proclaiming the virtue of its evasions even as it is converted in text. Knowing what the solitaire "goes out" from in human history does not exhaust the recognitions entered into through retreat. But even so, those recognitions are historically informed.

I will do no more than sketch impressions of the historical milieu from which Van Dyke's book effects retreat. It was an epoch culminating, in the years just before Van Dyke wrote, in what Higham calls a "reorientation of American culture," a shift the effects of which remain widespread in our time. This thorough-going turn against "the restraint and decorum" of Victorian society was manifested in "a demand for vivid and masterful experience" in numerous spheres of cultural life—in recreation, popular music, the circumstances of women—all in reaction to an "advanced state in the mechanization of life," emblemized by the introduction of the time clock into workplaces during the early 1890's ("Reorientation" 27). Events of the years preceding had been as frenetic and upsetting as "Gilded Age" mores were staid, marked by rampant urbanization, industrialization, corporate monopolism, cycles of boom and bust, and labor unrest, suppression and violence: Henry Frick crushing the Homestead Strike while Carnegie fished in Scotland (Painter 111–12). Large-scale immigration had swelled cities with strange new arrivals, who were met with proliferating bigotry, nativism, and the formation of "scientific" racisms: a hundred lynchings the year *The Desert* was published (166).

Folded into this setting is the cult of nature, of special prominence in the cultural reorientation of the day.[15] Nature's rejuvenative effects on a degenerating Anglo manhood were much touted. Museums of natural history were instituted, with anthropology and archaeology understood as continuous with the central project of "preservation" of nature through collection and taxidermy. Their boards of directors included scions and financiers prominent in two nascent "progressive" movements, conservation and eugenics (Haraway, *Primate* 55–57). Controversies over nature's representation could even command the front pages. When John Burroughs, celebrity nature-sage, unleashed to a national audience (and a president's approbation) his "Nature Faker" charges of anthropomorphism and fact-fudging among nature-writing rivals, one of his targets, Ernest Thompson Seton, opted to confront Burroughs in person—at a literary dinner hosted by Carnegie. He buttonholes Burroughs while the latter is chatting with Twain and Howells (Lutts 47–48). "John o' the Mountains" Muir goes cruising to Alaska with the august party of E. H. Harriman. "John o' the Hills" Burroughs camps out with the likes of Edison and Ford. And "John o' the Desert" Van Dyke fly-fishes in Scotland with Andrew Carnegie.

The difference is that there *is* no "John o' the Desert," Van Dyke bearing nothing like the public personae enjoyed, endured, or employed by these other literary naturalists.[16] Not that he'd have welcomed a profile so high—to the contrary, in fact, as we'll find as we venture out on the biographical turf I've roped off to this point. Considering the historical rifts and suppurations I've alluded to, to which this author was especially subject, it's no wonder Van Dyke *as* a subject in some ways sought to disappear into his books. He was accomplished at so doing, above all in *The Desert*, which is why it's been widely read and has persisted in ways his other works have not. In it, "the desert," while remaining alluringly indeterminate in reference, acquires the integrity of a single place recognizable as such both in factual terms and as the focus of a passion.[17] I have not much discussed the attention to landforms and effects of light, to plants and insects and animals, that make up the bulk of the book and constitute its enduring appeal. That appeal would be more circumscribed, though, were it not for the efforts of Van Dyke's commentators to narrativize the author's own history and character in ways the author himself is loathe to do.

The Van Dyke "lives" offered by Richard Shelton and Peter Wild comprise a telling exhibit in what Kenneth Burke calls "terministic screens," the "reflection, selection, and deflection" of reality through a given terminology or stance.[18] This process is inevitable—no term is transparent, no perception unscreened—yet it is also means-tested, so to speak, with terminologies turning maladaptive if they select too narrowly or deflect too widely. Critical scrutiny is needed to recalibrate the attitudinal calculus or melt down cracked abstractions to be recast in fresh metaphors. The narrative operations of reputation—of being "considered again"—are central to both the perpetuating and refreshing of terministic screens. As instances of reputation, these Van Dyke lives are instructive in several regards. They stand in high relief, for one thing, when compared with the author's own minimal self-narrating and with the paucity of such accounts in the intervening years. They contrast in the ways they narrativize the author's retreat and mediate its appeal to generations of new readers, especially those whose motives are participatory. Yet in reinscribing retreat with ideological entitlements by turns consonant with and incognizant of the author's own—"reflecting" and "deflecting"—they perpetuate suspect tropes for retreat and reimpose problems we've seen crop up in the interstices of the exemplary text. I offer these as cautionary tales in the double valence Buell finds in nature writing, how the same form can bear ideological content variously accomodationist or transformational, frequently all unwitting of such import, since filtered through a terministic screen.

I will start with aspects of the biographical subject that both Shelton and Wild incorporate; the character of their "selection" is such that we will not get far with this before splitting off into their divergent accounts. John C. Van Dyke, as we've already inferred, was indeed an aesthete of prominent stripe: a professor of art history at Rutgers College and head librarian at the neighboring New Brunswick Theological Seminary, a popular, much-published commentator on art appreciation, an Art for Art's Sake enthusiast and follower of Ruskin. These credentials were well established by the time he embarked upon the "two years of wandering" in the desert referred to in his preface. Both Shelton's introduction to *The Desert* and Wild's monograph study of author and book (*John C. Van Dyke: The Desert*) dramatize this embarcation, commencing their own texts with a scene and image thereof. Both openings capitalize on the evident incongruity of an art professor and librarian, over forty years old and sick with asthma to boot, venturing on horseback alone and directionless into fabulously inhospitable terrain. Introducing the scenario in this manner straightaway raises the questions of how the author survived and why he persisted in this courageous and incongruous undertaking.

Shelton's answers are partial in a way that is bound to color reception of the text. Any "introduction" will do this, certainly, by design; yet Shelton's "selection" effects a "deflection" of substantial degree, with regard to the question of how Van Dyke could persist in the strange terrain. It's a question that Lawrence Clark Powell, literary historian of the Southwest, heard another desert writer phrase as "how a desert tenderfoot could have written that book" (1976—unpaginated)—a question Powell set out to answer, the fruits of his search informing his introduction to a previous reprint edition of the book.[19] The very first thing Powell mentions about the author's life is something Shelton barely gets around to: namely, that Van Dyke, far from a "tenderfoot" notwithstanding his asthma and his academic cachet, had evidently learned his way around outdoors during a boyhood on the fringes of civilization in Minnesota. Despite a professed intent to fill us in on "the man" rather than the book (xxviii), Shelton does not mention this upbringing, except in a passing allusion (xix). He draws upon the same biographical resources as Powell had unearthed and offers a detailed reconstruction of the author's movements and habits in the desert. But in his account, the incongruous image of the sick librarian in the sticks is permitted to stand.

I am suggesting no chicanery on Shelton's part but rather an emphasis, or better, a narrative line to promote. Shelton narrativizes the author's wandering as a peak experience: the climax and culmination of a heroic life story, ascetic in its amatory and sacrificial overtones. In this story, the hero, "neither young nor in good health," seems equipped for his venture exclusively by virtue of a single, extraordinary feature: he wields "two of the most highly trained mechanisms for visual perception in America—his eyes" (xi). Rather like a comicbook superhero, his prior experience and present powers are distilled into a single potent entailment. Indeed, this hero's past is of interest mainly to the extent that it prepares him to purge the dross of his past, his life theretofore having been spent in the effort (here Shelton cites Blake) "to cleanse and purify the doors of his perception" so as to see the desert world "as it is, infinite" (xiii). He succeeds—on our behalf, as it were—at this work of seeing the place clear, his arrival "almost a miracle . . . as if he had been sent" to preserve for us in writing the once-pristine, now-defiled realm (xiv). Then he fades from the stage, leaving as relic his exemplary book, "a model . . . before which other writers bow" (xvii).

Detailing the author's exploits and illness, Shelton answers the question of how and what he survived. Why he persisted, Shelton answers by recourse to a core metaphor, a cultural commonplace he insistently pursues: a metaphor of romantic love.[20] Shelton takes up the author's remark about being not a poet but "only a lover" of the desert and parlays this into an argument, characterizing the wanderer's extreme behavior as "an enormous flirtation with death and a love affair with the desert's beauty" (xiv). The desert landscape is a woman, not a spouse but a mistress, infatuation with whom is as perilous as it is delightful.[21] The trials and attrition of this illicit affair amount to self-sacrifice, even martyrdom: Van Dyke's "affair with the desert was a love affair in the grand manner, to which he gave himself entirely and for which he risked his life each day" (xvi). There's even a sense in which Van Dyke *did* die for his beloved, Shelton implies, having sacrificed his old self. After illness and exertion, he returned to his home back East "a far different man than the one who had left" (xv), his youth effectually ended, his energy sapped. He is spent not just physically but creatively, his later books being distinctly lesser works than this one into which "he poured all his passion and sensitivity" (xvi) and to which others, in turn, pay obeisance. So seriously does Shelton take this metaphor of romantic love, he fudges its boundaries as metaphor, suggesting that Van Dyke's desert infatuation left him sexually spent in a literal sense as well. His desert stint, suggests Shelton, was Van Dyke's "last grand affair; and he never married" (xvi). This assertion, rhetorically potent as the "clincher" to the "grand affair" paragraph, is remarkable in what it overlooks and assumes. It overlooks that Van Dyke (as Shelton himself points out in his first sentence) was *already* forty-two years old when he ventured out on the desert, and had presumably had ample opportunity to marry before then had he been inclined to. And it assumes he must have been inclined to marry, had his desert "mistress" not wrung him out so, though there is no particular evidence of such inclination.

In sum, Shelton offers a life concentrated in a single experience and "converted" into a single exemplary text. What precedes this episode is preparation; what follows is fall-off, a descent and husk. To dwell on or even mention Van Dyke's prior life in nature would be to suggest the possibility of other "great loves" or amorous escapades—not the plot he has in mind. Shelton wants a desert that lures the unsuspecting professor in, slips his glasses off, makes him and unmans him. He sells *The Desert* as severest romance, the extract of a life reduced to a single passion. And it's *The Desert* that Shelton is selling. His tale of love and self-sacrifice, lodged between the preface and first chapter of the reprint edition, may mediate for current readers Van Dyke's own exclamation-ridden Victorian style and hyperdetailed attention to visual phenomena, unfamiliar to readers weaned on photos and film. These features may then be read as a sort of dialect, lines emitted by a particular character whose story of devotion Shelton has sketched for us. Shelton mediates as well this character's failure to tell the story for himself.

Peter Wild assumes a similar mediating function in narrating a life not eager to narrate itself. He has taken this narrating as a mission, offering "lives" of Van Dyke in articles, a monograph and forewords to other Van Dyke reprints, and squiring Van Dyke's own autobiography into print.[22] Like Shelton, Wild is committed to the notion that knowledge of this author's life enhances understanding of his work. But as the range of his activity indicates, the life Wild offers is not condensed in a single episode centered upon *The Desert*. Wild is invested in a narrative of Van Dyke's entire career, in the full sense of that word: his Van Dyke is an American picaro, an expert and flexible mover between cultural spheres, an adventurer and bon vivant, master of the varied situations he enters. This characterization is evident in the introduction to *The Open Spaces*, most autobiographical of the books Van Dyke himself saw into print. Wild begins with a stock depiction of the late-nineteenth-century West as a region of "colorful characters" drawn to "new lands" because of the "fantasies of childhood" to be enacted there: "a stage, not only for empire but also a place where individuals acted out their dreams and delusions" (vii). Not that Wild depicts his author as conqueror or crank: he allies him instead with a high-minded subset of this larger cast of colorful dreamers, "scientists, artists, photographers, and writers driven by curiosity, not greed or the aberrations of personality" (viii), as if the writer's curiosity may not be greedy or aberrant. Thus Van Dyke takes the stage as a picaresque idealist, his book an exhibit of this reading of the scene of the West. To Wild, the book's value stems primarily from "the man who wrote it, a man, on the one hand, who grew up riding after buffalo with the Sioux Indians, and, on the other, became, of all things, one of the foremost art critics of his day and a habitue of the East Coast's most fashionable salons" (ix). The myth Wild offers is here in a nutshell.

Neither the wild boyhood nor the heights of fashion prominent in Wild's myth are features of Shelton's account. And while Shelton distills the author's life and work to a single episode and text, Wild's more far-ranging version of Van Dyke entails valuing others of his works besides *The Desert*.[23] But these differences of emphasis don't mean that Wild discards Shelton's account: he both quotes (VDS 403) and emulates Shelton's dramatic opening, and like Shelton (perhaps following him), employs the metaphor of romantic love and sacrifice, ranking Van Dyke among "grand romantic lovers" (JCVD 25), one who "gives his all to glorify his mistress" (VDS 410), a feminized landscape that "lures her suitors on" into "her deadly arms" (WS 222). Yet Wild's image of Van Dyke turns finally not on romantic subjugation but on heroic omni-competence and power. This is a man who could have his way with others, who "could get the drop on a group of menacing bandits, or who could drop just the right quip to elicit titters and chuckles from the proper ladies and gentlemen" of the privileged class; one who even as a staid academic "could make collectors tremble" in the fear he might tab their Rembrandts as frauds (OS xii).

This emphasis on all-purpose prowess determines Wild's reading of one incident in particular: an episode in *The Open Spaces* in which Van Dyke, as a guest of Andrew Carnegie in Scotland, bests the magnate at a contest of fly-fishing, more than quadrupling the plutocrat's catch. Van Dyke reports that Carnegie had assumed that, as an expert on art, he (Van Dyke) "knew nothing about anything else" (106); and Wild would like to construe this anecdote as Van Dyke's own "telling comment on his whole life" in how it depicts his expertise and versatility in two worlds (xx). It may be, as Wild supposes, that Van Dyke felt that way—it's certain that Wild himself does—but the episode's aftermath, which Wild does not discuss, suggests another sort of "telling comment." It turns out the great man just plain hated to be beat, so Van Dyke thereafter "took pains in fishing and golfing to make no startling scores" (207). This epilogue could serve quite as readily as a "comment" on a "whole life": the life of a courtier, a crack fundraiser,[24] emissary for a wealthy benefactor whom he advises on art purchases, whose anonymous largesse he helps distribute—and to whom he is not above taking a fall in golf.

Wild's treatment of the Carnegie fish story points up a tendency in his commentary with consequences for much that I've discussed above. To broach this, we can review this statement Wild provides of his purposes for offering his brand of biography-based commentary, in preference to a "heroic" yet naive conception of the wandering aesthete of the sort Shelton disseminates:

To probe the realities behind the author of *The Desert* is to de-
mythologize Van Dyke somewhat, to deflate the chromatic
image of the author. . . . The gain, however, is to take Van
Dyke down from the rosy gallery of desert gods and see him as
a complex human of a dual nature, a rare combination of "an
indoorsman and an outdoorsman." Van Dyke was equally at
home, equally tough-minded, around the camp fire and in the
museum. Realizing this can be a first step in a more sophisti-
cated and a more enriching appreciation of the desert's early
champion. (VDS 407)

Yet Wild's own purpose remains "appreciation" of a "champion." His
procedure more than anything *re*mythologizes the author, instituting a
second "rosy gallery" for him to occupy in a rarefied social realm,
establishing for him a "dual" but not especially "complex" nature. A key
instrument of this remythologizing is Wild's tendency not just to point
out but to accept Van Dyke's self-assessments as his own. In his boasts
over fishing Wild reads the author's attitude toward his life — but it's an
attitude Wild holds as well. In his biographical excavations, Wild speaks
as though his human subject were a quarry to be flushed out; he calls
him "wily," talks of "tracking" and "catching" him. When the quarry is
flushed, though, it's a toss-up as to which, the biographer or his subject,
is the more thoroughly snared.

   This is especially the case in two interrelated matters crucial to our
reading of *The Desert*'s opening narrative: the screening of personal history and attitudes toward ethnicity and race. Wild follows Van Dyke
himself in seeing personal reticence as a trait of his Dutch ancestry. To
Van Dyke, though, not only his propensity to personal reserve is characteristically Dutch; his love of wilderness and his distaste for civilization
are themselves racial traits, literally inborn. His sixteenth-century ancestors in stormy northern Holland had been evolutionarily tried by their
severe, sublime surroundings, and as a result, Van Dyke insisted, both
"dislike of the crowd" and "love of the wild" resided "in his blood"
(JCVD 14). This "old Dutch love for the open air and the wilderness" is
an atavistic holdover from a prelapsarian life led back in the ancestral
landscape, a life which "was rational in that it fitted itself to nature and
was a part of it" (16). That this life may have been "fitted" the way that
dikes (from which the Van Dykes took their name) are fitted to the sea
does not, of course, enter the calculation.

It is not extraordinary that Van Dyke should have made over crowded, cultivated Holland for a personal mythology in this way. Such ethnic or "racial" mythmaking is a stock-in-trade of the era (and of course is not confined to it); Muir, for instance, makes nearly as much of his Scottishness. It is noteworthy that Wild should himself embrace this construct, though, not only reporting it but seconding it in his own explanations of Van Dyke's behavior, with rhetorical fillips like "Teutonic devotion to the outdoors" (17) and the "organic world" of the Dutch ancestors (VDS 413). More important are the character and the object of those explanations. Wild asserts that it is not the fact but the author's "perception" of his ethnic "heritage" that matters, and insists: "By gaining at least a rough idea of Van Dyke's intellectual and emotional struggles, we better appreciate the rewarding complexities of his writing" (JCVD 23). While an ethnic "heritage" is tacitly collective, what we are enjoined to "appreciate" here is not. The author's "struggles" of ethnicity are strictly individual. When Wild moves to evoke a historical context in which the "perception" of ethnicity might figure—when the nation in its "adolescent energy," having overwhelmed a continent, "continued right on . . . to create overseas empires" (37)—the author's "heritage" is nowhere in evidence.

An apparent exception is found in another aspect of the familial heritage, a class-based one: the "sense of civic responsibility" borne by the Van Dyke clan from colonial war heroes through the author's own father, a banker and New Jersey Supreme Court judge. Here Wild depicts the manner in which Van Dyke enacted the family legacy:

> From over the years, the civic pride would devolve on John, not in the form of an office holder or of a soldier, but as a teacher and writer, one who feels the moral responsibility to lead the citizenry aright. During an age when, in his view, hordes of uneducated and uncouth immigrants were overrunning the country, he felt pride, too, that the Van Dyke family still upheld the old, genteel traditions (*The Money God* 40–41). (JCVD 19)

Tucked between references to the pedagogue's "moral responsibility" and the aristocrat's "genteel traditions" is a subordinate clause about immigration. The entire passage is backed by a page citation from a book that constitutes Van Dyke's most determined attempt to "lead the citizenry"—*The Money God*. Tracking the citation down, one finds it says nothing about the Van Dyke family's "pride" in "traditions." It does, however, say quite a bit about immigration, and what it says drastically compromises the "rosy" picture Wild accepts of Van Dyke's "perception" of ethnicity.

In the pages Wild cites (40–41), Van Dyke is engaged in sorting the "hordes" of recent immigrants into two groups: "a minority contingent of exceptional quality" hailing from Northern Europe (except "Russia and its provinces, and the Jews"), and the majority, the "miscellaneous mobs" from the rest of the world—the "undesirable class." So the reader will appreciate the scope of the problem, Van Dyke provides a tabular breakdown of "the larger elements in the undesirables," the numbers of immigrants for 1905 in eleven categories of peoples from Southern and Central Europe and from Asia. The Northern Europeans, not incidentally, "have made excellent farmers," whereas the others "gather in the cities, in the factory towns, and about the mines." The "desirable class" prizes our traditions and assimilates easily; the "undesirable" is unassimilable, "knows little . . . and cares less" for our traditions, and basically "is after our money." Such an immigrant thus epitomizes the profligacy and greed that *The Money God* assails.

We find in this book the ugly flip side of Van Dyke's faith in his own blood-based "heritage"—and a fuller expression of the race anxiety that crops up in his nature writing. Van Dyke entertains the question as to whether "physically these hordes will help out our hollow-chested, nervous race," but dismisses the case, on the grounds that believing the better aspects of "undesirables" will come through in a blood mix "is as fatuous as to suppose that a good omelet may be made by beating up a half-dozen bad eggs" (42). After all, blood will out:

> And bad blood will tell just the same as good blood. Biology has proved the lasting quality of heredity. Unto the fourth and fifth generation the stupidity of the Russian, the cut-throat instinct of the Sicilian, and the moral obliquity of the Balkan hordes. Centuries have not, centuries will not, change the low cunning of the Jew, the treachery of the Greek, and the rascality of the Armenian. The less we have to do with them the better for us. (42–43)

Nor will education improve those deficient by blood; they are born as they are, says this teacher, "and education will not beat it out of them." Driving the point home, he offers a parable: "The camel that was allowed to put his head under the Arab's tent did not turn into an Arab; but he continued to occupy the tent to the owner's undoing" (43).

So Van Dyke, it turns out, is not just a snob. He's a bigot. Wild knows this—he's cited this book. What does he make of it? *"The Money God,"* he offers, "is not Van Dyke's finest hour" (JCVD 20). The reason: though the book excoriates the greed and waste of American life — including despoliation of the land—it regards this as in no way associ- ated with the activities of plutocrats like his companion Carnegie. Explains Wild, Van Dyke's "self-righteousness and valued friendship with Carnegie blind him to the implications of the man's march to riches" (20). While true as far as it goes, this formulation of Wild's indi- vidualizes a larger set of social issues, just as did his reading of Van Dyke's ethnic myth-making. It reduces Van Dyke's sweeping (and strik- ingly incoherent) commentary into a question of allegiance to a friend.[25]

Except for the passing reference to "uncouth immigrants" repro- duced above, Wild is silent about Van Dyke's bigotry. Is it possible that Wild is justified in this omission, that this evidence of Van Dyke's racism is incidental to his work on nature and art and thus not worth mention- ing? Or were racist, nativist attitudes so ubiquitous to this class and era as to pass as given, a denominator so common it may be factored out in individual accounts? In answer, we may recall Wild's assertion that learning about this author's life means complicating our understanding of his work. In pressing the biographical inquiry, he avers, "we are searching not only for the matrix of *The Desert* but for the shape of the whole man" (JCVD 11). But if, as Wild believes, "It turns out they are largely one in the same" (11), then ought not this misshapen aspect of "the whole man" have its bearing on "the matrix of *The Desert*"? Our reading of the book's opening suggests that it might.

Recall, too, Wild's assertion that what counts with Van Dyke is "his perception of the heritage" he believed he embodied. In the passage this is taken from, Wild proceeds to offer a second, less strictly individual reason for attention to myths of ancestry—a generic reason:

> the approach applies particularly well to authors of the Ameri-
> can West, a young land in Anglos' experience. The literature it
> has produced frequently deals with flight, with people leaving
> cities and families, and with personalities reacting to strange but
> rapidly changing landscapes. (JCVD 23)

That Van Dyke's book in particular and retreat narratives in general are instances of this literature of "flight" is clear enough; only Wild leaves hanging the lead he dangles of "Anglos' experience." Thus he neglects the possibility that Van Dyke may love the desert in part because it's not the lower East Side: teeming with Jews and Italians, paved and polluted and, above all, *loud*, largely with the talk of others. The desert he celebrates for its silence; and his Indians never breathe a word.[26]

If Van Dyke's attitudes are ubiquitous to his social circle, this hardly is cause to pass over them—not if such attitudes are implicated in the tastes and longings, the predilections and understandings typifying those who have given *The Desert* its enthusiastic reception. I do not suggest that it is a bigoted book pitched to bigots; it is more than that. But I am driven to wonder what the full compass may be of the "familiar facts" Van Dyke assumes shared knowledge of as he devises his prefatory myth of civilization. I am arguing for a reading of this author neither as Romantic isolate nor as heroic, picaresque individual but as a characteristic, if extreme, instance of a generic type. In part, it is a vatic type, this voice from the wilderness, bearing witness to the "fact" of his disembodied "impression." For there's an underside to this author's "noble" subjugation of self to "subject," to the unruffled certitude of his "I"-eschewing voice. Issuing from the desert, his "facts" seem solid and assured; but this same tone of assurance informs the "truths" he trumpets in his social, economic, and eductional pronouncements. And these appall; they are hateful and incoherent, not true at all. But this incoherence is the larger image of the half-submerged breaches of coherence we find in *The Desert*'s opening. It is ever the function of the vatic personality to take such breaches—irreconcilable impulses and beliefs, founded in clashes of cultures—and embed them in forms of resistance: to find ways to narrate them. The story is offered as fact, often in a voice not the seer's "own"; the measure of its success is that its "facts" are found "familiar."[27]

Both Shelton and Wild tell stories we find familiar in this way— variants of heroism. Shelton's version of Van Dyke reiterates a tale of fatal attraction to the Romantic sublime—a single overweaning desire. Wild holds for a more "complex" or at least various Van Dyke—both city and country mouse. But in his "appreciation" for this hero's seeming prowess, he has difficulty reconciling or contextualizing what he sees as his "dual" nature. Thus he chides Peter Reyner Banham for attributing "a strain of misanthropy" to Van Dyke like that of later "desert maniacs" (Banham 158), a remark he says is "not informed" since it overlooks biographical evidence of the author's gregariousness (JCVD 10). But Banham's observation *is* informed—by *The Desert* itself, its author's manifest intent (as Banham puts it) "to observe everything *but* his fellow

human beings" within "a desert absolute and unpeopled" (158)—the
very paradigm of retreat. Wild finds no way to integrate this central
aspect of the book with external signs of its author's bonhomie. When he
gravitates toward linking the author's performed misanthropy to anxieties of class and race, he is halted by his embrace of the very mythos he
identifies in Van Dyke, the "perceptions" of beauty and ethnicity. Thus
the author's major statement of racial and economic ideology Wild can
only call "not his finest hour," fundamentally unrelated to those hours
of his that *are* fine.

   I do not deny that Van Dyke had many fine hours and was an impressive man in many regards. Here, in sum, is what I do question. First,
I wonder whether familiarity with the author's biography does much to
"enrich" most readings of *The Desert*, which are place-based and participatory, undertaken by readers involved with what remains of the desert,
not with Van Dyke's own remains. I say this even while cognizant of the
temptation to conflate the persona with the place, in the belief that the
book's factual emanations, its palpable correspondance to place, are
foremost among its qualities. Assuming the productions of biographers
do affect participants, I question the emphasis on the seamless movement of a masterful individual between disparate, contradictory spheres
of desire—an emphasis shared by tropes of the romantic lover and the
picaro. Contradictory desires may be structured in relations of resistance, which like terministic screens are neither good nor bad in themselves but in some form inevitable. Yet we have reason to doubt that
these particular terms provide that helpful a perspective on our actions
and desires as participants in nature and culture, or in spheres we might
envision between these. And finally, taking the author's side (somewhat
perversely) against his own biggest proponents, I wonder whether the
biographers' investigations honor Van Dyke's own best impulses, or at
least his most ascetic ones, against such a focus on the primacy of the
biographical subject. The implicit testimony of his literary methods
might rather hold that (paraphrasing *The Money God*) "The less we have
to do with him, the better for us."

   It turns out that biographical restoration has in one sense sanctioned this impulse of Van Dyke's, that we or at least he would be better
off if we left him out of it as we read his best book. For it turns out,
almost as a punchline, that the author made it all up. Evidence indicates he never was a desert wanderer in the sense he imparts in his
autobiography and *The Open Spaces*, as in the interstices of *The Desert*.

He traveled not by pony or foot but by rail, spent most of his time not crisscrossing the wilderness but holed up at his brother's Mojave ranch or in hotels, and may never have spent a single desert night under the stars. His aesthetic effusions are pretty clearly his own, but his observations on plant and animal life appear mainly cribbed from his brother, an authentic outdoorsman, or from academic authorities, as is evidenced by factual lapses.[28] While this evidence of mendacity may, as Wild claims, "make little or no difference" from an aesthetic standpoint, it surely undermines the sense of testament such a generic production depends upon, raising the possibility that this is *not* "the one story this man can tell," that another, truer story has been suppressed. Though overlooked for years, the book's factual discrepencies were actually called to its author's attention right after its publication, by an Arizona professor who served as one of its sources. Apologizing for his "blunders" and promising to correct them in subsequent editions (though he never did), Van Dyke pleads: "It's the book of a sick man written to escape morbid mental anatomy and with considerable of the morbidity sticking to its pages" (Teague and Wild 26). Here, at least, I suspect him of telling the truth. I am trying to take him at his word.

A STORY OF READING

> Alongside the narratives I submit to analysis there
> remain others, unsubmissive. And if, at this very
> moment, I am "drawing the moral" of my history,
> it is with no thought of yielding up and "fixing" its
> meaning—a narrative is not reducible to a
> maxim—but because I find it more honest to
> formulate some of the impressions it makes upon
> me, since I too am one of its readers.
> Tzvetan Todorov, *The Conquest of America*

Early on I mentioned that, just as Van Dyke does not intrude on his "subject," which is the desert, so Shelton and Wild do not intrude on theirs, which is Van Dyke. I have observed the same injunction with regard to my own subject, which is all of the above. But to conclude I would like to butt in with some personal history of my own, a story of the reading that has eventuated in this chapter. I feel that otherwise I may fall into the very tone of certainty and prescription that disturbs me in Van Dyke's social pronouncements—this when I am far from settled on the consequences of my findings.

I did not seek out *The Desert* but came across it on a sale table (the paint stripe on the bottom of my copy indicates that I paid 89 cents for it) at a time when I was first acquiring cheap "nature" books and acquainting myself with the type. I had heard of the book, in asides by Edward Abbey, for instance, whose passing advocacy has had much to do with its revival (see note 1). I sampled the book as I was sampling many books then, in search of excerpts to teach; and I did teach a chapter (not the first or last, unfortunately), which foundered—too visually detailed, too exclamatory in style for my students. Later, I returned to the book and read it through with concentration, in an attitude of study. This chapter and this book are in large measure the outgrowth of that reading.

My impressions were threefold. First, I took to heart (or bought into) Shelton's narrative of the author, to an extent that I find it hard to imagine what reception the book might have *without* this potent introductory apparatus. I still find it appealing as a tale of retreat as Romantic trial, however much I've come to suspect that response. Second, I was struck by the shape of the book's opening narrative, noticing and resolving to elaborate a formal parallel to Thoreau's "Ktaadn," as I have done. The third sort of impression was and remains participatory: I associate the book with the desert at Anza-Borrego in California, the most significant extant parcel of the largely "reclaimed" Colorado Desert into which Van Dyke reports riding in his first "approach." My stay there was short but formative—a rare spell of solitude, the desert in rare bloom— and numerous passages conjure for me specific images of the place. I would not have come to write about this book if I had not been furnished with memories of that stay as a touchstone.

Tracing the faint library trails of the academy, I strayed across *The Money God*, the mere title of which seemed to confirm the positive impression of its author I'd derived from Shelton's story, from my own participatory engagement with the text, and from the vaguely formed comparison of Van Dyke to Thoreau I'd contrived. What a guy, I thought: a wandering naturalist and social critic to boot! But eventually I took up the book and turned to the chapter on immigration, discovering the sentiments reproduced above. Imagine my surprise. The desert solitaire was revealed as a racist; also, it turned out, as an apologist for robber barons, most likely eugenicists, too, with whom he seemed to differ over methods but not intents. In a flash, my appetite for my project vanished.

What avenues besides abandonment were open to me? My affection for the figure of Shelton's desert "lover" was gone; but it still seemed that the author's racism might be a stray trait, effectively (and technically) unrelated to his work on his primary "subject." Van Dyke's formal task—that of both establishing and effacing his own subjectivity through narrative—still held a formal interest. I began to reconstitute a "subject" of my own in this changed situation, negotiating a movement between the "affective space" of my reading experiences, both participatory and suspicious, and the "field" of the text as a formal assemblage. I could discount neither what I'd learned of the author as a historical subject "mobile" in time nor what I'd come to value of the book as a "fixed" and enduring entity—even now, I am trying to enact a state of resistance between these. I began to believe that, in this treatment of the desert, the writer's "life" is precisely what doesn't belong—as in some measure I still do.

At this point I came across Donna Haraway's *Primate Visions*. It dispelled for me the idea that Van Dyke's retreat and his racism might be altogether unrelated. In her chapter on "Teddy Bear Patriarchy," Haraway recounts the creation of the American Museum of Natural History, with its project of collecting and preserving animal specimens in dioramas—especially large male mammals like elephants and gorillas. This project, overseen and underwritten by the prominent industrialists and financiers of the museum's board of directors, was envisioned as an educational and spiritual defense against the threats to white Anglo-Saxon masculinity summed up in the notion of "decadence": "the threat of the city, civilization, machine" (27). The diagnosis and treatment of decadence—which Haraway deems "a venereal disease proper to the organs of social and personal reproduction: sex, race, and class"—depended upon three activities, "exhibition, eugenics, and conservation." As the museum's main business, these therapeutic activities "attempted to insure preservation without fixation and paralysis, in the face of extraordinary change" in social, sexual, and race relations—the reproductive "organs" the "venereal disease" of decadence attacked (55). The project of preservation, Haraway insists, depends upon a doctrine of realism; and realism, in turn, requires direct exposure to the object reproduced, in something of the manner of a photographic plate. What

Theodore Roosevelt called "the strenuous life," we might say, was lived
in despair of decadence and in quest of such direct exposure. The
collector's exposure to experience informs his production of "an exact
image" that will "insure against disappearance" and arrest decay (45).
The whole project is founded on an ideology of *organicism*, the "ruling
concept" of which is "an organic hierarchy, conceived as nature's principle of organization" and understood as extending through "a hierarchical division of labor, perceived as natural and so productive of unity"
(40). This unity is to be "authored" by the technical craft of white manhood, to which alone the organic hierarchy in its totality may be
exposed, and which alone can effect its reproduction.

Exhibition, eugenics, conservation, all three are present in *The
Desert*: conservation in explicit pronouncements, eugenics in signs and
stresses we've surveyed, and exhibition in the effort to transcribe desert
"facts" down to the finest visual differentia. The author's reliance upon
second-person pronouns can be understood thus, too, as a shift from
reporting to exhibiting situations. Subordination of self in landscape is a
bid for redemption, power of another sort. Says Haraway:

> Nature is such a potent symbol of innocence partly because
> "she" is imagined to be without technology. Man is not *in*
> nature partly because he is not seen, is not the spectacle. A
> constitutive meaning of masculine gender for us is to be the
> unseen, the eye (I), the author. (54)

Thus when Shelton speaks of the "trained mechanisms" of Van Dyke's
eyes, he employs a figure which is covertly of a piece with his core
rhetoric of sexual attraction and romance.

If Haraway's argument holds, the "dual" aspects Wild finds in Van
Dyke—the allegiances to nature and to corporate capital—may not
diverge after all. Prominent capitalists "were, with excellent reason, at
the forefront of nature work—because it was one of the means of production of race, gender, and class." Investigation and preservation of the
natural order, the special province of white manhood and its
authorizing craft, supplied "direct vision of social peace and progress despite the appearances of class war and decadence" (54). To go "back to
nature" was to return to order, as the doctrine of organicism understood
it. Van Dyke's patrons and companions acted in their own interests, to
be sure; but out of *principle*, not chicanery, by and large. Thus their
actions

should not be narrated as a tale of evil capitalists in the sky
conspiring to obscure the truth. Quite the opposite, the tale
must be of committed Progressives struggling to dispel darkness through research, education, and reform. The capitalists
were not in the sky; they were in the field, armed with the
Gospel of Wealth. (55)

"The Gospel of Wealth" is the tome on the social functions and
responsibilities of the rich authored by Andrew Carnegie.

I reduce the story of my reading, then, to three major stages. Before
reading *The Money God*, I understood *The Desert* as an act of prophecy
and advocacy, a beam of biocentric light levelled against the forces of
anthropocentric darkness—something of the way Shelton construes it.
After that, but before reading Haraway, I maintained this oppositional
model by resituating it within the author himself—rather like but more
strongly than Wild does in suggesting a split between Van Dyke's "finer"
and not-so-fine "moments." This character, I reckoned, was a visionary
in the sticks but a high-minded monster in the parlor, at least by the
standards we've since come to adopt. I have not and *can* not entirely forsake this stance, since it corresponds too well to my experience of reading *The Desert*, my vacillations between approval and opprobrium.
Since reading Haraway, though, I have been moving toward a conception of Van Dyke—and of retreat narrative in general—that accords with
the trend that Philip Fisher sees operating in recent critical work in literary and cultural studies: "the implicit rejection of this heroism of oppositional dissent and its replacement by collaborative and implicational
relations between writer or speaker and culture" (237). This trend is
instantiated for environmental literature in Lawrence Buell's recent
work, which similarly declines the simple choice between complicity
and dissent in depictions of nature. The impulse toward retreat in
nature is not pitted against but proper to our culture, as the case of Van
Dyke, among others, dramatizes.

What then does this mean for our projects of opposition now, our
judgments of what we should reject and accept? The Van Dyke stories
of Shelton and Wild, as well as my own, concern the "currency" of *The
Desert*'s dated text—its status in the present, its "cash value" in the
Jamesian sense. Many of us who oppose the despoliation of natural
places by a state-sanctioned industrial economy seek out representations
of those places—and believe that circumstances warrant our desire and

concern for them. But many of us are also white Anglo-Saxon males; and white males like us have a history of mistaking our own concerns for the world's.

It's here where I'd most like to avoid a tone of pronouncement that I will appear least able to do so. The "morals" I draw I would like understood as continuations of the movements I've been narrating, but they will still take the form of morals: recognitions, injunctions, too general and oracular. I offer them in the spirit Todorov proposes: as the upshot to a story as provided by "one of its readers."

First, most obviously, I draw morals for the analysis of retreat narratives. Following the critical turn Fisher cites against the "heroism of oppositional dissent," we might understand projects of solitary retreat as sustaining relations to modes of social existence, even as we insist—and this is crucial—they are not confined to them. Retreat addresses the ingrained "disquiet" Harpham refers to, one which is proper to culture *in that* it gestures beyond it: an ineradicable and generative gesture, "raising the issue" of culture in the recognition of its absence. This is the ascetic gesture, and if Harpham is correct, what's at stake in our discourse is not whether or not but rather *how* this gesture is manifested.

It follows that, especially in "literary" manifestations, we must investigate the forms of our desire for nonhuman scenes. Any reaction depends upon the configuration of what's reacted to or against: retreat construed as leisure, for instance, can reinforce the shape or purpose of our work as well as our desire to escape from it. Freedoms we seek follow the contours of our confinement and fears, just as Burke says a burden exposes a strategy of unburdening. Retreat configures a temptation, Janus-faced, to both attraction and flight; and flight can't be reduced to an urge for personal *Lebensraum*, even if it's primarily attraction that holds sway.

A case in point concerns the status of "strangers in the land." Higham takes this phrase for the title of his study of American nativism (1969), in which context it refers to immigrants and non-WASPs; but from an environmental perspective, it could be taken to refer to most any postconquest arrival and a great many colonized indigens as well. Nativism—and the movement of retreat in the likes of Van Dyke—is founded in part upon the sense of *not* being native, an uncertainty, anxiety, and bravado on that score. Much current nature writing, by contrast, is concerned with the conditions of our inhabiting, not just residing upon, "the land." In my judgment, this is why *The Desert* is not

only a better but more exemplary read than, for instance, Van Dyke's
The Mountain: the former feels like the work of a familiar, a would-be
denizen, with its first chapter even performing the temptation toward
such a state; the latter, which draws its illustrations from a bewildering
myriad of mountain ranges spanning two continents, seems the work of
a collector—a literary taxidermist.

A broader moral to my story concerns the need to rescue
organicism from the force of Haraway's critique. Muir's remark that
"everything in the universe is hitched to everything else," a much-
repeated credo of the ecological perspective, can as readily be seen as
expressing the organicist ideology that Haraway finds informing our
reproductive politics. This is not the place and I am not equipped to
argue the case; but it seems to me that Haraway's deconstructions of
biology as rhetoric need to be resisted, in Harpham's sense of the word:
kept in play, yet counterposed to constructions of rhetoric as itself biological. This entails negotiating recognition of *some* evolutionary inheritance—the "fixed" term of this configuration of resistance—with the
"mobile" recognitions of social construction. Social construction enjoins
us that the "facts" of our nature will always come down to "impression"
(as Van Dyke seems half-wittingly to allow in his preface); the evolutionary perspective insists that this process of "impression" is itself an element of our biological estate.[29] The aesthete and the indigen differ in
color vision, but it is their rhetorics that appear at odds; their organs are
strictly comparable, though only *through* those rhetorics. A slogan for
this stance may be found in Burke's credo that we humans are the "animal symbolicum": "Bodies That Learn Language."[30] The need, in any
case, is to divest organicism—the recognition of biological interconnectedness—of its hierarchical imperative, and this is a project proceeding on many fronts, not least in the work of many nature writers operating
from a posture of retreat.[31]

My final moral, which issues from the project of rehabilitating
organicism, is drawn from what I perceive as the shortcomings of the
Van Dyke commentaries I've reviewed. This concerns the need for what
I would style a "biopragmatist" critical orientation in the practice of
what Joseph Meeker has called "literary ecology": "the study of biological themes and relationships" in texts and the "roles . . . played by literature in the ecology of the human species" (9). Meeker proposes "to
identify some of those patterns within human art and thought which
hold most promise for a fully developed human cultural and artistic life

consistent with a diverse and stable natural ecology" (xx)—an undertaking that is pragmatist in its stress on how practice may be revised in light of identifiable outcomes. A biopragmatist criticism might focus, for one thing, on the conditions informing the "participatory" reading of generic texts—reading that entertains the prospect of conversion in the sense of imitating actions and recognitions depicted. This criticism would ask: What difference might it make in biological terms to take this text, this set of texts, or this mode of commentary as exemplary? What does it mean to seek and accept conversion upon the terms the work provides? What does it entail for the life of the place depicted and that of the places left behind?

One writer who poses such questions prominently and about whom such questions have been asked is Wendell Berry: it's to his work I now turn.

CHAPTER FOUR

Familiar Mysteries

The Exemplary Wendell Berry

If every fully realized story . . . is a kind of allegory,
points to a moral, or endows events, whether real or
imaginary, with a significance that they do not
possess as a mere sequence, then it seems possible
to conclude that every historical narrative has as its
latent or manifest purpose the desire to *moralize*
the events of which it treats.
　　　　　　　　—Hayden White, *On Narrative*

As we return from our visits to the wilderness, it is
sometimes possible to imagine a series of fitting
and decent transitions from wild nature to the
human community and its supports. . . . What I
have been implying is that I think there is a bad
reason to go to the wilderness.
　　　　　　　　—Wendell Berry, *Home Economics*

This chapter concerns some narratives of retreat in nature by Wendell
Berry, considered as further instances of, developments of, even correc-
tions to the narratives discussed in the previous two chapters. This
means I am claiming, first, some formal resemblance, second, a historical trend, and third, ethical implications among these texts. In formal
terms, my claim is familiar by now: that all these *are* narratives of retreat,
stories of movement from human to nonhuman spheres. Historically, I

am suggesting that these narratives reflect the elaboration of a genre over time, in addition to operating within cultural scripts active in their own times. As for ethical implications, these stem from the contention that not only these narratives but also the histories in which they figure, including any that I devise, enact the "desire to moralize" that Hayden White remarks upon—like it or not. Thus they offer background checks, if not outright guides, to human comportment of given sorts.

Thoreau's "Ktaadn," you will recall, I termed paradigmatic but not exemplary of retreat narratives. Formally "pure" but puzzling and much disputed over in its upshot, this narrative enacts a formal logic of retreat without much registering with later readers as an attitudinal and hence ethical model, for reasons concerning its historical position, its relations to prior and subsequent texts. Van Dyke's "Approach" to *The Desert* presupposes its own status as exemplary, a response to "familiar facts" authorizing the well-established generic activity of "wandering," even as it twists the paradigm of movement from human to nonhuman. But the generic legacy as Van Dyke employs and bequeaths it turns out to be riven with difficulties, which persist to the present day. Since after all, it's the present status of these tales that's at stake, my analyses have involved how recent commentators stake claims as to their continuing model status, claims advanced tacitly in narratives of the authors' lives. My argument to this point has a narrative trajectory of its own, then, including three stages. First is a formative stage, a fable of generic creation; next comes a crisis stage, where what had seemed settled is undermined, rendered uncertain. What follows is a stage of restoration, in which the ethical dimension projected all along advances in a fully (though never finally) exfoliated set of terms, enacted in narratives that perform relations in which solitude may be productively constituted. I am counting on Wendell Berry to play this role.

The narratives by Wendell Berry that I'll examine draw my attention because they are unusually thorough, detailed realizations of a formal paradigm of retreat and, a related attribute, are unusually forthcoming about and explicit in what Hayden White would call their "desire to moralize the events" they depict. They point out and dwell upon much that other nature writing presupposes. They employ the narrativizing resources that White mentions—allegorizing, pointing to morals, endowing events with significance beyond mere sequence—insistently, without qualm. And repeatedly: retreat in movement through landscape is a scenario Berry returns to, a habit of his, one by which he reenacts and retrieves morals in a mode of "in-habiting" both topographical and textual.

The poet, novelist, and essayist Berry (the farmer too, for that matter) is not primarily identified as a "nature writer," even in his essays: not in the sense of being a naturalist, a practitioner of "natural history." Yet what nature writing he does is all the more suited to my purpose for that, for it is the very impulse, indeed the imperative, to pursue "nature study" that Berry narrativizes. The shapes of his nature stories, the manner of his moralizing thereupon, and the terms of value he elaborates in the process thus can be widely generalized. And generalize them Berry does. He seeks universal terms to embody local interests; he narrates in the broadest ways what it means to seek and find limits. This is what makes his work exemplary.

I will discuss this exemplary character more fully in the conclusion of this chapter. That discussion will emerge from an account of the language of meaning and value through which Berry generalizes, moralizes, and narrativizes his experiences of retreat. Terms of this language will be drawn, in turn, from Berry's narratives of movement in nature, particularly those in *The Unforeseen Wilderness*, his one book devoted exclusively to stories of and meditations on wilderness.[1] Much of this chapter will be devoted to analysis of a single essay from that book, in the course of which I will advance my claims about this author's deployment of a formal paradigm of retreat.

The Unforeseen Wilderness, first published in 1971, is a collection of essays about Kentucky's Red River Gorge, accompanied by a portfolio of photographs by Ralph Eugene Meatyard. It belongs to a significant subgenre of nature books, those that feature photographs and text about a wild, often endangered place—a prototype being the influential collection on Dinosaur National Monument produced in opposition to the Echo Park Dam project there (Fox 285). Berry and Meatyard's book was issued at a time when the Red River Gorge itself was threatened with inundation by a dam intended for "flood control," with the book conceived to arouse and articulate resistance to that project. The resistance prevailed: the dam was not built and the Gorge has so far been preserved. This makes *The Unforeseen Wilderness* exemplary both in its artistic and polemical *raisons d'etre* and in the fortunate outcome of the controversy in which it figured.[2]

The phrase "terms of meaning and value" I appropriate from James Boyd White's *When Words Lose Their Meaning* (1984); it is drawn from

the third of "four fundamental questions" that White proposes for analyzing a text in a manner that will expose "the resources of meaning that
[the text's] culture makes available to its members" (10). The first and
second of White's questions interrelate in ways integral to the phenomenon of "retreat" as I've been describing it. In stories of retreat, the
realm of his first question—"How is the world of *nature* defined and presented in this language?"—tends to preoccupy the entire text, effectively
emptying his second question—"What *social* universe is constituted in
this discourse, and how can it be understood?" (10—my emphases).
This tendency makes White's third question all the more pivotal. In full,
it reads, "What are the central terms of meaning and value in this discourse, and how do they function with one another to create patterns of
motive and significance?" (11). Such "central terms," to White, are
those that cannot be defined by their equivalence to other terms but
exist in ordinary discourse as "words with a life and force of their own,"
irreducible, emerging in "the particular ways each can be combined
with other words in a wide variety of contexts" (11). These terms constitute a profound cultural resource, born of their repeated use—a
resource not fixed but capable of reconstitution in texts that redirect
their inherited life and force. Identifying and placing such "central
terms" is pivotal for our purposes because of the ways the terms move or
traffic between "the world of nature" so scrupulously represented and a
"social universe" apparently neglected in nature writing texts.

An approach through a language of "meaning and value" is especially warranted with Berry, whose longstanding effort has been precisely
to reconstitute and redeem such a language. For White's fourth question—"What forms and methods of reasoning are held out here as
valid?" (12)—in Berry is answered in part precisely in the use of such
terms: what is valid is reasoning conducted in a traditional language,
widely comprehended, renewed for present exigencies.[3] The "forms and
methods of reasoning" that most occupy me here, though, are those
conducted within or through narrative, by which the "essence" of an
argument or set of terms may be, as Kenneth Burke says, "temporized":
depicted as unfolding in time. And so it will be through considering narrative form in Berry's essays that I approach the language of meaning
and value configured therein.

The essay I will examine in detail, "An Entrance to the Woods," is
central to *The Unforeseen Wilderness*: literally central in that it is the
middle of the book's five chapters, functioning as a sort of rhetorical

fulcrum; and central to my purposes in that it alone of these essays depicts a single narrative, a single wilderness trip, from start to finish. The book's other essays also include and depend upon narratives of wilderness travel, but they are not "stories" in the same entire sense. Further, "An Entrance" is determinedly a drama of *solitude*, its import and "plot" hinging on the writer's being alone—a fact pertinent to the book's purposes as well as my own. What follows, then, is an account and analysis of this central essay, during the course of which I propose to flag certain "terms of meaning and value" at work in Berry's nature narratives generally.

DAY ONE: PACE, PRESENCE, AND MELANCHOLY

I read "An Entrance to the Woods" as unfolding in several movements, as I will call them. By "movement" I do not mean anything that technical nor do I refer to the obvious breaks of white space inserted between stretches of text; the movements I have in mind may coincide with, be bounded outside of, or lap over such section breaks. I think of a movement rather loosely as a sequence of events along with whatever "narrativizing" cues or maneuvers may impart a sense of having made a start then come to an end. The notion is tautological and begs the definitions of its parts; but I believe it will serve well enough as applied, relying upon no more than the word's usual entitlements.

The first movement of "An Entrance" extends for four paragraphs, from the writer's departure for the Red River Gorge to when he first hears the sounds of water in a ravine. Several "events" transpire during this movement that bear upon the whole narrative as it develops. The essay opens in what seems a straightforward manner, the writer noting time of day and year (afternoon, late September), the fact that he's leaving from work, and the various roads he drives upon, from freeway to highway to use road, en route to the foot trail down which he begins to hike. There is something so routine as to approach transparency in this scenario of driving away from work for a weekend outdoors. Yet this choice of a departure point is not inevitable: Berry might as readily have commenced his narration at the trail head or somewhere *in medias res*. His including the drive from work is a gesture not just conventional but purposeful, for as it turns out, the drive to the woods becomes part of what's at issue in his "entrance."

Out of the car, off and walking, the writer sets the scene, noting in particular the stillness of the afternoon and the relative silence of the place, in which "the steady somnolent trilling of insects," an occasional woodpecker's cry, and his own "footsteps on the path, are the only sounds" (230). Or so he says: a literal-minded hiker might wonder if there was no creak of pack straps, rustle of trouser legs, or for that matter, sound of breathing audible within the hushed milieu. But of course this would be impertinent; those reported are the "only sounds" present to the narrating awareness, any others being filtered out. The drone of insects, the sound of footsteps: these are *pertinent* details, the former figuring again in the penultimate paragraph, the latter evoking the writer's own entrance. Most pertinent is that the prevailing condition of silence is established so early in the essay, for *silence* is the first meaning-value term I want to cite in Berry, one operating in ways I will proceed to suggest.[4]

The story's action continues—but this is the action of solitary movement across a silent, "somnolent" landscape. Thus any line between narration and description is indefinite indeed in the writer's report of his progress, with features of the terrain effactually depicted as events as they pass into the writer's cognizance. What "happens" in particular is the change from "the dry oak woods of the ridge" to the conditions prevailing when the writer has moved, first, "down into the rock" below the lip of the gorge (a place ordinarily wet, as the plants there indicate, but dry this late in the year) and then to a point further down the ravine. The writer reports: "And here where the ravine suddenly steepens and narrows, where the shadows are long-lived and the dampness stays, the trees are different" (231). The shift between tree types, in a terrain that "suddenly" changes, has the force and status of an event. The trail itself possesses a certain agency, the writer noting that trails thereabouts "all seek these stony notches that little streams have cut back through the cliffs"—a "seeking" evidently purposeful. We may be reminded of what Berry, in "A Native Hill," says of paths: "A path is little more than a habit that comes with knowledge of a place. . . . As a form, it is a form of contact with a known familiarity" (86). Habit is repeated action: attributing action to this trail is not personification so much as a shorthand for the habitual "contact" of creature and place. While the path seems purposeful, the writer's own agency is confined within two uses of the expression "I pass" ("I pass down into the rock," "I pass a ledge"). Mostly it's the landscape that acts.

This subordination of the writer's action holds through the conclusion of the essay's first movement:

> Finally from the crease of the ravine I am following there begins to come the trickling and splash of water. There is a great restfulness in the sounds these small streams make; they are going down as fast as they can, but their sounds seem leisurely and idle, as if produced like gemstones with the greatest of patience and care. (231)

The close of a narrative "movement" is signalled by the adverb "finally," confirming that what trail and hiker have sought in the ravine has been located. The sound of water in the silent place thematizes this initial movement, in that water is the signal attribute of the place, its presence in varying degrees having formed the landscape in the "eventful" ways we've been encountering.[5] In the essay's second sentence, the writer has noted that, upon leaving the freeway, he's entered "the watershed of the Red River"; what he "finally" comes upon in the moving water itself is a first emblem of his arrival there, of the "entrance" the essay's title heralds. Yet it is the water's sound, not the writer himself, that "begins to come" into presence; and what might seem a commentary on the writer's own mental state—the "restfulness" the sound conjures—is cited as an attribute of the water itself, which has an aspect of motivated agency. The streams move "as fast as they can" yet evince "patience and care" in their productive activities—a contrast of paces that will soon figure further. I will flag *patience*, in particular, as another meaning-value term of Berry's, employed here in a way typical of his work, as applicable to natural processes and mental states alike.

The next movement begins by signalling a lapse in time: "A little later, stopping, I hear not far away the more voluble flowing of the creek" (231). There's a hiatus between the first recognition of water and this subsequent sound, indicating that whatever immediately precedes the writer's "stopping" is, in the story's terms, of no moment. Having entered and recognized the domain of water, the writer's logical next "move" is not to keep moving but to dwell within this place and recognition: the creek sound initiates this. The movement thus instituted proceeds rapidly from the writer's search for a campsite in the creek bottoms, through his brief camp chores, to what turns out to be the last physical action he reports for that day: with plenty of daylight left, he goes to a rock by the stream and *sits*. A lengthy disquisition follows—but an "eventful" one, in which the action of dwelling continues even though physical actions are not reported.

It's characteristic of this narrative that whenever the writer sits (or reports sitting), elaboration ensues: discussions of mental states, experiential stages, habitual recognitions. Three "sittings" in all are represented, each followed by such elaboration, several pages worth for the first and second. The discussion that accompanies each might be thought of as resembling, recounting, possibly originating in the actual occasion of sitting, perhaps even in writing "on site."[6] By this I mean, in a basic sense, that the elaboration taking place in writing is far more likely to occur in sedentary than in physically active circumstances. You can't readily write while afoot, obviously; in really wild terrain, without relying on the "habit" of paths and established routes, you may not even be able to *think* in "writing" while traversing a terrain your "contact" with which demands attention, stamina, and ingenuity. A walk down the river itself through the rugged, boulder-choked "Roughs of the Red," for instance, "resolves into a series of problems and solutions" in which "[t]he way is never clear very far ahead" (256) — one's mind has its hands full, so to speak, just locating and negotiating a route. In this sense, then, the writer's disquisitions while seated are "true to life." Further, they raise the issue of how an understanding is itself construed as an event, an issue that bears on discussions below of how the essay's and book's conclusions are narrativized.

Although as I've said, the writer's sitting down is the last physical action he cites for the day, what immediately follows his sitting is a key event in the narrative, though one occurring exclusively in the realm of attitude. He sits:

> And then a heavy feeling of melancholy and lonesomeness comes over me. This does not surprise me, for I have felt it before when I have been alone at evening in wilderness places that I am not familiar with. But here it has a quality that I recognize as peculiar to the narrow hollows of the Red River Gorge. (232)

The next several pages of the essay are taken up with a disquisition on the reasons for and meaning of this melancholy. What bears notice is the play between *strangeness* and *familiarity* in the sensation described. The writer is overwhelmed by a sense of being alone and out of sorts in an unfamiliar place; yet he is familiar with this reaction, can as much as predict it. He even recognizes in it "a quality" particular to a landscape already familiar to him—a specific manifestation of a generalized sensation, a stage in his solitary acclimation to the "wilderness places" he is accustomed to frequent. Articulations between strangeness and familiarity, and between the predictable and the "unforeseen" in wilderness, figure heavily in Berry's narratives and will figure again in this one.

The feeling besetting the writer is, in part, one of "lonesomeness"; the story of its onset and passing is a drama of solitude. The drama begins in ambivalence over the absence of other people. In part, what's "peculiar" to the Gorge are the "little rapids in the stream that will sound, at a certain distance, exactly like people talking." Sitting by the stream, the writer has the illusion of "a party of campers coming up the trail": "When I finally realize that it is only a sound the creek is making, though I have not come here for company and do not want any, I am inexplicably sad" (232). Later, this sadness will turn to pleasure and ease within the unpeopled realm; the story of this trip concerns the transformation. Passage from "lonesomeness" to solitude occurs through an "artifactual" domain: as usual in retreat narratives, it must negotiate signs of prior human presence en route to recognition of the nonhuman.

Thus as the essay shifts into a more "expository" mode of imparting general recognitions, the first of three reasons the writer cites for his melancholy is that such places as this one seem "haunted" by prior inhabitants: the white hunters, farmers, and loggers, signs of whom mark the land (including the creek bottoms where he's camped, former pastures); also the "ancient tribesmen" who, leaving fewer traces, "have disappeared into the earth" (233). The writer remarks:

> For though this is a wilderness place, it bears its part of the burden of human history. If one spends much time here and feels much liking for the place, it is hard to escape the sense of one's predecessors. (232)

"Human history" is figured as a "burden" here, something "to escape" from in the retreat to wilderness—predictably so. But the progress of this "escape" is not so predictable. To the outdoor "participant" in this text—the reader who would like to emulate an experience of the sort depicted—there's something both counterintuitive and tutelary about the realization here expressed, the expectation formulated and pronounced. One is led to expect that awareness of the artifactual realm—the sense of past inhabit-ants—will *grow* rather than diminish over time, developing in and through one's engagement with "the place." "For *though* this is a wilder-ness place": it's the place's status as wilderness that's present to immediate, untutored apprehension, whereas recognition of the artifactual, of history, emerges only gradually. It does not fall away but accumulates. In what does "entrance to the woods" consist, then, if not in progressively *losing* signs of the human? How is the nonhuman to be recognized and config-ured if not by the disappearance of history? Berry's story cannot proceed as Thoreau's does in "Ktaadn," as a charting of human signs that seem both dwarfed and magnified in the landscape until they disappear altogether; nor can it sequester human presence into a single point of departure, pre-suming and portraying an inviolate nonhuman landscape thereafter, as does Van Dyke. Instead, the story must contrive some "escape" from history notwithstanding the difficulty of so doing; or it must posit a point beyond which this difficulty ceases to mount with further exposure to the place; or it must otherwise "place" history's ineradicable signs with respect to wilderness so that they are contained, incorporated, or overcome. Per-haps *assuming* the place has the character of "wilderness" will itself pro-vide the seeds of a solution—even if, at this stage, signs of the human past spell only melancholy to the one human present.

The second of Berry's "reasons" for his unease is that his high-speed auto trip has whisked his body to this place while leaving his mind behind: "though I am here in body, my mind and my nerves too are not yet altogether here" (233).[7] The events related at the start of the essay— the routine departure by car on a weekend camping trip—the writer considers in retrospect as a literal change of pace, the body's drop from freeway speed through slower roads to a walk, and finally, to a complete stop, while the mind goes racing on. As Berry depicts it, a virtually direct correlation exists between the *speed* of bodily movement and the *presence* of mind to body:

> Having come here by freeway, my mind is not so fully here as
> it would have been if I had come by the crookeder, slower
> state roads; it is incalculably farther away than it would have
> been if I had come all the way on foot, as my earliest predeces-
> sors came. When the Indians and the first white hunters
> entered this country they were altogether here as soon as they
> arrived, for they had seen and experienced fully everything

between here and their starting place. . . . Our senses, after all, were developed to function at foot speeds; and the transition from foot travel to motor travel, in terms of evolutionary time, has been abrupt. The faster one goes, the more strain there is on the senses . . . and the longer it takes to bring the mind to a stop in the presence of anything. (234)

What bears attention in this quasimathematical formula is not really its "validity" as a proposition: it cannot be verified in any but experiential terms, of course, and upon a certain reading is absurd on its face, implying that to be "fully here" the "mind" must somehow contrive to back up and "sense" the spatiotemporal transitions that the body passed over too quickly. The formula recalls the car-lengths of "stopping distance" necessitated at different speeds: how far will it take at this speed for the mind to skid to a halt? Further, it's debatable whether "the first white hunters," despite traveling at a more evolutionarily appropriate pace, were "altogether here" upon their arrival in any sense that Berry himself would in general support—any sense that does not seriously beg what it might mean to "experience fully everything" along one's route. What bears notice, rather, are for one thing the formula's points of appeal as rhetoric, and for another, the narrative program it suggests. As rhetoric, this positing of an equation extends almost "naturally" from the terms of rate and distance at issue; it's an idiom conventional to the automobile culture critiqued, and persuasive as such. Figuring "mind" and "body" as following separate but correlated trajectories may presuppose a mind-body split, but it does so only to establish the grounds of their eventual reintegration. Berry holds no brief for a mind-body duality: this "equation" is a way to suggest that any split is a condition technologically, not evolutionarily imposed. As for the narrative program, it concerns the reintegration: the temporal process of "bringing the mind to a stop in the presence" of what's before it, of approximating the condition of those predecessors who were "fully here" as a literal matter of course.

Though the third of Berry's three reasons for unease comes next, the essay's first section break (a skipped line) intercedes at this point—and for good reason. As I read it, the present movement ends with this disquisition on the vagaries of "going out" into nature; the movement that follows focuses on "going in." As Berry reports, his final reason for unease concerns his having "made an enormous change: I have departed from my life as I am used to living it, and have come into the wilderness" (234). At this point, he is suspended between the poles of retreat, between departure from a human sphere and "entrance to the woods." This suspension is represented in the terms of strangeness and familiarity broached earlier and here more fully delineated. The writer reports "an uneasy awareness of severed connections, of being cut off from all familiar places and of being a stranger where I am"; he experiences "a pervasive sense of unfamiliarity" in a place devoid of the myriad "associations" he finds in the places he's "most familiar with" (234–35). What is familiar reinforces his sense of his own "history" and "hopes"; what is strange undermines these, impressing upon him his insignificance to a place that proceeds without him. In this place, says the writer, "I see nothing that I recognize." There's at least one thing he recognizes, though:

> Uneasy as this feeling is, I know it will pass. Its passing will produce a deep pleasure in being here. And I have felt it often enough before that I have begun to understand something of what it means. (235)

The feeling has *not* passed yet, of course; but the very sense of unfamiliarity is itself familiar, understood. And thus what follows is predictable: it can be foreseen. But what is foreseen is the state that comes with immersion in a wilderness that is itself "unforeseen"—surpassing human abilities to understand or predict. We begin to see what a complex business is this attribution of strangeness and familiarity, then, entailing at once a wilderness familiar in its mysteriousness, predictably unforeseen, and a civilization whose familiarity is a mode of estrangement and whose pretenses to predictive power are foreseeably maladapt. If there is something ironic or paradoxical about the way these terms double back on themselves, that is consonant with the shift of feelings, from uneasiness to pleasure, this passage forecasts and itself begins to enact. The shift comprises a turn of the plot, a sort of *peripeteia* or reversal of the action, in a narrative whose emplotment depends so much on "events" of attitude.

In expounding upon the meaning of this shift, Berry is at once recapping his story to date, forecasting the course of the story to come, and above all, drawing morals from what he clearly offers as a representative anecdote, an exemplar of the narrative type, "entrance to the woods." The central movement of this type Berry expresses in what could serve as a credo for what I am calling retreat:

> It is only beyond this lonesomeness for the places I have come
> from that I can reach the vital reality of a place such as this.
> Turning toward this place, I confront a presence that none of
> my schooling and none of my usual assumptions have pre-
> pared me for: the wilderness, mostly unknowable and mostly
> alien, that is the universe. (235)

We find here retreat's characteristic movement figured in terms that
virtually restate Thoreau's celebrated intent (in *Walden*) to "front the
essential facts": the "turning toward" the nonhuman (thus away from the
human) to "confront a presence" of "vital reality." What has transpired
in the narrative to this point explicates the "lonesomeness" the writer is
turning away from; what will succeed it is his passage into a "vital reality" that he knows from experience he "can reach."

There are clusters of attributes to the wilderness "presence" the
writer confronts. I will cite one in passing, another at greater length.
Berry's didacticism, his elaborate drawing of morals, bespeaks a pedagogical concern; yet what he "confronts" in the passage above is largely
the inadequacy of "schooling" to the experience of wilderness. In this
narrative, as with retreat narratives in general, wilderness is itself figured
as a scene and agent of instruction. Of course, its teaching is not
imparted in words. In fact, the writer has already stated that in this
place, he "will not speak, and will have no reason or need for speech."
He has reason or need to *learn*, obviously, but speech has no part in this.
Instead, *silence* (a meaning-value term I flagged earlier), with its cognate
"quiet," is to Berry the element and agent of learning in nonhuman wilderness. Silence is what most characterizes even *human* teachers who
would help conduct others into this realm, like the hired hand who
teaches the writer squirrel-hunting in "A Native Hill," "a good teacher
and an exacting one" precisely because of the way he enforced an attentive silence (99).

A central cluster of attributes concerns human *limits*, which wilderness reveals and in effect teaches. "Perhaps the most difficult labor for
my species is to accept its limits, its weakness and ignorance," the writer
insists. In wilderness these limits are indubitable—especially when
wilderness is construed as Berry now construes it, as comprising the
greater part of the universe. The figure he employs to this end can be
read as one response to the problem I noted earlier, that of recognizing
the nonhuman in a domain increasingly seen to be weighted with

human history. Berry describes his campsite as situated "within an enormous cone widening out from the center of the earth out across the universe, nearly all of it a mysterious wilderness in which the power and the knowledge of men count for nothing" (235). The figure of the cone intimates at once both centrality of place and nonhuman limitlessness; it incorporates human traces but relegates them to a single dimension transecting this vast expanse, which is at once contained and open-ended. The figure is triggered by the writer's spotting "an airplane now flying through this great cone" (the sole report of any external occurrence within this section), an image expressing not the expanses but the limits of human "power and knowledge." As long as the airplane continues to operate, "its behavior is as familiar and predictable to those concerned as the inside of a man's living room"; but if it fails, "it enters the wilderness where nothing is foreseeable" (236). Thus familiarity and predictability are linked to the imperative of limits in an intricate sequence of enclosure images: cone, campsite, airplane, living room, and mollusk shell, to which Berry next likens the civilization that "encases" us. The airplane, too, is a further tacit comment on accelerated modes of conveyance by machine. Earlier, the writer has said of freeway travel, "One might as well be flying" (233); here flight is reckoned as reinforcing the enclosures by which wilderness is "camouflaged" from human view.

If civilization is an obscuring enclosure—an airplane or room or mollusk shell—then retreat is a breaking out into the open. The writer claims, "what I have done is strip away the human facade that usually stands between me and the universe, and I see more clearly where I am" (236). We see, though, that this rhetoric of limits, enclosure and release is just as complex and paradoxical as that of familiarity and predictability to which it is linked. The function of wilderness, to Berry, is to impress upon humans recognition of their limits. Yet owning up to limits releases one from limits, at least of a certain order; it enables transcendence, a moving "beyond" to a "vital reality." Conversely, failure to acknowledge limits is tantamount to remaining confined in the shell, an occupant of the moving plane rather than the still cone. The preeminent feature of this enclosure is that, from within, it is taken to be *un*limited, continually expanding in "power and knowledge."

What recognition ensues when the "human facade" is removed and the writer can "see more clearly" his place and standing? In brief, he sees that "all wildernesses are one" and that he himself is "alone also among the stars." With intermediate enclosures escaped or erased, he is reduced to the single enclosure of self amid the vastness of the "one." Thus chastened, he prepares "to enact . . . the loneliness and humbleness of my kind" in the process of "growing used to being in this place" (237). The representative moral character of this solitary "in-habiting" is reinforced in the movement's final paragraph, in which the first-person pronoun gives way to a generalized "he":

> A man enters and leaves the world naked. And it is only naked—or nearly so—that he can enter and leave the wilderness. If he walks, that is; and if he doesn't walk it can hardly be said that he has entered. . . . In comparison to the usual traveler with his dependence on machines and highways and restaurants and motels—on the economy and the government, in short—the man who walks into the wilderness is naked indeed. He leaves behind his work, his household, his duties, his comforts—even, if he comes alone, his words. He immerses himself in what he is not. It is a kind of death. (237)

This is, to be sure, as lonely and humble as can be, though it's an amplified, even grandiose "humbleness," ascetic in the highest degree. This profession of utter sacrifice extends unto a symbolic death, and may even be read to include the passing sacrifice of the first-person voice itself—though of course the sacrificed "I" is transfigured in the protean "he." To Berry, humbleness or *humility* (another meaning-value term) is a high virtue—and one commentator in particular (Scott Slovic) remarks on how this virtue is manifested in his work (127)—but it bears notice that humility, as a posture of self-sacrifice, may constitute its own form of ambition. It may entail aspiring to a representative, transcendent status, that of a moral exemplar, a model for conversion. Naked and emptied of personal entitlements, I "enact" the core qualities "of my kind"; "I" become "the man," a mythic figure.

Berry's essays are notable for the way their attention to affective states (what Slovic calls the writer's "watchfulness") is parlayed into this ascetic impulse to interpret one's own experience as representative. The effect is both phenomenological and mythical, as in this essay, which moves by increments from cognizance and diagnosis of a particular discontent, to a symbolic death of the broadest sort, occasioned by withdrawal from the details of a particular existence. As it turns out, though, the "kind of death" the writer describes has a tangible correlative. The symbolic death, which concludes this movement and the trip's first day, is followed, after a section break, by this line: "The dawn comes slow and cold" (237). A symbolic rebirth is in the offing—and not incidentally, the writer is waking up (though still half-dead, in a sense: he has "not slept well" and rises "without much interest in the day"). The figurative "death," it seems, has stood in for the writer's getting up from his rock, crawling into bed (to a mummy bag, it may be), and nodding off—tangible events gestured at only in symbolic analogue.

DAY TWO: AFOOT IN THE WOODS

The symbolic death and slow, sluggish rebirth constitute the midpoint of the essay—and of the trip, and the book. The essay's second half follows roughly the same procedure or sequence as the first, through its initial movement at least. It begins with narration of the writer's movements through the landscape; then at a point where the writer again reports sitting down, it opens up into further discursive elaborations, again figured as occurring in temporal sequence with the more tangible events narrated. These elaborations replay the agenda of the previous "sitting," attending first to the presence of human artifacts and predecessors in the wilderness milieu, then to the pace and disorientation of machine civilization, then to the writer's own solitary condition. And a similar trajectory in attitude is charted, the writer reaching a nadir in recognition of history's "burdens" but then rebounding, this time through the realization, not just the prospect, of uplift in his "stripped," "quiet" state. In short, both of these "sittings" progress *through* a fronting of the artifactual, historical realm *to* recognition of the nonhuman through solitude.

Here, in sum, are the events of the movement I have just plotted in the abstract. The writer, having awakened listless in the chilly gorge, looks up, sees sunlight, and "suddenly" is "full of an ambition" to reach and be steeped in it (237). He sets off for the ridgetop, so intent on his mission he's "thunderstruck" by some grouse he flushes. On the ridge he finds a sunbeaten rock to sit upon, at which point, like the sun-seeking trees he's just likened himself to, his "mind begins to branch out" (238). He notes first the incessant noise of freeway traffic nearby, in contrast to the ravine he'd camped in, sheltered from engine sounds. He finds an inscription on the rock, a name and a date from 1903; and regarding the prospect from the ridgetop, he realizes that the scene betrays no sign of the passage of time—no visual sign, at least. For the "roar of the high-way" gives the lie to that timeless appearance: the place is categorically different from what the Indians of two or ten hundred years ago would have encountered, a realization that prevents him from fully identifying with these vanished others. This leads to a troubled musing on how "the machine of human history" is hellbent on catastrophe, followed by a reaffirmation of the "possibility" of "a better life" which he discerns, "as always," when he's "afoot in the woods" (240–41). Upon this uplifting note, he sets off again, moving back down into the trees—the end of this movement.

The movement has at its center a summit scene. Like Thoreau on Katahdin surveying an expanse which "did not look as if a solitary travel-ler had cut so much as a walking-stick there" (*The Maine Woods* 66), Berry is struck most by the nonhuman character of the view, the absence of human artifact, which he construes as a timelessness belying the dated inscription on the rock nearby. Both summits are scenes of culture-nature contention, a trial of perception and mood. In Thoreau, contemplation of the nonhuman prospect is infiltrated with an under-standing that this place, too, will be bound over to commerce: "It was a large farm for somebody, when cleared." With Berry, the human oc-cupation that Thoreau assumes and projects has been largely ac-complished, to an extent that thwarts much identification with past inhabitants. For while the visual prospect seems unchanged over time, what the writer hears is "the insistent, the overwhelming, evidence of the time of [his] own arrival"—not the "great ocean of silence," only sporadi-cally punctuated with machines, still prevailing in 1903.

In the reversal of that past condition, we find elaborated the figures of enclosure from the earlier "sitting." Here, an "ocean of silence" con-taining stray machines has given way to "an ocean of engine noise" inundating the continent, containing only stray and isolated "silences." From the "island of wilderness" the writer occupies, it seems the tables have turned:

[I]t has seemed to me for years now that the doings of men no longer occur within nature, but that the natural places which the human economy has so far spared now survive almost acci-dentally within the doings of men. The wilderness of the Red River now carries on its ancient processes *within* the human climate of war and waste and confusion. And I know that the

distant roar of engines, though it may *seem* only to be passing
through this wilderness, is really bearing down upon it. (239)

It's as if the "great cone" of the night before had been capped and
inverted, with "wilderness" and "silences" forced down into the funnel
end, the jet plane tamping it like a muzzle loader. In this reversal of
what is "within" what, a distinction between prepositions is proposed,
one that Berry amplifies elsewhere and that may be added to the
meaning-value terms we are compiling. To Berry, to pass *through* is
praiseworthy, as opposed to moving upon or over the land, or otherwise remaining detached from rather than coming into interactive
contact with the landscape. A path goes *through* terrain; a highway or
airplane goes *over* it.

In this matter of making contact and passing through a place, *water*
is the great exemplar and, as we have seen, the genius of the place. So it
makes sense that, unlike the summit scenes in any number of wilderness
stories, Berry's is not the climax of his narrative. To this denizen of a hill-
and-river country, the high spots of which are the loudest and most
settled and the slopes and hollows the most silent and wild, the summit
is not the *sine qua non* of the nonhuman. And so, after his grim meditation on encirclement and catastrophe by machine—and his recovery in
the recognition that he cannot despair when "afoot in the woods"—the
writer heads back down "under the trees," the way the water goes, eventually identifying the "heart" of the place down there. We will follow
him there momentarily; but first we must look at this recovery of his,
since it reconfigures the sensation of solitude that he has earlier
described.

The possibility of "a better life" that the writer envisions when
"afoot in the woods"—one "that would enlarge rather than diminish the
hope of life" (240–41)—Berry associates with his solitude, his growing
sense of "comfort" in this condition. No causal relation is asserted
between these; Berry does not say that being comfortable by oneself
causes better relations with others, nor is it clear how he could. Instead,
the association arises through this juxtaposition:

> I feel the possibility of a frugal and protective love for the cre-
> ation that would be unimaginably more meaningful and joyful
> than our present destructive and wasteful economy. The ab-
> sence of human society, that made me so uneasy last night,
> now begins to be a comfort to me. (241)

What connects these two sentences? There is no obvious reply, unless it's assumed that only individuals in isolation seek alternatives to our "wasteful economy" — an assumption not otherwise supported in Berry's work. In context, the connection between them depends on prior assertions about the "mollusk shell" blindness and encumbrance of civilization, the machine noise and breakneck pace that pull body out of reach of mind and mind away from the place and moment. Since the attributes of solitude are opposites or antidotes to these features of the machine economy, they must be entitlements too of an envisioned countereconomy. Alone, without machines, the writer is "alive in the world, this moment," his travelling on foot having "stripped away all superfluities"; only his "irreducible self" remains, able to "assume [the] quiet" of the landscape he moves through "as one of its details" (241). This is a state he could not attain were he to bear with him "all the belongings of a family man, property holder, etc." — the belongings, that is, not the values. For the *social* life he can imagine — the life of family and land — has to be one in which it is routine to be "afoot in the woods," in the sense of submitting to "the lay of the land and the capabilities of [one's] own body." To Berry, such solitude may eventuate in a social act, but it is prevented by its nature from being a social movement.

This "stripped" condition is the same as the "nakedness" described earlier, but it is no longer "a kind of death," rather the fullest sort of life. It's in this state, resurrected as a "detail," renewed by the relinquishing of centrality and the integration with place this trope implies, that the writer reenters the woods. Therein, "you can never see very far, either ahead or behind, so you move without much sense of getting anywhere or of moving at any certain speed" (241). The "unforeseen" character of the place takes precedence, and the pace proper to it approximates stopping altogether, mind having caught up with body at last.

This movement following reentry into the woods is the essay's most descriptive, tracing, in a pattern now familiar, the writer's passage through various features of landscape to a point where again he sits down. Only there are important differences in the way the pattern is reenacted, having to do with the state of recognition the writer has attained. Recognition of the nonhuman has occurred in the writer's accepting the stripped condition of solitude and assuming the role of "detail"; this subsequent movement depicts the mode of his dwelling within this recognition, which is to say, within the place itself. And so, like the writer himself, the movement is quieter, more attached to details of the place that enact rather than discuss that dwelling, virtually stripped of the discursive events his previous sittings have generated.

The movement unfolds in two brief submovements, the first following the writer from the ridge along a trail, the second effecting a new beginning at the point when he ventures off trail "down a small unnamed branch of the creek," where, as he reports, "I begin the loveliest part of the day" (242). The narration is chronological but not slavishly so: each submovement culminates in a cluster of animal sightings, brought together there, evidently, from the various times of their occurrence. Animal presences are most concentrated in this movement of the essay, especially here, in its climactic passage:

> As I walk up on a pool the little fish dart every which way out of sight. And then after I sit still for a while, watching, they come out again. Their shadows flow over the rocks and leaves on the bottom. Now I have come into the heart of the woods. I am far from the highway and can hear no sound of it. All around there is a grand deep autumn quiet, in which a few insects dream their summer songs. Suddenly a wren sings way off in the underbrush. A redbreasted nuthatch walks, hooting, headfirst down the trunk of a walnut. An ovenbird walks out along the limb of a hemlock and looks at me, curious. The little fish soar in the pool, turning their clean quick angles, their shadows seeming barely to keep up. As I lean and dip my cup in the water, they scatter. I drink, and go on. (243)

Here in "the heart of the woods" the writer has come to a full stop in a "quiet" purged of machines—and the creatures emerge and come before him. Before, birdsongs had been mentioned perfunctorily, startled grouse had rattled the writer, and the insects had been merely "somnolent," not dreamful and songful; now, the life of the place approaches and participates. It is a commonplace of birdwatching that if, like the writer, you "sit still for a while," the birds that have fled from you will "come out again"; we might presume that like reemergences had also occurred earlier, while the writer, sunk in melancholy, was sitting on a rock at his camp. But this "entrance to the woods" is narrativized in such a way that the writer's reconciliation to the place and to his own solitude is the condition, not the result, of such visitations. That is to say, in the terms of the story, it would not make sense for him to report such happenings earlier: that would imply that the place was reaching out familiarly when the writer himself was still strange. These contacts with the natural eventuate from the trial of separation that must precede them, the drama of passage through the artifactual. Having passed through to recognition, the writer is himself now recognized. His drinking—always a portent in Berry—is at once symbol and tangible fact of this mutuality.[8]

At this "sitting," with the human at last left behind, the place itself provides the commentary, occupying the temporal duration, the spell of awareness that in previous sittings the writer has filled in himself. Here at the still "heart," the place itself has its say; once the writer, upon drinking, "goes on," there's nothing left to relate, and the rest of his day's walk is a hiatus, unnarrated. After a section break, we find him "back in camp" where, having walked all day, he "read[s] and rest[s]." (He still does not say he writes.) From this final "sitting" he takes stock of his day's activities, configuring in general terms what has already been enacted in narrative: his having "slowed to a walk," lost his "strangeness and uneasiness," and "become a part of" "the quiet of the woods" (243). He'd slept poorly before; this night he "sleep[s] well." The story ends with him hiking back up to his car before dawn the next morning (it does not follow him all the way to the car, much less to the highway), still surrounded by the "singing of the insects" that has "continued without letup or inflection, like ripples" on the water that moves through and inspirits the place: an audible form of the prevailing quiet.

This likening of insect to water sounds forges a poetic closure, of course, completing a circuit with images from the essay's opening. The last paragraph effects closure of a more overtly moralizing sort:

> In a way this is the best part of the trip. . . . It seems to me that if I were to stay on, today would be better than yesterday, and I realize it was to renew the life of that possibility that I came here. What I am leaving is something to look forward to. (244)

This conclusion does not only bring about narrative "configuration" as Paul Ricouer describes it. In a sense, it depicts the configurational act itself, which Ricouer describes as "the act of the plot, as eliciting a pattern from a succession" of events, the "reflective judgment" by which "the whole plot may be translated into one 'thought'" ("Narrative Time" 174–75). According to Ricoeur, every narrative contains both episodic (as in chronological events) and configurational dimensions—with configuration, as we've seen, most prominent in this narrative of Berry's.

But this doesn't mean that the single "thought" a story configures should be taken as achronological, as opposed to events themselves. The two dimensions form a "temporal dialectic," a single "time of fable-and-theme" which "is more deeply temporal than the time of merely epi-sodic narratives." This dialectic effects a sort of time-binding, whereby in the story's *repetition* the "end is implied in the beginning" and the be-ginning is seen "as leading to this end." This comprehension, or recol-lection, in turn enables us to reverse "the so-called natural order of time" and "read time itself backward," retrieving through repetition "our most basic potentialities inherited from our past in the form of personal fate and collective destiny" (175–76).[9]

There's an explicit configurational act in Berry's concluding asser-tion that his story's beginning—his reason for setting out in the first place—is only "realized" at the end. What is more, this crowning real-ization itself constitutes a call for repetition of a sort that will retrieve and bind past potentialities to future possibility. "What I am leaving is something to look forward to": the writer is leaving the place and can look forward to returning, but he is also leaving the now-completed story, the full round of which can model the possibility of a fully rounded day. The meaning and value of his experience is prospective: as Ricouer says, in narrative repetition, "retrospection is reconnected to anticipation, and anticipation is rooted in retrospection" (178). What makes the end "the best part of the trip" is that past and future are *both* accomplished thereby, made proportionate and placed to either side of the fulcrum of the present realization. What has occurred has attained a form that enables it to stand—or "renewed," to stand again—as "possi-bility"; no possibility can have a "life" if it is not understood as bounded in time. Possibility is alive in *days*; each day "would be better," says the writer, "if I were to stay on." Yet in narrative terms, he does "stay on" in this place: his spell and circuit are completed yet interminably held short of the car, the drive home, all those circumstances that would mitigate the pure "possibility" of the finished prospect and actually *bring* forward the "looking forward" he is (yet is not) now "leaving."

Suspended in mid-departure, the story in a sense is always leaving but never leaves "the woods," instead making a hiatus of the time between what is ending and what is now anticipated. In a sense, what the writer is "leaving"—not departing from but depositing for others—is this story that he leaves for *us*, to be repeated in our reading. Then the hiatus becomes the time of reading, which issues in our looking forward to participating, to being renewed or converted, in a place and manner like those the writer configures.

Repetition is multiform here. There is, to begin with, the formal repetition we've observed in the story, the cycle of episodic walk and configurational sitting, of progress toward and recognition of the non-human place. This cycle is itself informed by those repetitions of prior experience with the place that the writer has alluded to, by virtue of which he could discern the character of his initial uneasiness and foresee its passing. Reading about this, we encounter a sensation that we too can expect to repeat—to undergo and overcome—in our entrances to the woods, provided the writer has identified aright the primordial sources of the malaise. We are not just led to expect this sensation but are rehearsed in the manner of its passing, as we are also scripted to anticipate the condition—the quiet—that follows.

The repetition of experience that makes strangeness familiar is further represented within the whole book this narrative centers. Stories of other "entrances" precede and follow this central one, so that what the writer both leaves and looks forward to are further narrative versions of this place he visits and revisits. If the writer, as I have suggested, "stays on" in the respect that the story stops short of full return, he does so further in that the whole book is a testament to a mode of dwelling within the place and not a description thereof. It is a testament both in being the singular product of its creator—the only one who can tell this story, the only story he can tell—and in being of use, exemplary to others.

Finally, there is repetition across Berry's books—other stories of solitary movement and sitting in nature that resemble these in their formal procedures and meaning-value lexicon, pointing up the exemplary character of the narrative of retreat to Berry's notions of ethical development through attention to place. I will remark on these further; but first it remains to draw together that lexicon—the meaning-value terms I have been flagging.

A LANGUAGE OF MEANING AND VALUE

In imagining an "ideal community" that attends to both the living and the unborn, Berry has envisioned "a language, not yet spoken in any of our public places . . . that would live upon the realization that no man can act purely on his own behalf," such action being not just undesirable but impossible. This language of community "would include the place, the land, itself," which we are "not merely 'in'" but are "part of." Our persistence as a species, Berry insists, requires that we "learn to say" this is our state (*Long-Legged* 63). Berry claims no such "ideal" status for the language he himself employs, yet this statement surely marks his own aspiration as a writer, what he hopes to "learn to say."

The consequences of this ideal are such that a "man" who seeks or seems to be "purely on his own" should by this language be describable as nonetheless acting on behalf of others in a community, present and future, *and* on behalf of "the place itself." Ideally, the language would observe no distinction between these "behalfs." In practice, though, in the absence of any *public* way of speaking this identity of interests, bridging maneuvers are called for: forms of "pontification," in the root sense that Burke reinstates of "making bridges" between terministic realms (*Language* 187). If Berry pontificates—and it's the feeling that he *does* pontificate that accounts, I think, for the misgivings some readers feel about his work—I read him as pontificating in this sense, developing a language of meaning and value to publicly represent a solitude sought on behalf of a not-only-human community—a *good* reason to go to the wilderness.

Two points bear reiterating about the language of meaning and value Berry employs. The first is that this language *is* public: it is recognizable and accessible, consisting in those rich, complex, flexible, irreducible terms J. B. White describes—a sort of terministic topsoil in age, intricacy, and fecundity, as in the care and attention required if the language is to be regenerated and thrive in subsequent uses. Second, this is a "bridging" or "transcending" language, meant to effect transformation between disparate states; and such passage between states is incipiently narrative, or is at least readily translated (or "temporized") in narrative action. Rudimentary "stories" can be constructed using the meaning-value terms alone; a matched pair of terms such as "strangeness" and "familiarity" can in themselves suggest a narrative, even a fairly particular one considering the valence they acquire over the course of their use in this author's work.

My intent here is to "recollect" the meaning-value terms I've highlighted in "An Entrance to the Woods" and, cross-referencing with uses of these and associated terms in Berry's other nature essays, delineate the ways they interrelate in a language that mediates the nature-culture opposition. I don't presume to elucidate this author's *full* meaning-value language, a wider, richer instrument than my procedure can convey. My analysis pertains strictly to Berry's lexicon of retreat—which still, as we've seen, ramifies considerably.

The pair of terms just recalled—*strangeness* and *familiarity*—are preeminent for this purpose. Movement from the one to the other comprises the broad "plot" of these narratives, though it does not get us far to say so, since the same could be said of quest stories generally. We get further once we recognize, first, that Berry's meaning-value language has a strongly dualistic cast, its terms tending to carry distinctly positive or negative intonations, and second, that the strangeness-familiarity pair is an exception to this, with neither term good nor bad per se. It is true that the familiarity with place one comes to in retreat is desirable, but there are forms of familiarity not so desirable; and more important, the strangeness that precedes is not a countervailing ill. Strangeness may be necessary and educative. Other terms must be brought into play to impart values to or elaborate a dialectic between these two.

Allied with these terms is another pair more strongly marked as value terms: *prediction* and the *unforeseen*. To predict is bad, as a rule; to appreciate the unforeseen is good. As we have seen, complexities ensue from the way this pair of terms interacts with the strangeness-familiarity pair. Conventional usage would dictate that what is unforeseen is also strange, yet liable to develop into something familiar and as such predictable; only Berry's discourse does not work this way. Berry connects prediction with strangeness, familiarity with the unforeseen, the former being the starting point, the latter the close of his narratives. The seeming incongruity of these alliances generates further distinctions, such as that, for instance, between strangeness and mystery. These are not synonomous as Berry employs them. Mystery is what issues from familiarity with the unforeseen: "A mystery can be familiar" (62).

So familiarity plus the unforeseen equals mystery. When prediction and strangeness are similarly conjoined, the result, roughly speaking, is what Berry calls *preconception*: the whole realm of civilized convention and conjecture that stands opposed to mystery. This is what the solitary walker moves away from in retreat. But how can prediction be associated with the very strangeness it is meant to dispel? The association depends upon images and notions of *enclosure*. As with the jet plane moving through the cone of wilderness, prediction's efficacy is strictly circumscribed—limited and limiting. Beyond the airplane, the capsule, the mollusk shell—"the enclosure of preconception and desire" (UW 17)—

lies the unforeseen, the limitless strangeness that may develop into mystery. Maintaining this enclosure as much as propagates strangeness, stifling mystery by preventing the growth of familiarity with the unforeseen wilderness of the creation.

Of all the oppositions associated with that between prediction and the unforeseen, the most important is that between the creation, figured in wilderness, and *abstraction*. Abstraction breeds prediction; it constructs and fills "the enclosure of preconception and desire." It causes destruction, an exclusively human phenomenon: the creation is never destructive, except as viewed in narrow human terms (257). Abstraction is related not to creation but to recreation, the spurious, quantified, commodified substitute for a bona fide attraction to the woods—a distraction from, not an encounter with a wilderness which "is the creation in its pure state, its processes unqualified by the doings of people" (UW 66). Not recreation but renewal is the proper outcome of the move toward solitude in nature: in a place grown familiar, "the mind goes free of abstractions, and renews itself in the presence of the creation" (63).

Abstraction's attributes include blindness, arrogance, avarice ("the most abstract of human desires"—UW 18), and in particular two others we've flagged: accelerated *speed* of motion and activity, and excessive *noise*—of engines, of human voices. These attributes plot on to each other in various ways: enclosure of vision is blindness; noise and blindness interrelate in arrogance; excessive speed of activity is haste, an attribute of greed. Planes and cars, we've seen, are figures of speed, noise, and enclosure all at once. As a car causes the mind to become detached from and thus not present to the body, so abstraction in all its forms prevents a condition of *presence*: "the presence of the creation," presence of mind, the presence that no education prepares one for, that one must "bring the mind to a stop" in order to apprehend. What one is present to—or the presence one occupies—is the place in all its particularity. This is a particularity one comes to assume oneself. Having come to a stop, one can proceed to "move in the landscape as one of its details" (241). One moves *through* it as by the slow "adaptation," the *contact* of a path, not over it at high speed by the "pure abstraction" of a road (86).

But attaining the status of a "detail" of the place may imply a certain containment to the moving self, reemphasizing what we have encountered before: the complexity of Berry's figures of enclosure. A person who is "stripped" of abstraction's accoutrements becomes present to the creation as an "irreducible self"—self as a sort of elemental unit, it appears, fit to assume the condition of a detail, which is similarly elemental (can a detail have details?). Yet a similar figure is employed to depict what Berry regards as the epitome of civilized abstraction: the "specialist," who in his "moral loneliness" is "a man out of control, an erratic particle" (61). The difference between these figures has to do, so to speak, with their relation to ground. Both are discrete and "irreducible" in their way, but a "detail" is discrete only *with reference* to its surroundings, a "particle" without such reference. The image of the particle belongs to the enclosure of abstract preconception. By contrast, the counterpart of enclosure in the realm of creation's presence is called *limits*. To be a detail is to assume limits commensurate with one's presence in a place. Limits are recognized through contact with creation's particularities; they cannot be recognized through the sheerly internal reference of abstraction, which in principle (through preconception) does not even acknowledge their existence.

An evident ambiguity in all this extends from the notion that the specialist, in the "moral lonesomeness" of his pursuits, is somehow "out of control." One of the most fertile aspects of Berry's language of value is the way he seeks to recover such terms as *control*—and "order" and "obedience," and so on—for unembarrassed use, by reversing associations these terms have acquired. To Berry, the presumed "control" of prediction—the "control of nature," the "flood control" of the proposed Red River dam—in fact has "nothing to do with the control of anything" but evinces instead "the lack of moral and social and economic control that made the need for 'flood control' in the first place" (UW 19). The demand for such illusory and destructive "control" is made from within the enclosure of preconception, in ignorance and neglect of the unforeseen—made "as if control would not exist if some human being did not invent it, and as if it were something people could cry out for and surely get" (UW 17). Authentic control is the self-control that acknowledges limits and comes into effect through contact with place. Thus it is a function of individuals in solitary retreat to the extent that "each must confront the world alone, and learn to see it for ourselves" (UW 27). Still, self-control does not spell self-centeredness but rather the opposite. Nature's "control" teaches interdependence, not individual power and autonomy. We can only "see" but we can never *speak* the world solely for ourselves.

These notions of self-control and interdependence could be traced into the broader realm of Berry's language for community and economy, including such terms as "discipline" and "husbandry," in consideration of which we would begin to stray from his depictions of the individual in retreat. Two summary remarks will restore our course. First, while to Berry, individual autonomy is a destructive illusion, individual freedom is not. Instead it is manifested in the individual's right to become "exceptional," a condition defined as "the right of escape" from "abstractions of . . . class or condition"—what "American liberty" was established for (*Long-Legged* 10). The narrative of retreat configures exactly such an "escape from abstractions"—though it must also be allowed that such escape may be configured in terms that reinforce the very "class or condition" putatively escaped. Second, the course of retreat seems to begin in something called "loneliness," a condition suffered by the "out of control" specialist as well. But with contact this becomes transformed to another condition, one of participation or even companionship with the nonhuman place[10] in which true control resides. Becoming a companion to or a pupil of the nonhuman place means entering into a state of community with it, to experience and learn control. Thus while Berry does not himself make this case or place much stress on the term "solitude," it seems fair to discern in his narratives a movement from loneliness to solitude, the former a state of isolation, the latter associated with community understood as a set of relations comprehending the nonhuman place. And the transformation from loneliness to solitude has to do with the recognition of limits and control—a recognition which, in a further fertile ambiguity, leads to freedom, and even more, to joy.

We can summarize this movement toward freedom and joy by constructing a progression between these meaning-value terms, one of a number of versions that might be made. This version departs from Berry's own act of summarizing, at the beginning of the fifth and final chapter of *The Unforeseen Wilderness*, entitled "The Journey's End." Recollecting the entire five-year span of his acquaintance with the Gorge, Berry reminisces about his first visits to the place, at which time he "experienced mostly its strangeness" (UW 61):

> I thought of it then as a strange place, a place strange to *me*. The presumptuousness of that, it now occurs to me, is probably a key to the destructiveness that has characterized the whole history of the white man's relation to the American wilderness.

It is presumptuous because it demeans the knowledge and attachment of native animals and humans to whom the place is not at all strange, and invites the imposition of a false familiarity "by the machinery of conquest and exploitation and destruction." Berry continues:

> The strangeness, as I recognized it after a while . . . , was all in me. It was my own strangeness I felt, for I was a man out of place. And I believe that only in that realization lay the possibility that I would come to know the Red River Gorge even a little. . . . But once I learned to look upon myself as a stranger there, it became possible for me to return again and again. . . . It became possible for me to leave the place as it is, to want it to be as it is, to be quiet in it, to learn about it and from it. (UW 61–62)

Then, in the final stage of this experiential progression:

> Slowly, almost imperceptibly, my experience of strangeness was transformed into an experience of familiarity. The place did not become predictable; the more I learned of it, the less predictable it seemed. But my visits began to define themselves in terms of recurrences and recognitions that were pleasant in themselves and that set me free in the place. (UW 62)

This summarizing progression reviews much of the meaning-value language I've been exploring. I'd like to retell it in a way that reemphasizes key terms therein and weaves back in related ones, with attention to the ways these terms are enacted in narrative.

In light of this summary, we can discern why Berry's narrative of "an entrance to the woods" is not only a spatial but a paradigmatic center to his book. That narrative recounts a small-scale "recurrence" of the larger transformation the author here recapitulates, from strangeness through recognition to familiarity. Whether or not strangeness is negative depends upon where and how it is located. To locate strangeness in the *place* is to locate familiarity *in* oneself, in the enclosure of one's preconception. This is "presumptuous" in that it presumes the familiar conditions of the enclosure prevail everywhere. It is the way of abstraction, a form of confinement that pretends to the opposite, to the expansive power of prediction. Its plot is that of conquest and destruction, for it insists the place be made over by force to correspond with preconceptions. By contrast, to locate strangeness within *oneself* is to come out of the enclosure and to follow the way of creation—to be humbled, to be quiet, which means to be taught. What's learned are limits and controls particular to the place, attributes thereof, not of the humans therein. This is the plot of submission, adaptation, transformation, which Berry's narratives model and espouse.

Thus an evident paradox is at work, manifested in narrative as a reversal. If like "the European conquerors" you don't think *you're* the stranger, you are all the stranger for that: you are an alien species, "like so many English sparrows or Japanese beetles, free of controls, cultural or natural" (UW 62).[11] Attempts at prediction and control betray a lack of control; dreams of limitlessness spell encapsulation and isolation. But to recognize limits and to learn controls *means* to step out of the shell, to move "free in the place," *through* and not upon it. The resultant sensation, called "pleasant" here, is more often referred to as joy.

What enables this freedom of movement is familiarity, manifested in the "recurrences and recognitions" by which visits "define themselves." If familiarity involves knowing what to expect, then freedom must require a form of expectation narratively framed—but not prediction. If prediction is the way abstraction is oriented to future time, what is adaptation's equivalent way? The term appears in the passage we are examining as it does in the conclusion of "An Entrance . . .": it is *possibility*. Possibility, as we've seen, binds the accomplished past with a desired future, through acts of configuration. Unlike prediction, possibility is not exclusively human; it does not even pertain exclusively to the future. With increasing "knowledge of [a] place" comes the recognition that "its possibilities lie rich behind and ahead" (110)—they are *the place's* possibilities, in a sense still enacted in its inexhaustible past. In strong form, possibility may not even entail expectation at all. The one whom "the wilderness receives . . . as a student," who "returns often and stays long," may eventually learn "to live *without* expectations" (247). As a sort of formula, then, we might say it is possibility that allows for familiarity without expectation.

Having formulated this, though, we may be accused, and may accuse Berry, of oversimplifying. Wouldn't relinquishing expectation in this manner amount to the squelching of narrative itself? If so, then Berry the storyteller has not fully learned the lesson he says wilderness teaches. Whether this is so depends on how you construe "expectations." The sense of the word as Berry employs it here runs closer to prediction than, say, to readiness, an outcome more of planning than preparation (to cite Whorf's distinction).[12] Even so, narrative must depend on expectation of some order, even if, perhaps especially if, it is the expectation of the significant unforeseen, the realization that what you've "planned is not happening, as if by some natural law" (248). We've seen just how particular an expectation of this order can be, in Berry's assurance that his initial loneliness will pass into joyful solitude. One may have no idea what will happen to instantiate it yet be certain enough of its general course—certain enough, even, to *seek out* the very "recurrences and recognitions" that will complete the expected course.

This business of seeking the unforeseen raises all over again the problem of narrative logic, since the form of expectation Berry *does* rely upon appears to be no more nor less than the expectation of story itself. The strongly narrativized final episode of *The Unforeseen Wilderness*— the last movement of "The Journey's End"—is most notable in this regard. The essay's title is exact, as the expectation of an ending pervades this narrative of a walk in December: strongly marked references to the end of the year, to the trip's "conclusive feeling," to a sense that "the ends are gathering" and patterns setting, crowd the opening paragraph (263). The account proceeds, as usual, through a trial of human presence (housing developments, this time) to recognition of the nonhuman place, pausing en route to report that the writer is carrying "only a notebook and a map" (264). I find no previous reference in this book to the writer's tools or writerly activity per se, and only one, earlier in this same essay, to his occupation *as* a writer—which he disclaims, declaring that his best time in the Gorge had been spent "not as an observer or writer but as a creature bemused by the creation" (UW 63). As for maps, they have been brought up several times before in the book, but not as items used by the writer. Rather, they have served as an emblem of or metonymy for abstraction, something *not* to be confused with the place itself in its presence. Yet here, notebook and map are both mentioned as emblems of the writer's near divestiture of artifactual encumbrances. As it shortly happens, the map becomes a way of making good on the promise of an ending that has seemed to portend from the day's start. The writer realizes that he has lost the map, and fixes on the image of its rotting like fallen leaves: "I suddenly realize that it is the culmination, the final insight, that I have felt impending all through the day" (265). The realization occurs "suddenly," as an event, but lingers as a moral, acquiring "the force of a cleansing vision" (266).

As a configurational act, this is masterful: the map, having appeared at several junctures as a "marked metonymy" for civilized abstraction,[13] is dissolved into the original presence it purports to represent. This closing move takes the two laces of prediction and the unforeseen and cinches them tight. But what interests me is not so much the choice of closure Berry has made as the unmarked possibilities that surround that choice and highlight its character as a narrativizing maneuver. What happens, I wonder, to the "impending" sense of "culmination" the writer has so insisted upon if he does *not* lose the map? Is this a bona fide case of prescience he's reporting, such that he actually if only dimly "foresees" losing the map and learning the significance of its loss? Or is the impulse to closure so vigorous on this trip that some other "event" would have to be constituted, happening just as "suddenly," to complete the narrative circuit? Or must the story of *this* trip in particular disappear if the map does not, to be replaced by that of some other trip in which an initial "conclusive feeling" is seen through, consummated in the recognition of an ending? Further, what if it's the *notebook* that the writer leaves behind, instead of or in addition to the map? Does the writer experience the same "cleansing vision" and sense of freedom in its loss, or instead head back frantically over the route he's just taken? How much of the present book, with its present-tense relaying of events over a five-year spell, has originated in this notebook, which is, with the map, the writer's last encumbrance? If the notebook goes, does the book vanish too, or become a different book, or acquire a different moral? Must the book as it then develops mark prior appearances of notebooks rather than maps, as a metonymy for—what? For the triumph of memory over inscription, or silence over speech? For the achievement of a life without expectation?

My point is that this "cleansing vision" of an end is an achievement born of particular expectations, after all, generated by a narrating will adept at devising what it seeks. It takes a considerable bit of mulling "suddenly" to configure five years of visits and a full-blown meaning-value language within a single event of this sort—something so seemingly arbitrary made over as so decisive an outcome. It's an outcome, moreover, that from a "participatory" perspective could be read as less portentous and more self-serving than Berry allows. Consider one more alternate set of events: What if, instead of losing the map himself, Berry comes upon a map someone else has lost? Does he attribute to it a similar significance, or read in it some emblem of artifactual excess and taint? Does he leave it to molder significantly in the woods, or pick it up and pack it out as litter like a good citizen of the wild?

On its face, this ending would seem to illustrate Hayden White's claim that narrative (or rather, narrativization), in its impulse to moralize, gives story-form closure to events that do not in reality (as it were) come to such ends. Do I suppose, then, that Berry stands exposed in an act of formal chicanery? I stop short of such a judgment for three inter-related reasons. The first is that, as Ricouer demonstrates, it is only through such formal measures, formal impositions even, that our experi-ence of time becomes available to us at all, "configured" for our under-standing and use. Second, it seems to me that Berry's narrativizing tends in important ways to resist itself, configuring continuation of process rather than closure in its preference for contact over abstraction. What the "cleansing vision" of the lost, rotting map dispels is exactly the presumption that the place itself comes to an end in its human repre-sentations. "What men know and presume about the earth is part of it, passing always back into it, carried on by it into what they do not know" (265). In this vision of a "journey's end," the journey itself is understood to take its place as "one of the details" of the unclosed, unfolding wilderness.

Finally, it would not and should not abash Berry that his narrative culminates in a "moralizing" closure, which necessarily enacts, as White says, "the *passage* from one moral order to another" (22). Noth-ing interests him more than the prospect of such a passage. It's in this respect that his essays are most exemplary of retreat narratives generally, which configure a passage between a moral order predicated upon a nature-culture split and an order proper to nature in itself, in which cul-ture has been either left behind or assimilated back into the natural order. These two avenues are not the same: leaving culture behind cor-responds, generally speaking, to Berry's "bad reason to go to the wilder-ness." Berry's interest is in reaccommodating our present cultural order (which to his mind is no order at all) to natural order: this is what he narrativizes. Thus in considering how Berry's meaning-value language mediates the split between culture and nature, I embark on the review of his exemplary characteristics with which I will conclude this chapter.

BERRY'S EXEMPLARY CHARACTER: SOME SOCIAL USES OF SOLITUDE

Berry's language, as "temporized" in narrative, mediates the nature-culture split by depicting a process of human transformation to a condition of participation in nonhuman virtue. Such virtue, though nonhuman, *is* virtue nonetheless, because it may be incarnate as well in human communities that, submitting to limits, escape the enclosure of abstraction. Attributes of a nature "not qualified" by humans serve as human value terms, too: the "patience" of water, the "free nonhuman joy" of a heron performing a mid-air loop (112). To Berry this identity of value terms is no imaginative overlay but essential, a matter of practice in the strictest sense. These are virtues left when preconception is stripped away.

This stripped condition, in which virtue may be espied and practice revised, is often denoted in terms we have encountered but not yet dwelled upon: "silence" and "quiet." The latter term is the more often used, with its overtones of physical stillness (counterposed to the frantic pace of machines) and affinity with "peace," to Berry the desideratum of social relations. Quiet is the distinguishing feature of nonhuman nature, nearly always evoked as an emblem of its presence. Having called it a feature, though, I must qualify: it is more nearly an element, or better, a medium, in the double sense of both substance and agent of the nonhuman. A person can both *be* quiet and *be in* quiet, as is seen in this depiction of Berry's great-uncle's isolated cabin site where Berry would later build his own home:

> It was a place where a man, staying by himself, could become deeply quiet. It would have been a quiet that grew deeper and wider as the days passed, and would have come to include many things, both familiar and unexpected. (20)

Such a quiet is not only a trait or behavior; it is a narrative medium that "includes" events both of repetition and disjuncture. One's own quiet, then, holds the promise of narrative, a transformative story of becoming "joined" to and "a part of" this greater quiet (243).

More particularly, as mentioned above, silence to Berry is a medium of instruction, not just the substrate but the agency of instruction that issues from the nonhuman landscape: the agent or teacher. In Berry's many references to "learning from" a place, the lesson learned seems invariably to follow from or be delivered by silence. I am reminded of how James Boyd White (in a discussion of Plato) makes a distinction between rhetoric and dialectic, the purpose of the first being to persuade, of the latter, to be refuted, corrected (109). If the nonhuman place is an agent of instruction, it may be thought of as a dialectical partner in this sense, its function the refuting of preconceptions and the correction of the one beset with them. In the language of dialectic, White holds, community is constituted, even if it be no more than a community of the two engaged in dialectical exchange or in a writing-reading relationship. Berry's dialectic of land and inhabitant might also be construed as a "community" in some such way. The notion of instruction through silence forces an obvious reversal, though: this community would be constituted not in an occasion but in an interregnum of language. If language, as White somewhere remarks, mediates between two realms of the unspoken, we might by contrast regard presence in the nonhuman place as the unspoken mediation between two occasions of speech, the before and after of one's life in the human community. To those enmeshed in preconception, it may not be evident that there even exists any unspoken realm, any occasion to which language is not wholly adequate: this, in part, is what the dialectic with wilderness corrects. In this case silence becomes the mode of articulation (in the full sense) proper to cultivating the community with place. And what we learn in silence we express in kind: "For the wilderness, which is to say the universe, we have no words. . . . Our words are for the way we have been" (257–58). Our language is sufficient to our stories; we no longer pretend it is sufficient to all we are not.

If White's extension of "community" to groups of only two seems extreme, the term's extension to include relations with nonhuman place might be thought altogether absurd were it not that the purpose of this learning, this dialectic, is clearly to reconstitute relations of human communities with the land. In a characteristic formulation from "A Native Hill," Berry considers how "a more indigenous life" than the one "we white people have lived" on this continent might be made:

> Until we understand what the land is, we are at odds with everything we touch. And to come to that understanding it is necessary, even now, to leave the regions of our conquest . . . and re-enter the woods. For only there can a man encounter the silence and the darkness of his own absence. . . . Perhaps then, having heard that silence and seen that darkness, he will grow humble before the place and begin to take it in—to learn *from it* what it is. (107)

Even rehearsing "his own absence," Berry is never far from issues of habitation. Let us note how this passage, though drawn from an essay and book (*The Long-Legged House*) about coming to be *at home*, in essence reiterates the terms and the trajectory by which, in his trips *away* from home, Berry comes to envision "the possibility of a better life." Berry, I am claiming, is exemplary in that his "away" behavior and "home" behavior are all of a piece, or at least are represented as such, as mutually and dialectically implicated. The need for individuals to "re-enter the woods" is a *social* need, in his estimation, if communities are not to remain "at odds" with their surroundings.

We can view this interpenetration of "home" and "away" from either direction. We find in the second chapter of *The Unforeseen Wilderness*—the "away" book—a passage on a family living in the Red River Gorge, occupying "an ancestral tract of farmland enclosed in that wilderness." The usual attributes of wilderness hold sway over the place: it is largely accessible only by foot, not by mechanized conveyance, and the house itself partakes of "the quiet of the wilderness," having "been cleansed of all unnecessary sounds" (UW 25). Both the threat to and the promise of the place are the same as those dramatized in solitude: "abstractions" imperil its "particularity," yet it affords "the possibility of a better life" (UW 26).

And just as Berry highlights this home in the wilderness, so he focuses on the wildness at home. The most exemplary of many instances of this, I think, is a retreat narrative of the purest sort placed at the center of "A Native Hill."[14] This is a classic outdoor "ramble," recounting a walk through overgrown fields and down a wooded ravine by his home, a narration employing much the same formal procedures and elaborating the same meaning-value terms as does "An Entrance to the Woods." Much the same narrative trajectory is sketched, extending through artifactual portents—a beer can, a rock-walled basin at a dry spring—and correlative trials of attitude to the ultimate recognition of possibility in a nonhuman sanctum sanctorum: here, a stand of original, unlogged forest beyond a last fence, the crossing of which effects a passage between states. So pronounced are the resemblances of form and purpose between this narrative and the one I have analyzed, the one could stand in for the other in my account. Though one comes from "home" and the other from "away," the primary purpose of both is the promotion of "a more indigenous life."

The possibility of "white people" becoming "more indigenous" relates to a further exemplary aspect of Berry's work: his posture toward past inhabitants both native and, to Europeans, "ancestral." In retreat, Berry invariably encounters signs of the presence of prior inhabitants; and while these encounters are eventful, grounds for contemplation and consternation in varying degrees, they are not torn by antinomies of indictment and approbation. While Berry acknowledges and in some measure hopes to emulate the lives of the dispossessed, mostly vanished native peoples of his region, he does not romanticize, slavishly imitate, or even much dwell on their ways. He is more concerned with his own white ancestors, whom he indicts and despairs of but will not disown. One section of "A Native Hill," for instance, relays an account of the destructive exploits of some pioneer Kentuckian men who, after hacking out a road in wilderness all day, build an obscenely huge bonfire at night and do battle with flung firebrands just for fun, damaging each other as well as the place. In the violent activities of these predecessors, who "represent the worst that is in us," Berry reads all our subsequent troubles and atrocities as a society; yet he admits to a certain "admiration" for and even "pride" in these exuberant fellows whose history is continuous with his own (83). The "survival" of their ways in our own is his and our problem in the most direct, familiar way.

Though he excoriates our prevailing culture, Berry avoids disparaging humankind in general after the manner of some environmental writing. Since he does not totalize humanity and depict it as equivalent to technological elaboration and/or white manhood in the first place, he is not so prey to the tacit self-hatred and split sensibility toward other human cultures characterizing much of the retreat narrative lineage. In fact, he seems increasingly *less* prey to such sensations, or more critical of them when they crop up: his limited-impact pronouncement of 1969, for instance, that "A man should be in the world as though he were not in it," is answered with this footnote in 1981: "Impossible. The problem calls for *practical* solutions" (68–69 — emphasis in original). In assessing such practice, Berry does not discard inherited terms of adaptation; characteristically, he inverts and reconstitutes them. The problem of his Kentuckian forebears, a problem which "Indians" and "peasants" (Old World indigens) did not have, was that "they belonged to no place"; thus their "abilities . . . were far more *primitive* and *rudimentary* than those of the Stone Age people they had driven out" (84–85 — my emphases). Their "practical solutions," this amounts to saying, were deficient by the very terms of complexity and sophistication that they or their apologists might have purported to hold. By extension, our own practices are just as "primitive," considered in relation to the latent sophistication of place.

One area where Berry is rather more subject to a split sensibility—
where his pontifications have furthest to span and, in my view, most
markedly fall short—is in references to and constructions of gender. The
breadth of the span to be bridged extends from the fact that escape to
the woods has normally been so masculine a domain: even solitary retreat is defined in part by its relation to the group activities of hunters
and adventurers, as it is in part by its status as an evasion of a domestic
economy riven with contradictions of gender. Even here, Berry's formulations are in many respects exemplary. His emphasis on adaptation,
cooperation, and especially peace both in solitary retreat and in domestic life helps reconstitute prevailing notions of masculine virtue and
prowess. And Berry does not overtly feminize the landscape or resort to
metaphors of romantic love, enthrallment, or possession to account for his
bond with it.[15] At times he will speak in terms of entering into a
"marriage" with the land and couch this relation in terms of the virtues of
"husbandry," but this is a figure for fealty to and interdependence with a
cultivated landscape; it is not present in his writings on wilderness, a
domain that remains essentially ungendered in his work.

Yet there are grounds for qualms over Berry's constructions of gender.
It is a topic he has written about at length, and it surpasses the scope of my
effort here to recapitulate his views in detail, but such aspects as pertain to
my subject deserve comment. There is the matter, for one thing, of Berry's
heavily gendered language: his universal preference for male pronouns
and the expression "a man" for representative human figures. If it smacks
of a litmus test to point this out, it bears asking what larger reactions are
indicated in the change of shades. What is indicated at a minimum, I
think, is that Berry has a preference for traditional language forms and
depends upon the resonances they command: we have seen how this is
the case with the language of meaning and value he employs. It remains
the case, and it remains a problem, I think, that gender-neutral forms, as
yet so relatively thin in accumulated instances of use, are hard-pressed to
achieve the rhetorical effects that Berry summons with his gendered general pronouncements. Yet those effects—the mellifluous ease with which
the monolith "Man" and its matching pronouns unfold in Berry's prose
rhythms—may lay a trap for their author. The measured tone, the
seasoned vocabulary of value, the equanimity of pronouncement and
purified scorn of reproach—all may be jeopardized if the reader begins to
suspect that, after all, this man may not invariably venture all that "far out
of himself" or recapitulate sacred myth in his every foray out of doors.

Such suspicion, in my reading, has been especially warranted in Berry's mythologizing of his marriage to his wife and his "marriage" to his home place. This is where the sorts of vexations attending his allegiance to the pronoun "he" seem most evident.

It's in "The Long-Legged House" that Berry most mythologizes his "marriages" and that grounds for suspecting his myth most crop up. For the myth Berry makes appears to gloss over and belie certain specific life choices he reports. In this essay, Berry somewhat mystically connects his marriage to his wife with his inhabitation of "the Camp," his great-uncle's old riverfront cabin—a bond formed when Berry brings his new bride there the first summer of their marriage. Later, upon the family's return to Kentucky—a return which is the primary subject of the essay—Berry reports, "the plan was that I would do my teaching at the university on Tuesdays, Wednesdays, and Thursdays, and then drive down to the Camp to write during the other four days," this in order to afford him the solitude necessary to finish his book (62). Unless I'm mis-reading this, it appears that Berry effectively abandoned his wife and two young children to their rented house in town, disappearing alternately into the academy and the woods for the duration of the composition of his novel. This period was pivotal for him, says Berry: a time when he "had, in a sense, made a marriage with the place" (69)—with the place, one might venture, instead of his wife.

This course of events—this "plan" that Berry reports not as some-thing worked out or dictated but as something that just "was"—compro-mises the myth of harmonizing "marriages" that Berry tacitly promotes in his narratives of retreat. The myth is further undermined by another myth Berry creates about "the Camp," one he intertwines with the myth of his marriage(s): that of the writer's emotional identification with the great-uncle who built the original cabin at the site, a man of whom Berry declares, "I am his follower and heir" (72). What are the lessons and legacy Berry claims? The lessons he finds at home concern mar-riage, as we've seen, and a certain sufficiency of situation manifested in the resistance to the allure of other places (not to mention other women): "I do not long to travel to Italy or Japan, but only across the river or up the hill into the woods" (72). Yet the great-uncle he admires, we learn at the start of the essay, was a bachelor, a silent and solitary man (though a good storyteller), and an inveterate wanderer as well, lacking "either a home or a profession," drifting about between relatives' houses when he happened to be back in the area (17). This is

the presiding genius of "the Camp," Berry's site of stability and marriage, though these entailments of rootlessness and discontent have been
largely enveloped in this long essay's bulk by the time Berry claims his
psychic inheritance at its end. We should note, though, how much more
closely this ancestral figure corresponds to the "marriage" with place
Berry consummates *in the absence* of his wife and children—right down
to the uncle's facility with story, in the ascetic pursuit of which Berry
enters into his union.

In the analysis of "An Entrance to the Woods" above, I noted how a
connection between individual solitude and social and economic possibility was proposed , not as a cause-effect relation, but by association and
juxtaposition. Something of the same effect is created, I think, in the
juxtaposition of the bachelor ancestor with the writer's dual "marriage."
As the most favorable entitlements of solitude in that essay are appropriated to the vision of an improved economic order, so the most favorable
aspects of bachelorhood are here implicated in the writer's vision of a
"marriage" to place. Adapting Harpham's phrase about asceticism—that
it *"raises the issue* of culture" in portraying its absence—we might say
that this dwelling upon bachelorhood "raises the issue" of marriage, in a
relation of temptation and resistance that the essay in certain ways configures. Problems arise with this relation when "practical solutions"
don't follow the contours of idealized formal correspondences, as seems
to be the case with this "marriage" of Berry's. I have no wish to diminish
the difficult choices Berry's family must have faced that resulted in the
solutions Berry reports, nor to question Berry's sincerity or his wife's
approval of their domestic arrangements then or now. On the contrary,
if the practical difficulty of those choices is *not* represented, as it appears
not to be here, so much the worse for the informing myth, including, in
this case, the social efficacy of solitude.

Having cited these suspicions and discrepancies, though, I will say I
view them as evidence mainly of the difficulty of the problems Berry,
with many others, configures in narratives of retreat, with forms of masculine desire prominent among them. If stories of retreat *do* contribute
to "practical solutions" to such problems, they do so by helping to
*re*configure desire and sensation, offering scripts for participation that
revise even as they depend upon inherited behaviors.

Berry's narratives are exemplary not just in what they hold as
desirable but in the narrative forms by which they enact desire and
fulfillment. In his essays, drama ensues not from conflict but from

"contact": from the relation of participant to place, not from a contest of "characters" in which aspects of the landscape stand in for allies or antagonists. Articulations of topography and vegetation are themselves eventful, suspenseful, as are sensations, recollections, recognitions of general import. These narratives are questlike in that the writer undergoes trials, obstacles to the achievement of contact and recognition. But the obstacles encountered mostly extend from the artifactual residue of human conflict and violence; they are not themselves figured as adversaries to be engaged and subdued. In a sense, it is enmity which is the enemy.

And in these quests, recognition of the nonhuman essential is inevitable; what's "unforeseen" is *bound* to reveal itself, if the place is entered in the correct spirit, in quiet and peace, which is to say, alone. Berry especially furthers Thoreau's project of preparing us for solitude, a condition that most nature writers take to be necessary to the realizations they depict[16] but that few depict as any hardship or trial. The essay of Berry's we've examined depicts or "emplots" a process of recovery from the estrangement the writer feels—a sensation he recognizes as necessary, a condition of entrance. Berry is familiar with this strangeness; rehearsed in it, he rehearses it for us in turn. In story, he leads us to it and sees us through.

Berry does not configure this desire for solitude as escape from society; this we've seen. But one final exemplary feature: neither do his narratives configure a desire to collect and possess the nonhuman place. They betray no impulse to reproduce the place in its every detail, fixing it on the page in a technical arrest of mortal decay. Gene Meatyard's photographs accord with this not anti- or non- but not-representational project: black-and-white, they stress contrasts of light and dark peculiar to certain moments and vantages in the Red River. They are not abstract but are not especially scenic. In this "picture book," neither writer nor photographer paints a picture of the place to be "seen" by readers; they prefer to evoke the feeling and substance of its being "unforeseen." Faithful to particulars of experience, both text and images comprise not a record of a place but a mode of dwelling therein. If the dam project had proceeded and the Gorge had been inundated and lost, this book would not serve as a museum of what is lost or "preserve" the place in any substantive way. There are "no words" here "for the wilderness" in itself: "Our words are for the way we've been." Thus it seems after all that the moralizer Berry acknowledges not one but two "bad reasons to go to wilderness": to escape from people, and to capture the place.

CHAPTER FIVE

Sites and Senses
of Writing in Nature

A typical opening move in nature essays has the writer in effect proclaiming, "Here I am! in the middle of nowhere! immersed at this very moment in some offbeat, hair-raising, or otherwise exceptional situation! Now here's how I got here and why." Though the present effort is no nature essay, I too would like to start with a scene from the middle of my story:

Four vans have disgorged the thirty-six students of the New England Literature Program onto the coast of Maine.[1] Unprompted, they distribute themselves over the terrain, metamorphosing from the cluster unloaded near camp into single figures dispersing over the ledges and boulders of the littoral slope. They settle onto the rocks and face the surf, the spectacle. Before long, almost to a person, their eyes drop toward their knees and laps. Fresh to the Maine Coast, they bend over journals, writing.

These students are not "nature writers" by any means, not even "writers" as the term is generally employed; yet they are in nature, and they are writing. There is something both stirring and peculiar about the scene. Their writing is at once the emblem of their absorption—in the place and/or in themselves—and the locus of an evident incongruity, that they should be facing the page instead of the place itself. Yet on second thought, what seems incongruous is not their behavior so much as their numbers, the fact that, however scrupulously they space themselves out on the rocks, these are not truly isolated figures. A single figure filling a notebook in such a place would seem eminently natural, recognizable to all. Here a group conspires to imitate that recognized condition—to go solitaire en masse, as it were. They are versed in the cultural script of retreat and are moving to enact it. They could not enact it so markedly without the instrument of their journals, their attention to which signals to themselves and those around them their resolve to approach a condition of solitude. They might otherwise be taken, or take themselves, to be simply alone.

The students on their rocks do not so much secure a place to find solitude to write as they write to create a solitude that will secure them in the place. In this, they differ somewhat from more typical depictions of the writer as an isolated individual. They seldom regard themselves as "writers" while they write. In this, they have a precedent in Wendell Berry, who claims to have undertaken his trips to the Red River Gorge "not as an observer or writer but as a creature bemused by the creation" (*Unforeseen Wilderness* 63). Why would Berry, who writes professionally in all major genres, wish to disclaim the identity of writer and contrast it with that of "creature" in his wilderness visits? And how does the picture of these human creatures scribbling on the rocks compare with and speak to more prevalent images of the solitary writer?

By way of doubling back onto the subject of this chapter—sites, scenes, and constructions of nature writing and writers—I plan first to review one prominent critique of the image of the solitary writer, one of several such critiques that have gained currency in the field of composition and literacy studies, concerned as it is with intersections of writerly identity and behavior (see, for instance, works by Brandt, Gere, and LeFevre). The critique I will examine, by Linda Brodkey, I want not so much to rebut as to test and extend, to employ as a springboard for consideration of the identity and behavior of the writer in nature. As I expect to draw terms from Brodkey's article, I will not otherwise forecast the direction my discussion will take, except to say that taking various nature writers as exhibits, it will eventuate in speculation as to why Berry might make the distinction he does between "writer" and "creature." It will consider, that is, how the terms paired within the expression "nature writing" might describe a system of "resistance" in Harpham's sense of the term—providing a "capacity to structure oppositions without collapsing them, to raise issues without settling them" (*Ascetic* xii)—related to the narrative logic of retreat and embodied in the activities, remarks, and figures (the identities, the metaphors) of the genre's practitioners.

THE SCENE OF THE SOLITARY WRITER

In "Modernism and the Scene(s) of Writing," Linda Brodkey describes and analyzes what she identifies as "the scene of writing": the popular, iconic image of "a solitary writer alone in a cold garret," cut off from all social circumstances. This figure, which she shorthands as "the writer-writes-alone," exerts an attraction that Brodkey finds treacherous and in some degree unaccountable, considering that "it is after all . . . an image of economic, emotional, and social deprivation." Its sway, in her estimation, is great, notably among those involved in teaching or taking writing courses; whatever our particular writing situations, she insists, "all of us try to recreate a garret and all that it portends." In its dominance the image tends to suppress other images of writing, ones that do not tacitly discourage readers from inserting themselves into the position of writer. The scene is a sort of timeless tableau in which "the writer is an Author and the writing is Literature"; the reader is excluded as an element of that "social life" which "must not be allowed to enter the garret" (396–97).

This formidable "scene of writing" has more particular attributes in Brodkey's account, several of which may be sifted out from the following passage, in which Brodkey moves to align the scene with the tenets of literary modernism in which she maintains it originates:

> Notice that the image privileges only one event in writing, the moment when the writer is an amanuensis, making transcription a synecdoche of writing. In such a freeze frame, the writer is a writing machine, as effectively cut off from writing as from society. . . . One implication is that writing costs writers their lives. Likely to terrify writers and would-be writers alike, it is a picture, sometimes the only picture, we conjure when we seek the solitude necessary for writing. In its extreme versions, writers are condemned to solitary confinement, imprisoned by language and condemned to write without understanding either why they do so or for whom. . . . Seen in this way, the picture of the solitary scribbler is taken from the album of modernism, where the metaphor of solitude is reiterated as the themes of alienation in modern art and atomism in modern science. (397–98)

Adding to earlier points about its essential deprivation and its quasi-official cultural status, we may identify the following among Brodkey's assertions about the "scene": that within it, writing is transcription; that such transcription is a mechanical function; that the writer is a prisoner and the scene of writing a cell; that solitude is largely alienation and victimage (though *some* form of solitude may be "necessary for writing" in some moments); and that writing is separate from and threatening to life.

Filing for later reference most of these attributes, I want to draw attention to the feature of Brodkey's argument most pertinent to my own. Let me reemphasize first that Brodkey holds no brief for this image of the writer. On the contrary, she opposes it vigorously, espousing models of writing in which the social is reintegrated, transforming even writerly solitude. Yet the vigor of her opposition is proportionate to the extremity of her claims as to the scene's ubiquity and entitlements. In her depiction of the "scene of writing," the "writer-writes-alone" is figured *either* as deprived, imprisoned, subjugated to mechanical functions and victimized by art, *or* as enacting a view of writing as a social, collaborative activity and thus resisting the presumptions of solitude. The counterexamples she provides to modernist depictions of the solitary writer consist of women writers (the garret holds only men) who just as surely seek out isolated, confined spaces but in some manner refuse the imperatives of the garret, viewing and pursuing their solitude in ways Brodkey regards as "pragmatic" rather than "romantic"—for instance, Woolf and the room of one's own (406). Among the sites of writing we are impelled to make over as garrets, Brodkey cites these: "a study, a library, a classroom, or . . . a kitchen table" (397). There is no mention here of the woods, the desert, the mountains—the outdoors. Yet it's the outdoors—or that associated space, the cabin—that in the cultural script of retreat is figured as the scene of solitude, and this scene, too, enjoys wide currency, if not "hegemonic" status. Though "romantic," it is not the scene of alienation Brodkey describes; "pragmatic" in any number of its depictions, it is not a situation she considers.

I am suggesting that nature writing offers both a further alternative to the modernist image of writing—such alternatives are what Brodkey is calling for, after all—and a corrective to or at least complication of linkages she assumes between the numerous attributes of this image of the "writer-writes-alone." The scene of the writer outdoors does not rehabilitate the image of "the writer-writes-alone," but it does prise apart its package of attributes. Nature writing offers a scene of writerly solitude associated not with confinement but with its reverse, freedom of movement; a scene in which creative process (or "inspiration") is associated not with machinery but with its absence, or at least its problematization (since writing itself, in some respects at least, is ever and anon technology); a scene not fundamentally tied to an understanding of the writer as occupying the exclusive office of Author in the house of Literature; and a scene in which the confinement and trying solitude of writing, so widely attested to by writers in general, may be understood from the start as responsive to other voices and undertaken at least in part for public purposes. None of this is to claim that the problems Brodkey describes are forthwith solved in scenes of nature writing; rather it is to suggest the ways in which these scenes recast those problems, or the ways those problems offer up terms for a consideration of these scenes—a consideration upon which I now embark.

THE NATURE WRITER'S ESTATE:
"WRITING" AND "LIVING"

There is no more detailed an account of the scenes of nature writing and of the activities and the estate, as it were, of nature writers, than Stephen Trimble's essay, "The Naturalist's Trance," based upon interviews with over a dozen nature writers whose work he anthologizes in *Words from the Land: Encounters with Natural History Writing*. While this essay revisits in quick succession several features remarked upon in Brodkey, two aspects especially pertain.

The first is the notion of "the naturalist's trance" itself. Drawn from the biologist Edward O. Wilson,[2] the phrase refers to a "mental set . . . by which biologists locate more elusive organisms," in which one's "mind [comes] free" and becomes extraordinarily attentive to "the hard workings of the natural world." Note that the passage itself depicts a retreat narrative of sorts, a fronting through "trance" of nonhuman essentials culminating in a climactic recognition of "the natural world." In selecting this "trance" as a way to thematize his discussion, Trimble commits to a figure of nature writing as an out-of-the-ordinary, half-conscious, solitary pursuit, a figure much in keeping with the one Brodkey critiques. The difference is that, in the figure Trimble uses, the naturalist or biologist thus "entranced" has yet to write a thing. Indeed, the condition seems the very opposite of writing, and is certainly far distanced from the confinement of the scene Brodkey bemoans.

A second aspect extends from this. Trimble, as it happens, finds the notion of "trance" expressive of *both* stages of the nature writing process as he proceeds to describe it: both the preliminaries of fieldwork and the aftermath of the writing proper, so to speak. These are the components of the dual activity of nature writers, which Trimble catchily sums up: "They write. They live. And they forge a voice by doing both" (2). As here formulated, to "write" and to "live" are not the same: the latter precedes and is separate from the former. While this formulation does not quite suggest that "writing costs writers their lives," as Brodkey says the modernist "scene of writing" does, it expresses the same presupposition that "writing" is separate and distinct from "living." This is a notion sufficiently widespread in depictions of nature writing—as of writing in general as remarked upon by Brodkey—that we must wonder what, beyond sheer conventionality, might warrant it. The distinction is prevalent enough that Wendell Berry, for instance, must evoke it while attempting to dissolve it: of writing before a window, he quips, "Why not write and live at the same time?" (*Recollected* 40).

Having casually appropriated this distinction for his two-stage model, though, Trimble proceeds to fudge it somewhat, in a manner that leads me to retain quotation marks on this second-stage "writing" and its opposite number, "living." His next two sentences read: "These writers make *journeys* into the landscape; they enter 'the naturalist's trance.' They weigh their *journals* against the research, spend long hours in libraries, and talk to the experts" (2—emphases added). The "journey"—what the writer "lives"—gives way to an aftermath of "writing"; except "journey" has been blurred into "journal," by which maneuver "writing" surreptitiously invades the domain of "living." After field and research, Trimble continues, the writers "translate all this into lovely prose"—"all this" presumably including the journey/journal which, it follows, was not previously "lovely prose." Perhaps it was not prose at all but that subspecies of inscription called "notes."

The tacit split between "writing" and "living," I think, reflects an unsettledness over the occupational estate of the "writer" in the case of nature writers. The "modernist scene" that Brodkey sketches figures the writer exclusively as "Author" whose function is to produce "Literature." Yet if the subject is "nature" and "living" is its quintessence, professional allegiance to "writing" may compromise the relation one seeks. Trimble, though, believes that nature writers—at least those whose work he has collected—hold the identity of "writer" as foremost. Of these writers, he insists: "Whatever else they may be—biologists, teachers, cowboys, bee-keepers, farmers, artists—these people see themselves as writers first" (2). He cites this as his main criterion for selection, omitting work by "biologists and anthropologists" because, he claims, "however elegant their prose, they seldom define themselves first as *writers*" (3—emphasis in original)—as indeed, the students on the Maine coast do not.

Straightaway, there's difficulty in determining how writerly self-definition is manifested. How do we say in the case of the biologist, for instance (an example cited in Trimble's statements as in Wilson's passage on the "naturalist's trance"), that such an individual defines him/herself *first* as a writer? Cannot such a person write appealing, jargon-free, "elegant prose" while cultivating the role of biologist as primary occupation and not as something "else" in addition to an identity as writer? What could it mean to regard oneself "as a writer first" while still discharging the professional functions of a biologist? How do we tell the difference? This criterion of self-definition becomes further vexed, considering the tiers of figures Trimble cites as predecessors in the hard-to-name "tradition" of nature or (his preferred term) natural history writing: the originary Thoreau, then John Muir and John Burroughs, then Henry Beston, Aldo Leopold, Loren Eiseley, and Rachel Carson (3). With Thoreau, Burroughs, and Beston, certainly, self-definition as writer comes first (and it is no accident, I think, that these are all celebrated cabin-dwellers—a matter to which I'll return). But with Leopold, Eiseley, and Carson, such a judgment is difficult to make: all three worked as scientists in academic or governmental capacities through most of their careers, and the very personae they devised as writers hinge upon their identities as scientists. Most problematic, perhaps, is Muir, who preferred to identify himself as a scientist and not a writer, but whose persona is predominantly neither, but rather that of an all-purpose sage and instantiation of wild nature. Even among the contemporaries whose work Trimble selects, writerly self-definition is not clear-cut. Becoming a "writer first" may hinge upon the success of one's writing, rather than the reverse—as it did with Sue Hubbell, the "beekeeper" to whom Trimble alludes, whose first book, published after she'd turned fifty, followed upon her past identities as librarian, wife, divorcee, and professional honey producer (213). An extreme example of the act preceding the identity is Ann Zwinger, whose coming to be a writer actually originated in someone's request that she write a book, an undertaking she had never before considered (15).[3]

My points are, first, that while primary self-definition as a writer *may* be established by a nature writer's *own* direct testimony to that effect, it is more often an inference drawn from texts that do not directly make such claims. Such "self-definition" is a question of genre and reception: biologist, beekeeper, or any others who write about "natural" things in such a "poetic" or "popular" manner may be presumed or invited to regard themselves as a writer above all else. But—second—if the generic "core" of nature writing is a narrative of retreat, as I believe it is, then writerly ethos may actually be served through a self-definition that is *not* primarily that of a writer, or at least is indeterminate on this score. The drama of Aldo Leopold, of Sue Hubbell, above all of Muir, resides in the sense of their having come to writing out of needs and recognitions originating in their fronting of nature, and not the reverse. Even Thoreau, who Edward Hoagland says "lived to write"—as opposed to Muir, who "lived to hike" (45)—dramatizes in his own persona one whose primary business is "living."

Could it be, then, that in this literary realm, being a "writer first" means precisely to make a cipher of occupational identity? Then occupation would represent one further artifact to abandon in retreat, in the divesting of which one would act, as Berry says, "not as an observer or writer but as a creature bemused"—entranced, as it were—with no more specialized a standing than that. Except that writing itself issues in artifacts of the most literal and obtrusive sort, notably books themselves. Not otherwise visibly occupied, the primary "writer" is the one preoccupied with the making of books—precisely the business of the "writer or observer" that Berry, while a "creature," disclaims. Thus there is this tension, thus this insistence that these people who write nature are, in fact, writers above all. Of what other "literary" practitioners must this claim be advanced and supported? It must be insisted upon because it cannot be assumed.

I think it no accident that the contemporary nature writer who least evinces any occupational identity or even affinity *besides* that of "writer" is the one who most vigorously depicts a "scene of writing" like the one Brodkey critiques: Annie Dillard. Dillard is not a scientist or naturalist who writes, nor a writer so affiliated with naturalists as to be taken for one, nor a writer who accompanies scientists on their rounds; nor does she come to her writing from a working relation to land as farm or ranch or bee field. Even Edward Abbey, who vehemently rejected the label of naturalist and embraced that of working writer, made a reputation by writing out of his work as a park ranger, linking land to "living" in specific ways that Dillard has never so much as hinted at. Dillard is adamantly a writer foremost and exclusively. "Your life is literature," she avers; it consists of "hard, conscious, terribly frustrating work," not the "dream" that people envision in which "you just sit on a tree stump and take dictation from a chipmunk" (Trimble 32).

While this gibe about dictation may mildly contravene one aspect of the "scene of writing" Brodkey depicts, Dillard's views of writing confirm Brodkey's image in almost every particular, so much so that Dillard's book on the subject, *The Writing Life*, can be read as one long, fabulous embrace and elaboration of the image of the solitary, agonistic writer that Brodkey rejects. Particularly striking are Dillard's variations on the split between "writing" and "living," the range and ingenuity of the ways in which she pursues the assumption that, as Brodkey puts it, "writing costs writers their lives." Dillard quips about it: "The written word is weak. Many people prefer life to it" (17). She waxes phenomenological about it, speaking of the writer's "sensory deprivation" and asserting that, contrary to talk of "the life of the mind," whatever it may be that goes on in the writer's mind, she "would be hard put to call it living" (44). Since writing effectively kills you, she suggests, you might as soon die as write: "Why not shoot yourself, actually, rather than finish one more excellent manuscript on which to gag the world?" (12). Or if it's not the writer it may be the book that's near death: "I do not so much write a book as sit up with it, as with a dying friend" (52). The insistence, the enthusiasm with which Dillard equates writing with dying suggests the competitive dimension of asceticism that Harpham remarks on, expressed in "the far from idle boast of one monk to another: 'I am deader than you' " (*Ascetic* 26).

Characterizing the scene of reading in a similarly morbid image—"You can read in the space of a coffin" (26)—Dillard recalls, too, the confinement of the modernist garret. She is pleased to tout the virtues of a "cinder-block cell" as a study (26) and to describe as "solitary confinement" the days spent therein (48). Yet her posture depicts no single-minded zest for incarceration but rather a structure of *resistance* in Harpham's sense, ascetic in essence, formulating without resolving relations of opposition and temptation between "two apparently antagonistic terms" (xii)—in this case between freedom and constraint, that is to say, "living" (linked with "nature") and "writing." In this sense, not just Brodkey's and Dillard's evocations of writerly experience but also "nature writing" at large depends on resistance, and what is at issue is not whether writing should be construed as "solitary" or "social" but how the relation between these might best be structured.

One limpid fantasy by which Dillard illustrates her experience of writing evinces clearly the "ambivalent yearning" that resistance structures: "Every morning you climb several flights of stairs, enter your study, open the French doors, and slide your desk and chair out into the middle of the air" (10). This halluncinatory ascent seems a version of the climb to the garret, and the activity pursued there has as mechanical a character as the "transcription" Brodkey describes: "Your work is to keep cranking the flywheel that turns the gears that spin the belt in the engine of belief that keeps you and your desk in midair" (11). Yet this mid-air study is comically situated in nature, "between the crowns of maple trees," with a winter view "clear to the river" and in summer a complement of birds working the branches below and above the desk (10–11). Thus the utmost servitude is required to maintain a state of ideal, thus impossible freedom—if this mid-air vantage *is* an image of freedom (any more than the Vantage cigarettes Dillard reports smoking as she writes). For it is an image, too, of immobility, and of weightlessness akin to the ineffectuality she finds, by and large, in acts of writing. "Putting a book together" may be "life at its most free"; but this "freedom is a by-product of your days' triviality," the fact that "your work is so meaningless" to anyone but yourself (11).

The image of the mid-air desk is strikingly replicated in the cover illustration of Trimble's *Words from the Land*, which shows an old-fashioned, curve-legged writing table superimposed on an idealized mountain-forest-river landscape, not settled within it but hovering before it. The "field" and the "study" seem juxtaposed yet incommensurable. Yet it's "words from the land," not from the house, that the book is supposed to contain. What could the difference be? Why should it matter where the words are "from"?

BEYOND DOORS: WRITING ON SITE

Anne Ruggles Gere has proposed attention to the alternate sites, the "kitchen tables and rented rooms," in which the "extra-curriculum" of composition is enacted beyond the classroom ("Kitchen"). Her call echoes Brodkey's concern with writerly location, her asking what the upshot for writing practice might be if it's considered to occur in the kitchen as opposed to the garret or cell. I propose to devote a similar attention to location, but to attend instead to a more elemental distinction, between writing within humanly constructed enclosures of *any* sort—any "indoors"—and writing outside them.

Differences may exist, for instance, in the technology the scene depends upon and the modes of attention and participation it authorizes or obstructs. Aldo Leopold has remarked on the technologically mediated needs and leisure requisite to nature appreciation: "These wild things, I admit, had little human value until mechanization assured us a good breakfast" (vii). We might consider the genre of nature writing as itself derived from the possibility and habit of writing outdoors thus enabled. Genre in this case would be understood not as a collocation of set features but rather as Stanley Cavell views it, as a group of texts inheriting and enacting common "conditions," such that "each member of . . . a genre represents a study of these conditions" (28). Such enabling conditions include not just certain conceptual shifts, like that from "mountain gloom" to "glory" in attitudes toward wilderness that Marjorie Nicolson tracks, but also technical, material changes relating to these, from the very broad, like Leopold's "mechanization," to the specific: the development of lenses for microscopes, binoculars, and eyeglasses; the changes in paint bases and pigments that made landscape painting en plein air a feasible pursuit; the evolution of the lead pencil, which Thoreau was instrumental in advancing; and so on.[4] The questions I would pose are ones such as these: how are such technical-cum-experiential aspects of writing "in the field" represented or resisted in texts originating in and concerning the field? How is it that we come to think of writing as a mode or component of *being in* and not just reporting about a place—come, that is, to a scene such as the one I began with, the students with their journals on the coast?

These students, I have said, are enacting in their way a cultural script of retreat in nature. Such retreat will likely entail a drama of passage from or through the artifactual—as with Berry's account of becoming "stripped," first, to what little you can carry in a backpack, and subsequently of the conceptual artifices of what he calls "preconception" (*Unforeseen* 31–44). The functions and attributes of the devices one carries may come to stand out in sharp relief, before they fall away from attention (if they do) in the recognition of the nonhuman. The devices may even be fetishized, as so much is in the modern recreational "gear" industry, so that one's experience is configured by one's equipment, and one only goes out *in order* to handle the gear. The same goes for writing (as for modes of recording in general) in its capacity as technological activity, intervention, and wellspring of "events." What, how, when, whether to write (or sketch or photograph or otherwise inscribe)—these decisions to wield gear may become highlighted when set in the experiential frame of what Thoreau would call "unhandselled" surroundings, places sought expressly for the absence of such interventions. In my own experience, as one not professionally inured to "fieldwork," they are heightened: the prospect of writing "down" a sight or event or phrase as it materializes can occasion at least a hitch and at worst a crisis of selection and procedure, of preparing, executing, representing, coming to a stop, reconciling the demands of the inscribing activity with the larger, ongoing character of my conduct in the place. Any inscribing I end up doing will become ipso facto eventful, if for no more complex a reason than that I cannot both hike and write, paddle and write, even gawk and write, not in the strict sense. The equipment does not permit it.

This "materiality of the writer's life" (Dillard's phrase—46) in the scene of writing *en plein air* has been most dramatized to me not by any writer per se but in an exhibit of the work of an artist named Tony Foster, which I viewed in 1987. Foster, who hiked a fifty-one-mile route through the High Sierra from Yosemite to the Whitney Portal along a route previously taken by John Muir, prepared large watercolor landscapes constituting a visual diary of the terrain he traversed, each accented by side sketches of flowers and wildlife, small specimens of bark, granite, sand, seeds, pine needles, and so on, affixed directly or in clear plastic pockets to the surface, tiny relief maps marking locations of sketches and specimens, and assorted notes on names, route, events, and his exemplar and predecessor Muir, entered in a draftsman's precise hand. Foster's work—which when I saw it was exhibited not in an art gallery but at the California Academy of Sciences—comprised not only a remarkable representation of the landscape and the expedition, but also one most conscious of its status and procedures as representation. It sought not to conceal but to highlight the artifactual devices of its creation, with the effect that its participation in the place appeared all the more direct. It was clear both where and how this was made.

In the middle of the hall ringed with the paintings stood a plexiglass display case containing the artist's gear: backpack, ensolite roll, drawing board, aluminum paper tube with five-inch cork stopper, plus brushes and a tiny watercolor box, the middle of each color deeply dipped into where the fine brushes had bored a hole, as if by drip erosion. And there was a thin journal, pocket-sized, red paper–covered and staple-bound, with a thin pencil like an elongated version of the ones that used to come in the envelopes of newsmagazine subscription solicitations. There was something striking about the way that the weight-consciousness of the long-distance trekker, the backpacker's minimalism, had been brought to bear on those very instruments by which the exhibit hall had been filled—with people as well as images—and the way these instruments had taken their place among the artist's "outfit," the total array of devices by which he had made his way. A virtual economy: it was manifest how everything he had carried back out with him was now on display, and how this was the same as what he'd taken in, minus some food and plus that surplus that comprised the show and the story.

This sort of economic as well as artistic self-sufficiency is a powerful element of nature writing's appeal. What most outdoor equipment is meant to permit, after all, is one's very survival or at least comfort in the nonhuman milieu. Writing may be as prone as any activity to the romance of self-sufficiency, which figures in nature writing's ethos from *Walden* on; there may even be inscriptional equivalents to "living off the land." Robert Finch alludes to this prospect in lampooning a popular image of nature writers "as people who are out there writing down their essays on scraps of birch bark"—an image he contrasts with his own practice of foregoing field notes and instead entering "the experience with no preconceptions . . . then let[ting] the experience settle out" (Trimble 7). In denying that his inscribing activities are undertaken on the spot, Finch acknowledges the appeal of the idea that they might be. Yet there is no necessary contrast between the relinquishing of "preconception" that Finch and Berry both seek, and the image of composing *in situ* on birchbark, except as resides in the misapprehension that the written product arrives fully formed, like Dillard's chipmunk dictation. The birchbark conceit, in fact, reveals something about the larger realm of "preconception" involved in retreat, in which the material and experiential are not so readily differentiated. Even if the *essays* on birchbark are thought to arrive complete, it's clear from their primitive mode of inscription that the *situation* was yet unfinished. The "gear," the manner of inscription, was not all "preconceived." The devising of a manner of inscription consubstantial with the place itself serves as correlative to the situated event as original, authentic, "lived" within and not just "written" about: a material testament.

I offer two exhibits of this, one tending to absurdity, the other to hagiography. In one of the more popular and less durable nature books written, *Alone in the Wilderness* (1913), Joseph Knowles enacts Finch's quip, reproducing notes and sketches done with burnt sticks on birch-bark, executed during his highly publicized naked plunge into the woods of Maine, where he had resolved to live as a "primitive" for sixty days without any implements save those he devised himself. Knowles's birchbark missives, deposited in a hollow stump for pickup by reporters, were seized upon not only as the reports but as the emblems of his occupation of the wild domain. When one newspaper published evidence that Knowles had prepared his texts not in the open but in a secret cabin, their stock (along with their author's) plummeted, quite as much as if they had been forgeries (Nash 141–43).

Knowles is an oddity but not an anomaly; his survivalist stunt exaggerated a mode of retreat for which John Muir, most eminently, was celebrated: solitary, extended, undertaken with the barest of possessions. And as Knowles had his birchbark dispatches, so we have for Muir the story of an ink he made from sequoia cones: "native ink—the blood and body of the forest" (Ehrlich 1988, viii). More importantly, we have the eloquent material remains of his journals and notes, as depicted for us by his biographer and the editor of his journals, Linnie Marsh Wolfe:

> Having shared in the hardships of his wanderings, his notes, mostly written in pencil, are not easy to read after the lapse of years. Many were scribbled by flickering campfires when his body was numb with fatigue; or in the dark lee of some boulder or tree while the storm raged without; or tramping over a vast glacier, his fingers stiff with the cold, and his eyes blinded by the snow glare. Often before the notes could be carried home to camp or hut, they were smudged by ferns and flowers pressed between the pages, or water-soaked in bogs that had to be waded through. (xi)

Wolfe offers this as commentary on the difficulties confronting the editor as she attempts to decipher Muir's notes; but if the words themselves "are not easy to read," the "hardships" of their composition and passage are eminently legible in their material condition — a condition which includes the words.

My point is that, whether for the sideshow Knowles or the main event Muir, the materiality of their textual "effects" (i.e., remains) is a warrant to the actuality of their narratives of retreat. If they *wrote* there they must have *been* there, where they say, in the ways that they claim — tangible ways. Yet these "effects" are reproductions — photos of birch-bark surfaces in Knowles's book; Wolfe's account of the drama she's deciphered in Muir's half-legible texts — second-hand testaments to a primary materiality. In a sense, they attest to no more than the "presence" of the present-tense assertions the original, "situated" texts contain. They depend upon and buttress a faith in the possibility of asserting "I am here" in writing and having it mean substantially what I (no longer) say.

Let me demonstrate. I'm looking out a window. (Or I was, before I wrote that, since I cannot both write and look.) To the extent that I am "noticing" (preparing a "notice," preparing to inscribe) what I see, it is all reportable. I mean that I can dictate whatever I happen to or resolve to see, after a fashion — I can identify, list, chronologize. But only in principle — in the character of my yet unwritten attention. For when I actually begin to *do* anything like this in writing, a great deal is changed. The move to the page, at once purposeful and stray, disengages me from the running sense of accounting to myself for what I notice. And this transforms the character of the noticing. It alters the rhythms of attention, introducing the page as home depot in the wandering commerce of the eye. If it does not stand to make me a liar outright, it at least enforces a duality upon what I may presume in print to be the present. I mean that I can write "I am sitting" or "I think" and be truthful; but if I write, "I see a bird," as I write this I am already either lying or appealing to a version of present truth that is additional, perhaps rival, to the first.

I do not claim that this change in noticing through writing must violate or diminish either. Nor do I believe such a change is peculiar to acts of writing in the scene of nature; clearly it is not. But the shift is less acute in its effects, I believe, when it comes to recounting exclusively *human* figures and actions. It's as if these were so storied already that no stretch or displacement is entailed in the move to transcribe them. We are used to emplotting humans; we regard them already in terms of such transcription. We tend not to regard nonhuman features and event in this way, though — especially if our intents in viewing the latter include eschewing "preconception" and letting the place itself dictate to our attention.

TRANSCRIPTION AND ENTRENCHMENT

I am suggesting in part that the very act of transcription may be narrativized in nature writing—storied in the hiatus or "conversion" between seeing and making seen. Let me relate this to what I said earlier about one's equipment configuring one's experience and about a "living"-"writing" split. Configuring experience through the material conditions of writing *en plein air* may place writing in an altered relation to "living"—not necessarily less mutually exclusive, but different in that the rhythms and postures of both are changed. The outdoors "scene of writing" itself, no garret or cell, cannot exercise the same exclusive sway over your way of occupying it; there is no question of "sensory deprivation" suffered or sought. Nor are you liable to sink deeply into transcription from the scripts of memory, not if your present circumstances are compelling or discomfiting enough, or if you assume your business is to front and formulate—or even memorize—the presence of the place before you. To do otherwise would be to remain within the grip of "preconception" and to abrogate your office as the land's own amanuensis, or in a related metaphor, its student.

Recall that *this* scene of writing depicts not the second-stage "writing" that occurs back at home but rather a variant of the first-level "trance" Trimble posits, the "journal" that slips out of "journey" and is scarcely associated with "writing" at all. Gary Nabhan's remarks about note-taking "in the field" demonstrate how such writing may function not just to record but to embody one's presence in place. Nabhan reports, what "I *want* to record in my notebook" are instances of the " 'Eureka!' moment" common to both scientists and artists—moments of creative intuition "when we notice something new that we haven't encountered before, . . . because we've jarred ourselves out of our normal world view. We've thrown ourselves into the chaos of [a wild place], and then discovered a greater pattern" (Lueders 75). This account of "the creative process" takes the form of a narrative of retreat, a shedding or upsetting of the habitual leading to recognition as a climactic experience which rounds out and defines a sequence of events. *This* is the sort of thing that belongs in his notes, Nabhan insists, and his insistence emphasizes that the act of transcribing is integral to the apprehension of a "greater pattern." The habit of note-taking seems part and parcel of the procedure by which "normal world view" is relinquished in the first place. Another aspect of Nabhan's note-taking reveals more concretely how he views his notes as embodying his experience of the field. Says Nabhan:

> When I take a lot of notes in the field, there is a chance that some of the sounds I hear in that landscape will carry over into the sounds of the words I use to describe a place. I work hard on that because I can't do that again later. (78–79)

Nabhan suggests that these on-site sounds are not only noted but somehow reflected in the language composed on site. He claims for this language a virtue borne of its origin in the place itself, a qualitative difference from any language he can generate elsewhere.

Nabhan's sensations correspond to the larger pattern that Scott Slovic identifies for nature writing in general. Slovic comments on how "literary naturalists" emulate the notebooks and logs of scientists, explorers and travellers, doing so, he asserts, "in order to entrench themselves in the specific moment of experience." His theme is "awareness"; he claims that "verbalization" enhances awareness as "passive assimilation" does not. While Slovic denies that this awareness is equivalent to a romantic "sense of harmony, even identity, with one's surroundings", what he describes is still a relation of identity, in which not place but time ("the specific moment") coincides with the account ("verbalization") (4). This binding of time with account is the essence of narrativity.

The difficulty is that while nature *writers* may produce notebooks, ✓ nature *writing* mostly emulates and does not reproduce those notebooks. Slovic's formulation commits him to the myth of Thoreau's *Journal*, which he accepts as "an example of nature writing at its purest, with no conscious attempt having been made to obscure and mystify" the relation of writer to "natural surroundings" (5). Once fused to "the moment of experience," "verbalization" is dissociated from "conscious attempt." But reading itself—including the writer's own reading—qualifies as conscious attempt, and this myth of the moment is in large part a myth of writing without reading. "Nature writing at its purest" is purified of readers, or at least, as with the *Journal*, of the writer's obligation to acknowledge and provide for how he is read.[5] As the act of writing is invisible to its readers, so reading is out of sight and timeless to the writer. Could it be the "purity" of its insulation from reading that makes such writing least like "writing" and most like "living"?

The *Journal* may be the "purest," but it is far from the most prevalent nature writing. Nabhan's notes are more typical in their purposes, marked as they are for eventual import into public texts. The reason he "works hard" at cultivating the induplicable virtues of sound on site is because he "can't do that again later"; rest assured he's tried. Both Nabhan and Ann Zwinger (his partner in a dialogue edited by Lueders) attest to moments when the writing in their field notes acquires an exceptional quality and integrity—moments of real "entrenchment," in Slovic's term—resulting in passages that are usable pretty much as composed, around which whole essays and book chapters can be built (Lueders 81). But there is no question in either writer's mind where these passages are headed: straight for the gradgrind realm of "writing," en route to the likes of us.

Thus there is a certain reciprocality at work here between far spheres—a shuttle system of motives and expectations. The relinquishing of preconception, the submission to "chaos" in the field, is meant to net narratable experience for export to the eventual "scene of writing." But that eventual scene also partly dictates or "preconceives" the character of notes composed on site, and thus the pattern of activity and attention. Ann Zwinger recalls Edwin Way Teale quoting William Beebe to the effect that he takes fieldnotes with a mind to what he'll want to know when he's back at his desk (Lueders 78). Along with the intent to preserve experience and the presumption, as with Nabhan's sounds, that some things can't be otherwise recovered, this advice imparts a sense of being "not all there," of having one foot back in the writing room, a site which to these writers spells mostly isolation and toil. Projection to the scene of the desk may be thought of as contaminating the experience of the field; or it may be felt that the habit of projecting such expectations conduces to enhanced participation or "entrenchment" in the moment on site. One who tends to the former view may fall in with Berry and disclaim the public identities of "observer or writer" before nature; one embracing the latter view may embrace those identities and, like Zwinger, produce fat information-laden books. Both, in my view, write narratives of retreat, underlain by structures of resistance between such options; it is not necessary to choose between these attitudes, the elements of which circulate through any public account of encounter with nature.

Is it necessary to choose between these sites, though, to occupy them alternately and in mutual exclusion? The site of "writing" at home — the computer screen, library, notecards, stretches of tedium — is by all accounts quite divorced from the "living" of the field; and in many accounts, these are the only scenes deployed. But there is a further scene that demands to be mentioned, a "writing" space that *fronts* the realm of "living" in nature. This is the scene of the cabin.

THE CABIN AS THE WINDOWED SITE OF WRITING

The cabin is an intermediate space between unmediated outdoor "living" and the entirely mediated space of manufacture and preconception associated with "writing," the elaborate human dwelling that the garret is presumed to top. In the cabin, it is presumed that the events of "living" may be simultaneously undergone and reconstituted in "writing," so that no clear distinction persists between stages of composition or levels of conversion into memory or text. It is no coincidence that the genre of nature writing originates with occupancy of a cabin. Indeed, Thoreau's habitat at Walden remains the prototype, in the sense of permeability between structure and surroundings, the fact of the three books composed there in whole or in part, and the emphasis on an ascetic "economy" that highlights the drama of the artifactual in access to the nonhuman "essential." The many other cabins in the annals of the genre by and large share these related traits of being permeable, writer-friendly, and materially ascetic: John Burroughs' celebrated Slabsides, Henry Beston's "Fo'castle" in *The Outermost House*, Aldo Leopold's Sand County "shack," and any number of other homesteads, cottages, out-buildings, or what-have-you.[6]

Consider the relation between the three traits I've just mentioned and the modernist "scene of writing" Brodkey portrays. Where the cabin is permeable, the modernist scene is hermetically sealed; where the cabin is writer-friendly, the garret bespeaks writerly torment and morbidity. But both share an ascetic economy in which the character and prevalence of possessions are at issue. The poverty of the garret scene, to Brodkey, spells deprivation both material and sensory. But the cabin's austerity is a function of renunciation, not deprivation, and the fact that material goods are renounced means that they are not withheld but remain in principle available. The cabin may even take the form of the "second home," the jewel in the crown of material accomplishment in American society, the very reverse of deprivation. Its isolation may be an emblem of social privilege sought or renounced: you can't "get away from it all" unless you've been *in* it all. In this regard, it correlates with the very occupational standing of the writer, that creation of economic surplus, to which a dozen highbrow Auchinclosses flock for every lowlife Carolyn Chute.

The enormous desirability of the cabin resides, then, in its combining the attributes of the garret, the tent, and the private estate. It may tend to any of these as extremes. John Muir's hut at Yosemite was as rustic and permeable as possible, "with floor slabs spaced to permit the unfolding of ferns," its total cost of four dollars "one-seventh the cost of Thoreau's" (Wyatt 41). Wendell Berry's place, "the Camp," evolved from occasional retreat to permanent dwelling, his primary and secondary residences eventually merging in a unified estate or "household" in which his family pursues its ascetic economy. Annie Dillard's cabins—her pine-shack study at Cape Cod and coastal cabin at Puget Sound—are classic approximations of the garret in the sense Brodkey disparages, incongruously sited in these expansive locales. I want to contrast these last two writers to the end of depicting the cabin as the windowed site of writing, with the entitlements and the relations of resistance that attend the presence of a view.

In "The Long-Legged House," his narrative tracing the transformation of "the Camp" into a home place, Berry connects his preferences in a scene of writing to his early years of habitation at this cabin, when he "would carry a card table out into a corner of the little screened porch, and sit down to write," remaining as he worked "conscious always . . . of the life of the river" below him (*Recollected Essays*, 39). Of the routine, Berry remarks:

> That confirmed me in one of my needs. I have never been able to work with any pleasure facing a wall, or in any other way fenced off from things. I need a window or a porch, or even the open outdoors. I have always had a lively sympathy for Thoreau's idea of a hypaethral book, a roofless book. Why should I shut myself up to write? Why not write and live at the same time? (40)

Berry's rejection of the garret scenario could hardly be more explicit: not only does he refuse confinement and the split between "writing" and "living," he even deigns to speak of taking pleasure in his work. Yet he is far from renouncing the image and practice of writerly solitude. On the contrary, elsewhere in the essay, it appears he ducks off to the Camp alone every chance he gets, at one period during the writing of a novel fleeing wife and kids four days out of every seven for an entire year, thus intimating why the kitchen table remains the primary site to those so abandoned (62).

As for Dillard, I have noted already how closely she resembles Brodkey's image of the "writer-writes-alone." She is the opposite of Berry in regard to the presence of windows in the scene of writing: where Berry requires them, Dillard theatrically refuses them. "Appealing workplaces are to be avoided," she insists; "One wants a room with no view, so imagination can meet memory in the dark." Consequently, upon occupying her Cape Cod cabin study she promptly "pushed the long desk against a blank wall, so [she] could not see from either window" (26). Berry favors "a roofless book," in effect making a window of the sky; Dillard quotes with favor a West African proverb: "The beginning of wisdom . . . is to get you a roof" (27).

Other contrasts with Berry's "hypaethral" practice of writing fall into place behind this one. There is the materiality of the writer's space requirements: where Berry takes a card table to the porch, Dillard recalls employing "the mechanical aid of a twenty-foot conference table" in constructing a book, and quips that "to write so much as a sonnet, you need a warehouse" (46). As for the materiality of high-tech equipment, Berry shuns it; he eschews computers, writes in pencil by daylight, and has his work typed on a manual typewriter by his wife, with whom he shares what he calls a "cottage industry," a cabin as an economic unit (*What Are People For?* 170–72). Again, Dillard differs, in metaphor of production as in material practice. No cottage industrialist, she tells a neighbor how much she hates to write, and eagerly concurs when he likens her attitude to the bitter alienation of a factory worker (53). Of the "pine shed" study with the windows she doesn't use, she remarks: "Like a plane's cockpit, it is crammed bulkhead to bulkhead with high-tech equipment. All it needs is an altimeter; I never quite know where I am" (25). Compare this with Berry's image of the plane crossing the "cone" of wilderness above him, an emblem of technological enclosure, and we see how Dillard relishes what Berry despairs of. Berry regards himself as "a placed person," unlike most American writers (*Recollected* 42); Dillard insists that she never knows where she is.

Yet there are grounds to question Dillard's insistence, and not just in her propensity to exaggerate. One hint can be found in the photograph of her with which Trimble prefaces his selection from her work (32). The camera, positioned inside her cabin study, aims toward an open door and window, and outside the window, elbows on its frame, stands Dillard, facing the camera. Pine woods are behind her; below her is a desk with scattered papers and a gooseneck lamp. This is one desk, evidently, that she did not turn to the wall. It may be the blank walls were taken, perhaps with a barge-sized conference table.

Or recall that passage where she reports pushing her desk to a windowless wall, while expressing her preference for a viewless workplace where "imagination can meet memory in the dark." As we read this we know already, because Dillard has told us, what is available to view from these windows: the pines, dunes, tideflats, and flocks of warblers she has just catalogued. For all this visual richness, she maintains that the "cinder-block cell over a parking lot" she once occupied was preferable as a study, though the cabin with the view "will do" (26). Perverse and presumptuous as this may seem to those of us who lack such perquisites, still there is method to Dillard's maddeningness. What impact can the renunciation of windows possibly have if the scope of the temptation they present is not depicted? It must be a great sacrifice to forego such a view in the service of art. But then the question arises of how the view itself crops up in the piece. It must be written in there, presumably at the site of her writing, this very shed. In cataloguing the view, did Dillard function at the junction of memory and imagination in the dark? Or did she turn and sneak a peek? Where is memory and where is *she* as she writes this out?

The fact is, Dillard rejects windows out of a fixation upon windows, with a vigor proportionate to the temptation she resists. Her opposition to Berry on this score is founded upon a similarity: namely, a preoccupation with the availability of the natural scene to the writer. This is the source of cabin narratives of all sorts.

The window is a presence ascetically refused by Dillard, a presence the more desirable for opening onto extraordinary prospects. Her essay on composing *Pilgrim at Tinker Creek* in the aforementioned "cinder-block cell" contains a parable of this. The view from this enclosure features considerably more than a parking lot, enough that its contents preoccupy her, transfixing her, luring her outside to snag turtles or join a baseball game—until the day she finally shuts the blind and tapes over it a drawing she'd done of the selfsame view. The drawing stands in for and wards off the view it reduces, and Dillard is able to work—at creating in words what she regards, in effect, as "a *trompe l'oeil* mural view of all the blinds hid" (29). This riddle of resistance and conversion is near-perfect in its involutions, the more so for its status as a testament, something she claims she actually did.[7] It's also more than a little creepy, like so many of her parables of writing—extreme, like hairshirts or bulimia. Hyperbolic though she may be, Dillard is perfectly reasonable, I believe, in advising that others should not rush to emulate her behavior—the very point Brodkey makes with regard to the modernist "scene of writing."

Yet Berry too, though inviting, not discouraging imitation, is prone to exaggerate in depicting the availability of nature to the scene of his writing. Cannot some hyperbole, however unwitting, be discerned in Berry's statement that while writing on his cabin porch, he was "conscious always . . . of the life of the river"? How could he maintain such vigilant consciousness and continue to write? For Berry, the temptation, the reverse image match of Dillard's, is the possibility of *losing* contact with his place through writing, of ceasing to regard the informing place itself and becoming absorbed instead in the verbal simulacra he conjures. It's a temptation he narrates having long since faced and resisted, but one so endemic to his profession (as writer, not farmer) that it is hard to imagine it does not repeatedly crop up. Berry's saga of coming to inhabit the Camp is one of going to California, to New York, to Europe, always as a writer, all the time writing about the home place in Kentucky he has left. At that time, early in his career, he is the very image of the writerly displacement Dillard cites (approvingly, of course) in which the scene of writing is always *elsewhere*: Dublin depicted in Paris, the prairie in New York, the Mississippi in Connecticut, as with Joyce, Cather, and Twain, respectively (68). Since returning and recovering from the displacement his occupation is presumed to demand, Berry's constant business has been to enact the identity of his subject and his site of writing. By the logic of resistance, his being "conscious always" of enacting this identity is the measure of the vigilance required to stay in place.

The cabin is the scene where this identity of subject and site is ideally transacted, with the window emblematic of the sought-after simultaneity of "living" and "writing." In practical terms, neither the elements of nature nor the machinations of writing need be diminished in their contact across this boundary: the paper stays dry and the trees stay wild. And in experiential terms, the drawing does not replace the view:

presence intertwines with memory, in a manner which the journal models generically.

I find it telling that Dillard, although she keeps a journal (she mentions "trying to explain Whitehead to my journal" as an example of something she does to *avoid* writing [54]), refers to it nowhere in her accounts of writing process and in fact seems loath to have her writing in any way linked with it.[8] I think this is related to her separation of subject and site, her pulling the drapes on the windows of her cabin. Berry, again by contrast, marks in his essay on "the Camp" the point at which his journal begins to figure in his account. It is not only a source, it is an event in his narration, a milepost in the transformation by which his subject and site come into synch. Berry's having made his household and career over in the image of his cabin shows the extent of his commitment to this ideal of simultaneity, of "entrenchment in the moment."

This *is* an ideal, though, one tempered by the many nature writers who unabashedly employ a rhetoric of stage and sequence, not simultaneity, in the traffic between "living" subject and "writing" site. If the process is conceived of as a shuttle of information and experience between the terminals of field and study, it may be that what the cabin site does best is to shorten the cycle, close the distance, at times to so infinitesimal a span as that between seeing and writing "I see." Or if this metaphor of shuttles seems too mechanical, we might resort to this one of Thoreau's, which figures the dwelling as an insect's nest: "While I am abroad the ovipositors plant their seeds in me I am fly blown with thought—& go home to hatch—& brood over them."[9] This movement, too, is reciprocal: as Thoreau's next sentence continues, thought that is "too discursive and rambling . . . for the chamber" requires him to "go where the wind blows on me walking." A typical, practical account of this interchange might be this from John Hay, whose two residences both have the attributes of cabins:

> On Cape Cod, if nothing happens at a dirty desk—just a hell of a lot of bad writing and lousy notes—you can always go on a walk. That's made all the difference, to be able to walk out to the tides, see the ocean, as I can walk out here in New Hampshire and see the mountains. It frees you. (Trimble 11)

Continues Trimble: "After the release, though, it's back to the desk." If in no other respect, the cabin is not a garret in that it does not sentence you to a fixed term at the desk. Periodically, it lets you down from mid-air.

LOOKING UP

Not all who write are about to acquire cabins, any more than we're ready to rent garrets. But if, as Brodkey claims, we feel compelled to reproduce the image of a garret in any writing scene we occupy, we could well afford to trade in that image for one that fronts some larger prospect, that construes "the solitude necessary for writing" as not just necessary but in some moments pleasurable and therapeutic. For while actual cabins may be few, there are many "windowed scenes" available, worth cultivating in senses both literal and figurative.

Of what good is a window? That depends on the view. What people see from their windows can materially affect their well-being, with hospital patients recovering more quickly and prison inmates seeking health care less often if some "nature content," rather than other buildings, interiors, or people, happens to be visible from their quarters (Kaplan and Kaplan 1–2). Some would say that a preference for living environments is essential to the species; others would insist it's a leisure-class atavism, a matter of constructed taste. On this issue, these patients and inmates vote with their feet—and hearts, and lungs, and other such gross corporeal entities.

Though less circulated than the garret image, the image of the writer in retreat holds appeal for many people, as the success of nature writing in the Thoreauvian vein amply demonstrates. It is an image of writerly solitude that invites readers to occupy the position of writer, to "go and do likewise" in their own discursive and *excursive* practices. This aspect of participation, of modeling and sharing exemplary scripts of behavior toward nature, highlights the social, ethical import the genre's practitioners insist upon. Their remarks on their work raise a "refrain of moral concern," in Trimble's view, a directing of attention "out of yourself" toward "what's more important" in the greater world (28). In their practice, solitude is not framed as alienation and atomism but refigured as affinity and integration within what Leopold calls the "biotic community," recognition of which comes to inform the human communities in which acts of writing are situated. If as Kenneth Burke asserts, "Form . . . is an arousing and fulfilling of desires" (124), the form of retreat in nature may prepare readers and practitioners to enact desires proper to the biotic community.

It need not necessarily do so: the shift in tenor I am heralding hardly invalidates the critique of modernist individualism that informs Brodkey's efforts to refigure writerly solitude. There are cabins and there are cabins, as we have seen; there may be, as Berry says, "a bad reason to go to the wilderness" (*Home Economics* 17), one that reinforces patterns of separation, self-involvement, and consumerist appropriation with which the pastoral tradition, or what Lawrence Buell calls "pastoral ideology," is itself in some moments associated. But just as Buell, in the most important book yet written about nature writing, reviews the "vulnerabilities" of this ideology in order to make a "positive case" for its oppositional and regenerative potential (33), so does the scene of writing outdoors qualify aspects of that critique, demonstrating that solitude need not recapitulate an ethos of individualism, complicating easy equations between the person alone and the culture of loners. In certain of its moments, nature writing shows another permutation: solitary writerly invention associated with resistance to elaborated technology and a critique of modernist individualism. And if retreat in nature in itself is not sufficient to the purposes of any community, biotic or other, neither is a more "social" view of writing, stressing collaboration and shared invention, bound to conduce to improved social and biotic dispensations. The shortcomings of this view are demonstrated in Karen Burke LeFevre's references to collaboration in organizational writing: the thoroughly collaborative Manhattan Project, a prime example of LeFevre's, shows social "invention" allied with a "modernism" of the most virulent order.

Versions of writing process follow stories of people writing, with students' own unfolding stories narrativized after accounts of successful predecessors, whose behavior is deemed worthy of emulation. What further lessons, then, might we draw from the behaviors attested to by nature writers? A modest one would be to baffle yet again facile distinctions of the sort that much writing process work has sought to complicate. We can confirm, for instance, that "writing" might indeed be felt as distinct from "living," for tangible reasons concerning the nature of the work, with "living" to be preferred but "writing" not necessarily denigrated on that score. But this "writing," in turn, is not a single activity, reducible to a single scene: if "writing" is not always "living," neither does it necessarily entail the making of books or essays or anything public at all. Yet writing for nonpublic purposes may still end up conducing to the good of some community. These sorts of writing may help constitute one's occupation, one's identity all the same, as they do for those who come to grips with recognitions of nonhuman nature through writing.

A more significant lesson is a narrative one, which is that writing has an end. As Walter Benjamin finds all story to be oriented toward death, so nature writing finds all acts of writing to be angled toward something not written or read. Says Gary Nabhan, "the trick of nature writing is to stimulate the reader to put the book down" (Lueders 74). What other "literary" writing has anything like this intent, to induce readers to relinquish the book? Examine John Muir's much-quoted statement of purpose—"I care to live only to entice people to look at Nature's loveliness"—and you will find that it reflects a double desire, to write and be read to effect ("to entice") and to effect an end to reading ("to look"). Both students and teachers experience this desire in both its aspects. Writing in nature, I believe, puts our expectations of form in relief, reenacting the relations of what we look at in the world to what we look for in words and writing. The students on the rocks cannot indefinitely bow to their books; when they bend their paragraphs to a close and reemerge, the waves will have remained. At times, the most helpful counsel is to look up.

CHAPTER SIX

Writer or Rhapsode?

Iconic Metaphors for Literate Identity

There is writing and there are writers: the two are not coterminous. For all the diverse competencies the term "literacy" may entitle, not all literate behaviors render a person a writer, not even by casuistic stretching of the idea of "composing." Compose a grocery list, a thank-you note, an understanding of the text before you—you are not rendered a writer thereby. It requires no valorizing of the title to assert this, no presumption of exalted status or higher cognitive operation, only the commonplace recognition that in some activities, intention is a condition of accomplishment. There is much one can write without being a writer, but no one can be a writer for long who does not entertain the notion that that is what they are being.

This does not mean that one need entertain the notion for good and always: a person can act as a writer briefly, sporadically, impulsively, reluctantly—even under duress, or perhaps especially so, as in the preponderance of writing classes not dignified as "creative." A mainstay of writing process pedagogy is to induce students to assume the role of writer, and a major means of doing so is to model what writers do. No one will write that readily or effectively who believes that what writers do is wait till they think of something to write and then write it out in a single unhindered motion. The process teacher is intent, rather, to dramatize the fact that every written text eventuates from a range of tangible actions performed under specific material conditions. The rub is, since these conditions *are* specific, we *are* dramatizing, not simply transcribing them—making images or lessons of them, images that are necessarily selective, despite process study's chimerical project to make visible every element of textual production. It may be that iconic metaphors[1] of the writer's role will serve just as well as any litany of process particulars in inducing students provisionally to assume that role. Such metaphors, after all, are what eventuate from the litanies, as morals emerge from stories. For the account of process is itself a product, as narrativized in instruction—one that in its imitable character embodies an image of the writer's condition.

We have reviewed Linda Brodkey's efforts to refigure that image by debunking the iconic metaphor she finds most prevalent and troubling. Her work comprises just one of the ways that writerly image has been subject to revision in recent years, part and parcel of a broad shift from individual to social conceptions of literacy, which I refer to in aggregate as the social view. Karen Burke LeFevre has rebutted the notion that writerly invention must originate in solitary inspiration, asserting that writing issues best and perhaps exclusively from acts of collaboration. Anne Ruggles Gere has substantiated this understanding in the activities of writing groups, and has further critiqued the understanding of writing as a technology. Deborah Brandt extends that critique and disputes as well the idea that writing is "decontextualized" in ways that speaking is not, insisting that every communicative act emerges from a context that is irremediably interpersonal. Recognitions of these sorts originate, I think, not just in the sense that our images of writing are insufficiently "accurate"; they emerge from the desire to refigure the role of the writer in ways that will enhance the existences of those who embrace it.

Laudable and enabling as it is, the social view still overlooks some factors that nature writing puts in relief, as we have been seeing. On one hand, it tends to discount the still-overwhelming testimony of many who embrace the label of "writer," to the effect that the work they do is solitary and difficult in the extreme. When William Styron moans that for him, writing is like dragging himself from the Crimea to Vladivostok by his elbows, the sentiment is no more hyperbolic than many others that might be cited—not least by Annie Dillard. On the other hand, the social view tends to neglect the possibility that some who write may take pleasure in solitude, finding in their work a relief from social conditions that may oppress as much as they enable. Asserting this, I am far from wishing to reinscribe in its totality the Romantic image of the writer's isolation. For a further neglected possibility I have raised is one that complicates the equations between individualism and writerly solitude, social consciousness and collaboration: the possibility that some writers seek solitude not just for themselves. In a sense, this possibility is acknowledged in an influential tenet of the social view, one derived from L. S. Vygotsky, the idea that since thought is internalized social speech, you couldn't really write alone if you tried. But for all its ingenuity, this perception does not exhaust the distinction between being alone and being with others, nor the sense of what might be accomplished for either self or others under such conditions.

I do not mean to reassert either a social or an individual image of the writer but rather to dramatize the interpenetration of the two, and to do so in a way that is still dramatic, that means to be taken as exemplary. My vehicle remains the figure of the nature writer in retreat, one whose very ethos involves attending to circumstances that are *not* social, characterized by the absence or seeming irrelevance of other people. The nature writer I will discuss, John Muir, remains a paragon of the role he assumed, a status both stemming from and enabling the social efficacy of his writing. But as I will show, the role of writer was not one he assumed readily or without distress—or alone. The manner in which he resisted that role, along with other ambivalences over writing and speaking, economy and technology configured in his person, make him useful as an iconic metaphor that comprehends such ambivalences. These issues will lead us to reflect on the character of literacy from the standpoint of its absence, through the figure of the indigen, the nonwriting inhabitant of wild places, upon which nature writers in some moments fixate. And these reflections, in turn, will lead us to speculate on other iconic metaphors with potential for resisting the depradations that literacy, broadly speaking, has long authorized.

JOHN MUIR: NATURE WRITING'S "NATURAL"

The version of John Muir's story I offer is that of a person who wrote voluminously for apparently private purposes yet disrespected and abhorred writing—or "the making of books"—for public purposes, even though increasingly he seemed marked for that work. It seems clear that Muir struggled against assuming the identity of a writer, and appeared to accept most any pretense to avoid "writing" in the latter, "bookmaking" sense. Even his compiling of a fortune in agriculture can be interpreted, says Stephen Fox, as an excuse to evade the making of books (73). Yet for private purposes he required no pretense or even much of a procedure to wield his pen. *That* writing, by all accounts, was integral to his way of being in a place, part and parcel of the "living" he made. If, as Engberg and Wesling maintain, "Muir's story continues to fascinate us" because there is something "profoundly representative" about it (5), this devotion to "living" and ambivalence toward print may be part of what makes it so.

Since I am concerned with Muir as someone who wrote and whose writing is widely read, I will begin by asking whether or in what degree we should attribute to him the identity of "writer." Those who write the introductions to books have a particular need to establish this, at least as a warrant that a person's work qualifies for "literary" reception. So it is with the introductions to books of Muir's by Edward Hoagland and Gretel Ehrlich.[2] Both are well-known nature writers in their own right; both find it important to qualify Muir's writerly identity, enough so that a disclaimer of some sort is among the opening moves each makes. In Ehrlich, the hedge opens the second paragraph: "Muir was a walker first, a writer later" (vii). Ehrlich is thematizing the prodigious distances Muir walked, including the figurative distance he'd traveled from a hard upbringing; but the further implication is that he did not walk right into the estate of a writer, and ought to be read or discounted accordingly.

This hint of a purpose becomes distinct in Hoagland. More than Ehrlich, Hoagland seems out to excuse Muir for not being a more proficient literary artist than he was. His essay opens with this disclaimer:

> We must go halfway with John Muir. He was more of an explorer than a writer, more confident of his abilities in botany and geology than of what he could do with the eagle-quill pens he liked to use, while encouraging a friend's year-old baby to scramble about the floor, lending liveliness to the tedium of a writer's room. (45)

To "go halfway" suggests to give the benefit of doubts to a not-quite-writer whose lack of confidence redeems his lack of competence, implying it wasn't *him* who said he could do this work in the first place. (Which it wasn't—of which more later.) What business do we have reading this man, then? He has other abilities, clearly, but more than that, he has an eagle-quill pen and a baby on the floor—natural talismans and new life as counterweights to the tacit artificiality and death of the study. The opposition of "liveliness" to "tedium" is a version of the tacit split between "living" and "writing" in general that we have been exploring: even in writing, Hoagland implies, Muir veers toward living, leaving us as readers "halfway" away.

Hoagland evokes further aspects of Muir's nonwriterliness and liveliness: the books published late in life, the notetaking done heedless of eventual publication, the preferences for spoken over written language and for direct rather than vicarious involvement with nature. He strikes a running comparison with a kindred figure who *was* a writer: "Henry David Thoreau lived to write, but Muir lived to hike" (45). This seems true enough on its face, yet since Thoreau hiked constantly and Muir compiled heaps of on-site writings, in what does the distinction reside? It presumes, of course, that the two are rival activities, which is true in the trivial but definite sense that you can't do both at once. But more than anything, it must concern the resolve to publish and disseminate one's writing, and to be socially defined thereby. In this regard, what each man "lived to" do gets less clear-cut and more bound to shifting life trajectories, with the resolve to publish initially strong but progressively blunted in Thoreau, and absent at first in Muir but developing under encouragement and pressure from friends and eased by the remarkable reception his efforts enjoyed from the start.[3] For as remarked earlier, writerly identity may issue from as well as lead to success, and Muir's success was immediate, his articles "always accepted" and handsomely paid for by prominent Eastern magazines, much to the author's surprise. Yet even this reception serves mainly to confirm Muir's status as anomalous: "Most young writers believe in themselves extravagantly in order to endure early rejections; Muir deprecated himself but was an immediate success" (Fox 56). *Real* writers don't make it this way.

As it happens, what Hoagland and Ehrlich, among others, hold out as the alternative to an identity as a writer for Muir—that of a walker or hiker—is central to the appeal he exerts as a writer. In every sense anyone could discern, Muir was a natural. What it might mean to be a natural as opposed to a writer can be discerned in his biographer Linnie Marsh Wolfe's account of how Muir came to write. Says Wolfe: "Apparently he had no wish to become a writer, hence there was no *conscious* playing of 'the sedulous ape.' " He distrusted writing but loved "rhythmic language": poetry and the Bible "lent an *unconscious* music to his spoken words." As a teen he did compose metrical letters and verse, but

Wolfe calls these "simply the effervescence of high spirits moulded by an *innate* law of rhythm" (ix–x). The above emphases—all mine— sketch a Romantic tension between conscious intention and unconscious emission, the latter thought to be more "natural." Even when Muir is writing what are apparently extended verse efforts, Wolfe shields him from the onus of intending to do anything especially writerly by characterizing his behavior as "innate."

Muir is natural, and successful, because the persona he projects seems as musical and spontaneous as his language. It is common to note that the appearance of effortlessness in writing results from arduous effort—and Muir did work hard at making books—but it is less remarked that an effortless quality may result, too, from the absence of effort. Or at any rate, from its irrelevance, as seems often to have been the case with Muir. Consider his writing habits in the field: per Wolfe, he took "two or more notebooks" on treks, "tied to his belt whichever one he happened to pick up," and "wrote his notes, sometimes in the front, sometimes in the back, often not dating the entries" (xi). Consider the volume and character of his output: sixty journals in forty-four years, plus "a mass of notes scribbled upon loose sheets and bits of paper of all shapes and sizes" (ix). Despite this habitual and prodigious output, no one supposes, as many do with Thoreau, that these journals may be Muir's primary work after all, outstripping his published works.[4] The reason is that Muir's reluctance to assume the identity of a writer is manifest even in the disorderly, random, chronologically neglectful— the effortless—manner of his journalizing. There is no suspense or complexity to the question of whether he expected these writings would be read: he appears to have been oblivious to the prospect. Of Thoreau, Sharon Cameron claims that the wooden box he built to house his journals evinces his "cogent wishes for literary posterity" (93); Muir's journals and notes end up in piles which he likens to "moraines on my den floor" (Wolfe xv). They are not boxed; like gravel, they are deposited.

This does not mean, though, that in these disorderly texts Muir may not have been enacting what Cameron sees Thoreau as up to: that is, "writing nature" as its direct manifestation, not (or not only) representation. Certainly Muir's readers attest to a sense of identity between the writer and his subject. "Neither above nor apart from nature, he merged so fully with his subject matter as to become indistinguishable from it" (Fox 57). To Ehrlich, the tale of his writing with an ink he made from sequoia cones bespeaks his consubstantiality ("the blood and body of the forest") with what he writes about (*Mountains* viii). The sense of identity is such that Muir's "descriptions . . . might have been written by the subjects themselves" (ix). Not Muir but the place itself seems to do the writing. But the place ends up writing Muir, too: more than one writer comments on implicit self-portraits in Muir's depictions of certain animals (the water ouzel, especially). Nobody suggests he *intends* to portray himself, though, or is conscious of having done so.

This is the key to his appeal. Muir seems as unconscious of himself as of his materials. Of the quality that made his work immediately popular, Fox says: "He had gone alone, usually, and *thought nothing of it*" (56—my emphasis). His full attention seems drawn to his surroundings, and as a virtue of this, they cease to surround him. By a sort of compositional jujitsu, he redirects the force of what most "literary adventurers" had depicted themselves as confronting, so that it moves instead in his own direction, sweeps him along to where he would have meant to go if he could have meant to go anywhere particular, which he cannot, because his own prerogatives are dissolved in the process of being taken. This, at least, is the effect, one of passionate engagement and personal reticence or self-effacement all at once.

Given his evidently effortless, un-selfconscious facility with language, and the immediate success this bred, what are we to make of Muir's distaste for writing? It's certainly true that books and their making were to Muir inadequate and suspect in the extreme. In a journal he writes: "I have a low opinion of books; they are but piles of stones set up to show coming travelers where other minds have been" (Wolfe 94–95). This image suggests a gulf between an animated presence and the inert remains of its writing. The disparity is more graphic yet in this figure in which Muir, citing the poor resemblance between his drawings and their referents in nature, notes the same "infinite shortcoming" with writing: "The few hard words make but a skeleton, fleshless, heartless, and when you read, the dead bony words rattle in one's teeth" (Engberg and Wesling 143). And while he does hold a grudging hope for what those "dead bone-heaps called articles" may suggest to "living souls" for whom they "contain hints," it appears that only a few "know how to find" those hints (143–44). It is cold comfort to think that only select, skilled paleontologists of experience might reconstruct the living creature from its stripped remains.

In thus disparaging "dead bony words" in comparison to direct living experience, Muir hews to the "writing"-"living" rift by which

Hoagland, among others, narrativizes this author's activities. One of
these others, John P. O'Grady, extends this complaint of Muir's to the
author's attitude toward language in general. O'Grady claims:

> Nowhere in [Muir's] published or unpublished writings does
> he mention the sheer joy of writing, the pleasure that so many
> other writers attribute to the pen. Unlike Thoreau, Muir never
> felt the thrill of desire in the cascades of language, but only in
> actual mountain streams, peaks, and earthquakes; thus his
> affinities for singing the wild hover closer to a bird, the water
> ouzel, than to any literary precursor. For Muir, writing was
> always work, never release; never did it consummate his
> desire. (66–67)

There are two false steps here, I believe, which I will dispute to make
points of my own. The first resides in O'Grady's presuming that, since
Muir does not *mention* his pleasure in writing, he must not have *felt* any.
This is surely wrong: there's a great deal that Muir found joy in yet does
not mention in his writing, his family and friends especially; and too
much of what he *does* mention embodies his "thrill of desire" in prose
for this diagnosis of joylessness to hold true. What O'Grady is assuming
for Muir is an equivalence between "book-making"—which indeed
seemed to entail "special tortures" for him (Fox 73)—and other writing,
especially writing composed, we might say, on site. Muir's writing on site
itself attests to his attitude: he wrote voluminously, with obvious pleasure
and verve. If he nowhere mentions taking pleasure in *this* writing, this
must be in part because it was not in the writing proper that Muir
located his pleasure, but rather in his presence in the wild place, to
which the act of writing was impressed.

Second, it's presumed by O'Grady that Muir's posture toward "writing" reflects a resistance or numbness to "the cascades of language" in
general. But if it is wrong to presume Muir's joylessness in writing, it is
doubly wrong for his *spoken* language. For by all accounts, Muir was a
gifted, prodigiously voluble talker, one for whose output the metaphor
"cascades of language" was a natural, as it were. O'Grady leans toward
acknowledging this when he likens Muir to a bird that "sings the wild";
Muir's own remarks cited above reflect this yet more strongly. A book,
he notes, indicates "where other minds have been"; if we read this as
contrasting with *speaking* situations in which it's clear where these
"other minds" *are* at this moment, then it is an observation akin to that

of Socrates in Plato's *Phaedrus*, that writing, unlike speech, cannot answer to its present auditors. And when Muir complains that while reading, "the dead bony words rattle in one's teeth," it is the sentiment of one accustomed to having the words in his teeth emerge full-fleshed and alive. "I like the feel of words in my mouth better than bread" (Fox 77): here is a declaration of pleasure in language.

I have remarked on Muir's immediate, uncanny success as a writer, attributing it to an un-selfconscious facility with language that echoed the writer's appearance as a "natural"—a manner meshed with its material. However this facility may have developed, it must certainly have been related to the writer's knack for extemporaneous spoken address— an arguably more natural facility and one to which Muir certainly attached greater value. If it is further the case, as I've noted, that Muir's success stemmed from the support and exhortation of friends, this exhortation, in turn, arose largely in response to Muir's powers of speech. His friends urged him to the solitary labor of writing for publication because they were so awed by "the nature-struck verbiage that cascaded from his mouth" in company, a torrent which they believed ought to "be preserved in print" (Fox 19). Thus while several commentators reasonably attribute Muir's distaste for writing to the fact that it would detract from his time outdoors,[5] it just as surely took away from the time he spent holding forth in the parlor.

Fox describes how Muir would monopolize conversation at social gatherings for as much as eight hours at a stretch—and how chagrined he would be if it were pointed out to him that he had done so. In Fox's view, Muir's volubility was not due to any self-centered wish to dominate or dictate to others—formal addresses such as lectures terrified him, after all— but instead "acted as an unconscious defense mechanism against the mystery of social intercourse" (78). Without disputing this interpretation, which fits well the particulars of Muir's social development, I would add to it the observation that in this behavior—spontaneous, "unconscious," extended in duration, situated in intimate gatherings—Muir resembles nothing so much as a *rhapsode* in the traditional, oral sense. The implications of this shed light on a seeming contradiction in this sketch, by Ehrlich, of Muir the writer in old age:

> Even at age seventy-three he struggled with the translation of experience into language. He preferred to talk, enchanting listeners with stories of his adventures until his wife, Louie, or

a friend shunted him upstairs into the grim solitude of the
writing room. (xv)

Here "language" is differentiated from and even opposed to "talk"—an
inadvertent yet telling breach of common usage in which talk is just one
form of language. The breach is easy to miss, though: Why is this? If it
seems apt to consider "language" in terms of struggle and isolation inap-
plicable to enchanting "talk," it must be because "language" is primarily
understood as writing. In fact, according to Illich and Sanders, this primary understanding of "language" is its historical sense as well, since
"language," strictly speaking, is a nonentity in cultures without writing:
"Only the alphabet has the power to create 'language' and 'words,' for
the word does not emerge until it is written down" (7). To the bardic
rhapsode of nonliterate societies, even memorization is foreign, modelled as it is upon the tangible, persistent traces of written "language."[6]
In his verbal fecundity and his disregard for the preservation of his emissions, Muir resembles that bard; though he strives to fulfill the wishes of
others for preservation, there remains always something grudging and
equivocal in his acquiescence.

THE MISSION TO ENTICE

Thus Muir enters his "grim solitude" upon the urging, even the
injunction, of a community—one that values his spontaneous vatic
emissions but cannot fully privilege what is not preserved in print. In
this situation, "writing" is a lonely, laborious undertaking precisely
because it answers to social circumstances: it is spouse and sponsors that
"shunt" Muir to his room and lend him a baby to enliven it. But then
what of that solitude that is *not* grim, and that writing on site which is
not the "writing" of the room? Even this writing springs from an identifiable social milieu, in the sense that Muir's journal-making habit
stemmed from a habit of correspondence—in particular an "exchange
of thought" in letters proposed by Jeanne C. Carr, the wife of a professor
of Muir's, and pursued voluminously for many years (Fox 45). I cannot
broach here the many dimensions of Muir's relationship with Mrs. Carr,
who acted variously as his confidante, soulmate, mentor, sponsor in society, and de facto literary agent. I would note only that it was in correspondence with Carr that Muir developed not only the prose style and

the turns of mind but also the habit of spontaneous writing that marked the journals he soon began to keep—and that of those who urged Muir to take up a public pen, it was Carr who urged longest and loudest, and who indeed was primarily responsible for Muir's acquaintance with those others who echoed her exhortations.[7]

We may be noticing by now certain complications to the picture of a Muir split between the joy of "living" and the toil of "writing." There are gradations between the most private and most public forms of his writing, with Jeanne Carr a mediating figure between these extremes. Muir's journals, his most unstudied, even expendable writing, may be thought of as his form of "talk" in solitude, a sort of solo gregariousness. Not that he is talking to himself, exactly, or particularly to others; but his journals at their most forthcoming are a sort of direct emission seeming to keep an undifferentiated company quite as much as to record and recount. The more locquacious entries share manner and substance with Muir's letters to Carr. And many of Muir's early articles, in turn, originated in epistolary reports to Carr, dispatched upon his correspondent's urging and revised after her suggestions.[8]

The relation between letters and publications is quite close during the first stage of Muir's writing career,[9] his first published article, for instance, having been pieced together out of passages from letters to friends (Turner *Rediscovering* 99; Engberg and Wesling 76). One piece shows especially well the various levels of address and modes of writerly siting from which his earlier works originated. This piece, given the title "A Geologist's Winter Walk" upon its 1873 publication in the *Overland Monthly* (Muir's usual publishing venue at the time), was like his other articles of the period sent first to Jeanne Carr, who relayed the piece to the magazine. A difference, though, is that whereas his other articles arrived with the request that Carr have them published (or with the understanding that if she could, she might), "A Geologist's Winter Walk" was sent as a letter alone. Muir did not request or intend that it be published, though he deferred to his intermediary's judgment when he learned that she had placed the piece.[10] While the circumstances of its publication are different, then, they more extend than depart from the standard operating procedures of these two. Muir was accustomed to addressing Jeanne Carr in order to address the larger public she both represented and served as a buffer against.

The letter/article is a narrative of Muir's return to Yosemite after a stay in the city and of his subsequent trek into the difficult recesses of

Tenaya Canyon. A striking feature of the piece is that, while itself a
letter from Yosemite Valley, it includes a letter within it, written on site
in the canyon itself. The composing of this letter-within-a-letter is presented as an event in the past-tense narration of the letter proper, the
writer reporting: "I reached the upper end [of the canyon] in a little over
a day, but was compelled to pass the second night in the gorge, and in
the moonlight I wrote you this short pencil-letter in my notebook" (147).
The "pencil-letter," written in present tense, describes in intense, de-
lighted terms the peaks, domes, rock walls, and cascades that surround
the writer as he perches on "a big stone, against which the stream
divides" (148). It is loosely tied by the conceit that the writer is instruct-
ing the "you" he addresses to look about the scene, too: "Do you see the
fire-glow on my ice-smoothed slab, and on my two ferns?" (149). The
on-site letter culminates in a nightfall epiphany, then the past-tense narration resumes, until it breaks off into a further second-person address,
most suggestive with respect to the relationship, working and otherwise,
between these parties. Muir imagines his auditor's response: "Now your
finger is raised admonishingly, and you say, 'This letter-writing will not
do'"; and so imagining, he resolves to recount but part of his "homeward
ramblings" and then to "cast away my letter pen, and begin 'Articles,'
rigid as granite and slow as glaciers" (150). Across the distance from
Oakland to Yosemite, Muir imagines himself being shunted upstairs by
a dear one.

Three levels of address are represented here, including this last one
that Muir does not intend and in fact construes in opposition (ironically, it
turns out) to the more fluid, less "rigid" and "slow," narration of his "letter
pen." These levels correspond to three modes of inscription, so to speak:
the journal entry (which the "pencil-letter" orginates as), the personal letter, and the published article. And they register as emanating from three
distinct sites: field, cabin, and civilization. In this, the formal sedimenta-
tion of the piece reflects the substance of the narration, for the story Muir
recounts is a retreat narrative of leaving the city, shaking off its pernicious
effects, and in stages reentering the wilderness fastness he recognizes as
home.[11] The letter-within-a-letter is embosomed, as it were, both thematically and emotionally at the center of the narration. The expressed conditions of its inscription are correlative to this state: seated on one of the
"talkative" rocks that he recognizes as "dear friends" (145), Muir contem-
plates that other friend who can decipher the human script of his repose
in, indeed his discourse with, nonhuman creation.

These various sites and levels of inscription exemplify how a thread of textuality shuttles loomlike across the apogees of Muir's travels between wilderness solitude and human households. This thread is oral and rhapsodic at its source—the root of "rhapsode" being to stitch together (Illich and Sanders 18). What Muir increasingly stitches together is an identity bearing an ethical purpose at once self-effacing and self-assured. His central pronouncement of this purpose, oft-quoted as a single clause—"I care to live only to entice people to look at Nature's loveliness"—itself comes not from any public statement but from a letter to Jeanne Carr. The entire paragraph from which it is taken is worth examining. Muir has just mentioned his latest solitary excursion, during which he has gathered "ouzel tales to tell," and has relayed his renewed conviction that he is "hopelessly and forever a mountaineer." He continues:

> How glorious my studies seem, and how simple. I found a noble truth concerning the Merced moraines that escaped me hitherto. Civilization and fever and all the morbidness that has been hooted at me has not dimmed my glacial eye, and I care to live only to entice people to look at Nature's loveliness. My own special self is nothing. My feet have recovered their cunning. I feel myself again. (Engberg and Wesling 159)

Restored to context, Muir's much-vaunted mission to "entice" appears as the outgrowth of his "studies," which involve the recovery of "noble truths" in nature. Such "truths" are discerned by a "glacial eye"—a visionary organ consubstantial with its material object—which is jeopardized by a "civilization" allied with illness and death. By this sequence of associations, the solitary retreat from civilization's oppressive, even persecutory force acquires ethical purpose. The stance is ascetic, solitude being productive of a true (unfevered) view of one's inconsequential "special self" and leading to its renunciation through ethical commitment. But note that this declaration of purposive self-abnegation occurs in a passage the thrust of which is a celebration of the writer's own rejuvenation, prowess, and success. While the "special self" may be "nothing," there is another, authentic identity that is not the product of fever and morbidness, not tethered to personality; and this identity Muir does not renounce but exultantly recovers in his "studies." It is not an exclusively mental entity, not a mind steering a body: it incorporates a glacial eye, feet of cunning, a self he can feel and need not merely reflect upon.

Finally, note that Muir's declaration extends from a refreshed resolve over his vocation, his social role; and the role he declares is not that of writer but of "mountaineer," albeit one with "ouzel tales to tell." Further, his resolution to "live to entice" others comes on the eve of four further years of solitary wilderness travel extending well beyond the orbit of Yosemite; the paragraph that follows announces his plans. How can Muir assert a mission to entice others even as he is planning to disappear even further from their midst? Only through his writing, we might say, but even more, through the nonhuman "tales to tell" he gathers, the "noble truths" turned up in the cunning movement of his feet. The social function of Muir's "mountaineer" is more nearly akin to that of the storyteller, as Walter Benjamin describes it, than of the writer.

Per Benjamin, storytellers come from two overlapping groups, those who have "come from afar" and those who have "stayed at home" (84); the mountaineer is clearly one bearing stories from afar. Whichever the point of departure, "In every case the storyteller is a man [sic] who has counsel for his readers," counsel meaning "less an answer to a question than a proposal concerning the continuation of a story which is just unfolding" (86). Counsel cannot be sought or used by those who do not recognize the unfolding story; the threat to storytelling, which Benjamin regards as a dying art, comes with the diminished value and communicability of direct experience in the industrial era. For storytelling relies upon oral tradition and transmission; its opposite number, the novel, depends upon the printed book and extends from the status of the writer as a solitary individual, who in isolation can neither give nor receive counsel. In Benjamin's terms, what Brodkey calls the "writer-writes-alone" is the image particularly of the novelist in this age of industrial technology, an image extended to subsume writing behavior of any sort.

I am claiming not that Muir is a storyteller in any unequivocal sense but rather that the role of the storyteller *as opposed to* that of the "maker of books" is one that figures in his occupational identity. It does so in several of the characteristics that Benjamin attributes to it. For one, Muir continually espouses the virtues of direct experience—especially of nature and implicitly of the speech of others. His resistance to writing stems not just from the drudgery of the work but more from his recurring anxiety over the communicability of his own peculiar experience in the cold medium of print. He bemoans the static, moribund quality of books, whose makers have absconded and left their dry bones behind, and decries the quality of the counsel to be found therein, so inferior to the counsel of the mountains. And of course, he himself was a most spellbinding storyteller in person, his written works by all accounts paling beside his impromptu spoken performances.

THE BREAD PROBLEM

Why does he do it, then—why make books? We've mentioned the social pressure, the exhortation of friends to conserve, as it were, the natural resources of his speech; and we've reviewed Muir's own resolution "to entice people" to develop a "glacial eye" of their own. But there is a further motive most pertinent to the question of occupational identity in the conventional sense. Muir needed money, and he wrote to make it. Ascetic as this wilderness recluse was in his needs and habits, in his stints of wandering he was leashed by a factor more unyielding even than the desire for human company—what he called "the bread problem." In the wild, he subsisted on bread and tea, if necessary could forego the tea; but the need for bread kept bringing him back in. Bread, in turn, cost money. For his first published piece, Muir received $200: this was a lot of bread.

Muir refers to "the bread problem" at intervals in his work, but nowhere more insistently than in the chapter of *My First Summer in the Sierra* entitled "A Bread Famine." The book narrates Muir's early excursion to the high mountains in the company of a herd of sheep and their shepherd, whom Muir was retained to oversee; the chapter recounts their having run out of flour and beans and being forced to subsist on disgusting mutton while awaiting the overdue arrival of the flock's owner, who would replenish their stores. Galled by this diet, Muir bemoans his consequent indisposition and inattention to his studies, "as if one could n't [sic] take a few days' saunter in the Godful woods without maintaining a base on a wheat-field and gristmill" (77)—an entire economy, in effect. Significantly, this chapter is one of the few places in Muir's work where he mentions the native peoples of the regions he traverses in any but disparaging terms. He muses: "Like the Indians, we ought to know how to get the starch out of fern and saxifrage stalks, lily bulbs, pine bark, etc. Our education has been sadly neglected for many generations" (79). This dream of an indigenous existence, passing in Muir, becomes a refrain in some later nature writers, in ways we will remark.

The question of how a suitable education (and thus a fit subsistence) might be secured, though, was of more than passing interest to Muir, since it had set the conditions under which he could escape from the toil and deprivation of his upbringing and solve "the bread problem" on his own terms. Without reviewing all the biographical particulars, suffice it to say that Muir, largely an autodidact, schooled himself most thoroughly in the intricacies of machine technology. His bent for mechanical invention, if anything, exceeded his facility with speech. Through its exercise Muir was able to flee the family farm and his tyrannical father, enter the university, then secure paying positions at various junctures in his travels, including the post as a sawmill operator in Yosemite Valley by which he contrived to finance his mountain wanderings.

Making this point, I am coming around to a further respect in which Muir, formulating an occupational identity, shows affinities with the figure of the storyteller as Benjamin describes it. Muir's posture toward industrial technology—which Benjamin, recall, finds antithetical to storytelling—embodies complex relations of temptation and resistance. Not easily parsed, these relations are readily evoked in the character of the inventions by which the young Muir first distinguished himself. This rhapsodist wont to proclaim the timelessness of days in nature was at first an inveterate builder of clocks, the parts hand-whittled out of hardwood. These clocks, in turn, were associated with labor and especially literacy in his thinking, as demonstrated in his two most celebrated timepieces. One was a bed designed to tilt up at a set time and eject its occupant onto the floor—generally at one o'clock in the morning, the only time Muir's father allowed him time of his own to read. The other was a desk that by a system of gears would present and remove at set intervals the books loaded into it, inducing the student to read expeditiously the book set before him before it was snatched away. Thus the mechanical acumen that would lead Muir, in later machine shop jobs, to become, as David Wyatt puts it, "one of America's first efficiency experts" (43), was from the start connected with his efforts at self-improvement through hard labor over books. His later antipathy toward labor over books and his vehement preference for settings devoid of any article of manufacture whatsoever must surely be connected with these predilections.

As Wyatt remarks, "Muir's opting for wilderness ensured that labor and leisure would be consigned to separate realms"—this in contrast to the likes of Frost, for instance, whose location "in semicultivated nature" ensured the continual interpenetration of work and play (43). Yet under the dispensations of an industrial economy, these "separate realms" are the general reality. Writing as a complex of technologies undergirds this dispensation; as an occupation, a mode of specialization, the role of the writer depends upon the separation. This is a situation at least half-acknowledged in nature writing as a rule, one in which it can even be said to originate. Stories of retreat in nature chart passages between the realms of labor and leisure as these are commonly con-structed—of "writing" and "living"—in the process dramatizing issues of economy and subsistence, the terms by which various living entities, including but not limited to humans, may be said to be or not to be at home. The mountaineer as storyteller travels afar *in order* to be at home, to take and lend counsel on that score, having learned something of what it means to "make a living" at the leash ends of the technological, literate dispensation—or to fail to, if the bread runs out. If Muir is repre-sentative, I believe it is this dramatization of leisure and subsistence—their separation, their relation—that in his work and life he represents.

My reading of Muir's story, then, eventuates in this moral, among others: that what's at issue in writing is in part what's at issue with technology. This is a notion widely rebutted in social view discussions of literacy. The rebuttal is an element of a larger denunciation of oral-literate distinctions, the so-called "great divide" between nonliterate and literate conditions out of which such notions as the oral "rhapsode" grow. The next section discusses further the pertinence of this "divide." Suffice it to say that, in discounting writing's dimension as technologi-cal, it seems to me that some social view theorists may foreclose avenues for inquiry consistent with at least some aspects of the perspective they promote: the belief that being "literate" is *not* tantamount to being exceptional or improved per se. In the same way, not all technological changes are "advances": it is a matter of moment whether Wendell Berry, for instance, writes with a pencil, a computer, or not at all, just as the clay tablets of the Sumerians were associated with tangible attributes of their schooling and social dispensation.[11] If we don't totalize, neither ought we neglect writing's character as technological intervention.

I am not claiming that Muir's antipathy to writing was based upon any such view, only that in his relations to nature, industrial technology, the making of books, and the writer's role, he presents a figure that can be taken to raise such issues. I take Muir as a fable to express this assertion: that considering technology as an issue in people's existences *as writers* does not entail its entire embrace or rejection but rather involves judgments of efficacy and appropriateness to situation. Should we assume, for example, that desktop publishing or the Internet tend more to democratize than dissipate? In some instances, we may be better off talking, or scribbling on whatever scraps come to hand.

Also present in Muir, though, are the temptations to extremes that make his case dramatic. Muir the clockmaker eschewed the fortune he might have accrued analyzing human movements for industrial "efficiency"; he chose to move freely and proclaim holism instead, with enduring repercussions. His choice remains exemplary, but we must not overlook how the very form of his choice of "leisure" keeps suspended and even depends upon the possibilities of the industrialized "work" he ultimately spurned. So too does his mania for speech, his character as a "rhapsode," exist in relation to his agonies and capacities as a writer. Muir is not "oral" *or* "literate," any more than he is for or against technology, but neither does it make sense to collapse these distinctions in his case, not when he so markedly enacts them in his conduct.

Similarly, while Muir's activities as a writer cannot be rendered simply in terms of "individual" or "social" behavior, neither can the categories be simply erased or conflated, not in a figure so habitually alone, for whom solitude provided grounds for the recognitions he felt impelled to express to others. Muir's case dramatizes how writerly solitude is incomprehensible outside a social context. But it also suggests that an adequate account of writerly behavior cannot efface solitude with the recognition that language is social. In the perspective of ecological holism, as Karl Kroeber notes, attention to the individual is not antithetical to social motives or sympathies. On the contrary, the study of individuation is a study of the interrelations in the ecosystem or "community" that constitute its members.[13] Evolutionary holism *requires* individuals. This is not to say it requires a doctrine of "individuality," the capitalist abstraction that rightly draws fire. We may indeed do well to subordinate our "special selves" and regard them as "nothing" in comparison to "nature's loveliness," social justice, or whatever greater entity or good we feel might encompass them or us. But it cannot help us to renounce the "feeling" self in which the sense of interrelation itself is manifested—the individual creature that has not just a tongue but feet of "cunning." A view that conceives of people solely as bundles of "particular Discourses" (Gee xviii) maligns the body's cunning while only deferring the problem of particularity, of individuation, that it's bound to encounter and at some level embraces anyway.

THE INSTRUMENTS OF LITERACY
AND "INDIGEN WISDOM"

In the case of Muir as in preceding chapters I have posited a social function, an exemplary ethical character to the nature writer's activities—a character not inevitable to retreat, but one evident enough in a number of its sites and senses. Nature writers themselves are not reluctant to claim a public, ethical function for their work, their remarks raising the "refrain of moral concern" that Trimble remarks upon (28). They maintain that this ethical character is not vested in them personally, that the places they frequent are themselves equipped to give counsel. "Nature counts as a model, a guide," says Gary Nabhan in a typical formulation (23). You need only "live in a place and let it tell you how to live," Gretel Ehrlich insists (10).

It is in speaking of this public function, the transmission of the land's own dictation or counsel, that nature writers tend most to speak in terms of storytelling. Barry Lopez, who presses furthest the genre's claims to ethical and political import, is also most insistent that its practitioners function as storytellers. His essay "Landscape and Narrative" takes up the subject in detail, and in Trimble's book he further remarks on "the storyteller's responsibility," which "is not to be wise" but to function as one "who creates an atmosphere in which wisdom can reveal itself" (29). This meshes with Benjamin's credo, "Counsel woven into the fabric of real life is wisdom" (87), which similarly locates wisdom not in individuals but in the storied situations they inhabit. Nor is Lopez alone in claiming such a responsibility. Robert Finch, for instance, speaks of nature writers as representative figures who "story the landscape" and "shape our understanding" thereof: "Through stories, we literally identify with the land" and learn "to recognize home" (Lueders, *Writing Natural History* 41–42).

Yet nature writing is recognizably more descriptive and expository a genre than it is narrative—not so driven by plot and conflict. Why should nature writers claim this storytelling function, then, when they could defer to novelists on this score? Following Benjamin's distinction between storytelling and prose fiction, we may hazard some answers. For one, there is nature writing's reliance on the writer's direct experience and the expectation that the reader's own experience will answer to it in point of practice—the offering and taking of counsel. There is the circuit of field and study, wandering and cabin, the ethos of having "come from afar" to lend counsel about the character of home as it unfolds. And there is the fact that part of this work, the central part, involves the impulse to elude the orbit of industrial civilization to recover the circumstances that in Benjamin's view make story, as distinct from fiction, possible. All of these aspects are in some measure epitomized in Muir, as we have seen.

This last factor, in particular, helps explain the interest many nature writers evince for the figure of the indigen, the cultural being from beyond industrial civilization. Nature writing, like environmental writing in general, is enamored especially of Native Americans, perceived bearers of the "Indigen wisdom" (in Oelschlaeger's phrase) that comes with direct contact with place. To some, such situated wisdom is understood to be specifically embodied in narrative, with Terry Tempest Williams, for instance, relating an experience with Navajo children that "changed [her] life" by showing her how story delineates not just human but natural interrelations (Lueders, *Writing* 46–47). As an iconic metaphor, the indigen is everything Brodkey's garret dweller is not: not mechanical, not isolated and alienated, not confined to the recesses of a grim manufactured dwelling, not vexed by experiential deprivation or sacrificed to the demands of any art. The indigen is not the spare part of an industrial dispensation as the "modernist" writer is.

Furthermore—though this part is mostly unmentioned—the indigen does not write. No "traditional" people does; this is the effectual criterion for an otherwise variegated class. Finch comes close to allowing the appeal of nonwriting when, in responding to Williams's Navajo children story, he bemoans the absence of a surviving "oral native tradition" on Cape Cod, where he lives and writes (47). The place is somehow less storied for being more written: this is the implication. Indeed, the very notion of "nature writing" may lend support to this innuendo. If "nature writing" as a formula signals a relationship of resistance between its constituent words—one narratively configured in ways I have been suggesting—then the appeal of native peoples may consist in their affiliation with "nature" as precisely that which does not write but which transmits its situated wisdom even so.

It smacks of the noble savage to even breathe this much, of course, suggesting distinctions of spurious sorts that have informed the museum collector's mentality Haraway critiques, among other ills—anathema to postcolonials. Attempts to generalize about a "divide" between literacy and so-called orality may indeed take a crude form, projecting wholesale cognitive advances or economic "take-off points" supposed to result from expanded literacy, projects discredited both practically and ideologically.[14] Subtler forms may be seen as Ruth Finnegan sees them, more generously but still disparagingly, as marked by "a kind of romantic nostalgia, in 'the world we have lost' tone" they adopt toward nonwriting peoples, a tone counterweighed by the impression "that such losses were worth the sacrifice and that our own fate lies upwards and onwards through literacy" (6). Finnegan astutely renders the mingled affection and condescension characterizing some discussions of the subject—or subjects, human ones.[15] But not all treatments betray the "nostalgia" Finnegan decries, nor must the notion that some peoples have been "closer to nature" than others upon *some* terms lapse into irrelevance, not if those terms concern sustaining relations to place. In sheerly material terms, this would be so even if it were presumed that "noble savages" would do the same damage as literates, if given the same instruments. But the correlations run deeper than this, as efforts to reinstate "Indigen wisdom" attest.

In assuming the relative virtues of lives without writing, such efforts reverse the usual tenor of oral-literate distinctions. It's the notion that such distinctions must end up privileging literates that drives much critique of the oral-literate "divide." The charges leveled frequently involve determinism, especially of the technological sort: the notion that writing (or any technology) must inevitably bear consequences of sorts projected by the researcher. With so complex and overdetermined a cluster of activities as those entitled by "writing," it's not difficult to rebut such a notion. But these critiques are prone to their own sorts of determinism, in the slippery-slope contention that versions of the "divide" must necessarily disparage orality, and in the conviction that differences between writing and nonwriting can never have explanatory force but rather must be regarded as aspects or outcomes of other factors, ones that are often less concrete, more ineffable than the appeal to instruments of literacy. Yet to remark that events *did* happen in certain patterned manners— that division of labor, social hierarchy, religions of conversion, money, ecological crisis, and writing have arisen in league in one venue after another[16]—is not tantamount to saying they *had* to. No single causal chain need be posited to find such correlations significant. Upon Berry's terms, we needn't claim powers of prediction in order to admit these phenomena into the realm of accomplished possibility—to "prophesy after the fact," as Burke would say.

Nature writers' reasons for so doing would be less retrospective than prospective—preservationist, after a fashion. The efforts in literacy studies that resonate best with theirs are not those that swap a eulogistic "take-off" theory of literacy for a mirror-image, dyslogistic view of writing's ills, regarding literacy as an oppressive overlay upon an otherwise more-or-less original oral condition. More resonant are approaches that stress the varied methods, capacities, procedures, and understandings of nonwriting peoples—*active* virtues, not those (like "innocence") figured simply as the absence of something else.[17] Such approaches still observe the possibility that a state of nonwriting may be a condition of some peoples' achievements.

Differences of opinion on this subject do not come down to issues of evidence: learning more may not mean learning better how to explain these relations. Ample data exist to debunk the most facile "great leap" theories of literacy's effects; but beyond such pipedreams of national planners, nothing is clear cut. Researchers at both ends of a spectrum of response think their cases quite well established already, with "divide" proponent Eric Havelock, for one, convinced that with literacy-orality as a conceptual axis, a thousand odd facts coalesce that had floated loose before, and social view theorist Brian Street adamant that central tenets of the "literacy thesis" in even its weakest versions are insupportable, not just untested but untestable. Differences need not hinge upon the *type* of evidence taken as relevant, either. M. T. Clanchy's research on literacy's spread in the Middle Ages, for instance, has been pressed into service for both sides, with "divide" advocates Illich and Sanders reading "a society . . . turned inside out" (51) where critic Graff finds gradualism and "continuity" (28).

The differences, rather, are rhetorical: they concern the purposes for which inquiry is undertaken in the first place. Social view critics of oral-literate distinctions, as I've said, quite reasonably fear the slippery slope of determinism: such scholars as Graff, Street, and Brandt mean especially to discredit too-easy equations of literacy with enlightenment and progress, assumptions that, when vapidly observed, conduce to the "violence of literacy" exercised by educators and policy makers.[18] Illich and Sanders, on the other hand, wish to expose features of our terministic deep structure, our categorical makeup, so to speak, by demonstrating how such evident givens as "identity"—or for that matter, history itself—are founded upon script literacy. The motives of the social view critics are noble: by disputing that writing is in any important way distinct from speaking, they hope to undermine conceptions of the "literate" as a separate, exalted realm of behavior discontinuous with ordinary existence. The effect, they hope, will be democratizing, empowering to students from a diverse range of backgrounds. What comparable motives might the likes of Illich and Sanders hold? Appreciating these, I believe, will entail returning to the dynamic by which solitude can be said to "raise the issue" of culture in retreat: an ascetic dynamic.

I have suggested that "nature writing" may entitle, in part, a relation of resistance between its constituent terms, with "nature" associated with "living" and in some moments counterposed to "writing." Then retreat in nature may entail a strategic evasion of writing as well—a possibility that Finch, at least, observes in eschewing on-site notetaking on the grounds that he would as soon forego this form of "preconception." As the longing for the precultural or noncultural is part of cultural experience, so the attraction of the prewritten or nonwritten may be integral to a culture so writing-imbued as ours. It need not smack of "nostalgia" to honor this impulse, or even to contemplate the provisional escape from history, when as Paul Shepard explains, history itself is a specific ideational formation and arguably not a sustainable one.[19] One motive for exploring oral-literate distinctions, then, parallels motives for retreat in nature: that of "raising the issue" of writing in its absence.

A catch in this formula arises if it is considered that nature itself *is* written and can be read in a manner analogous to the decoding of a book. This is an extraordinarily commonplace notion. Muir, for one, frequently elaborates upon the old trope of the "Book of Nature," especially in his earlier work: he depicts it first as a volume that is mostly legible despite frayed edges and missing leaves, and later as an endlessly overwritten palimpsest, the deciphering of which demands more-than-human discernment and must thus be continually deferred.[20] A far more elaborate version of Muir's palimpsest metaphor might be gathered from Derrida's notion of writing as "trace," the (illusory) originary condition for spoken language or sign use of any sort.[21] In literacy teaching, there

is Paolo Freire's slogan of "reading the word, reading the world," as relatively accessible as Derrida's "writing" is inscrutable. And so on: in fact,
much of what gets summed up as "social construction" might from one
perspective be taken as an extended gloss on the notion that the world is
a legible text.

Whatever the appeal and practical applicability of this notion, it
must be allowed that it would never occur to nonwriting peoples. In this
respect, it is a notion of limited usefulness to those who would also assert
the situated integrity, even the relative superiority, of indigenous points
of view. For this is the practical dimension informing the speculative trajectories I've sketched: the motive of specifying what indigenous peoples
have achieved at entering into dialectical relations, relations of community, with nonhuman creation. Just as the most useful elements of much
nature writing consist in the particular features of natural processes that
get plotted along the narrative trajectories I've sketched, so specific
aspects of human relations to place may be conveyed through the
vehicle of oral-literate distinctions, through which these relations are
placed in relief.

For those who write and are steeped in writing, though, it is anything but simple to reject a view of the world as essentially written, or
rejecting it, to also reject the opposition between "nature" and "writing"
that this view arises in part to dissolve. For the "implications of literacy"[22] appear to ramify endlessly once their tag ends in our thinking
are picked at and unravelled. Without claiming to be comprehensive, I
will offer some instances of the ways these perplexities may trace out,
relative to notions I have been exploring. Say, for instance, we would
prefer to consider neither that the world is writing nor that writing
stands in opposition to nature, but rather that the world is nature and
includes writing as a sort of exfoliation thereof. We might arrive at a formulation like that Joseph Meeker offers, in which literary creation is
regarded as an adaptive trait of the human species, one implicated in
our biological welfare and our relations with other species. Thinking of
literature as adaptation leads Meeker to view writing upon a scale of evolutionary processes generally—to remark, that is, on the briefness and
paucity of the written record relative to the scope of evolutionary time.
But by what devices and along what lines is this evolutionary expanse
revealed to us in the first place? A circular account culminating in a
mode of transcendence is here implied: the forms of writing, seen as
adaptive, equip us to regard the world itself as readable text or story—

and the "deep time" story, whether eked out from vestiges like a singed scroll or blatant as a billboard to the eyes of the geologically "literate," in turn exposes the ephemeral character and ultimate paucity of the methods upon which it is founded. Letters are short-lived and limited; we know because they say so. To evoke, as Meeker does, "the novelty of consciousness as an evolutionary device" (4–5) is to cite a recognition predicated on the very "device" it discusses—or even more, upon those devices by virtue of which we come to regard consciousness as a "device" in the first place: our instruments of literacy.

Following Muir, who decried the shortcomings of writing through a comparison to the inadequacy of his sketches, we might draw an analogy to art to press this point. As *plein air* landscape painting, eventuating from specific technological innovations, has altered our understanding of what a landscape might consist in, so must the development of painting in general have affected our modes of differentiating among and determining functions of colors, which other peoples, particularly some "traditional" ones, are far from sharing. (Recall what Van Dyke made of this disparity in color perception.) Analogous factors apply to modes of differentiation that writing in general and specific applications thereof have encouraged. Most notably for writing in the field, there is the impulse to "preserve" or "capture" experience. People of pronounced literate cast may feel that they have not truly seen or been through anything that has not been "captured" in writing. Thus a nature writer like Ann Zwinger may truly "write just for pure self-indulgence" in a very immediate sense (Trimble 79), all the while contemplating the mass publication of her every realization, which presumably will be all the more "realized" for its dissemination.

Some of the widest and most vexing considerations in this regard extend particularly from the matter of publication. Of considerable import in environmental terms, publication appears nearly invisible to most people of pronounced literate cast. In some quarters of literacy education, there seems even the tacit assumption that most democratic of all would be a world in which everyone published, with no one then silent or silenced. Of course, the direct material effects of publication industries—trees cut, chemicals discharged, fuels spent, landfills crammed—are widespread and troubling enough. The perceived solution to this—electronic publishing on the World-Wide Web—entails resource costs of its own, hardly appears to be reducing the printed paper trade, and depends on effects that vanish when the plugs are pulled. Beyond these obvious effects, all sorts of indirect or covert implications attend publication as well. As elaborated by Illich and Sanders, for instance,[23] not only such relatively clear-cut concepts as reproduction and reputation depend on print literacy. Notions of personal "identity," as I've said, and the autonomous self are themselves deeply connected with print and thus implicated in any number of evidently estranging understandings that some nature writers, as promoters of "Indigen wisdom," think it their business to reformulate. Contemplation of this boggling prospect brings into view the far curve of another big circle myth like Meeker's assertion of the "novelty of consciousness." The myth of literacy that some, like Illich and Sanders, would promote envisions the conversion of writing from a tool of industrial totalization and alienation to one of "conviviality" (in Illich's term) and participation in local community and place. But for writers, the promotion of such ends must involve an acute double bind: it requires publishing the resistance to publication, at least as it is now constituted. The shape of the "success" one might have at this is at present scarcely conceivable, though this ought not to rule out the prospect.

All the prospects I have touched upon highlight the broad use to which oral-literate distinctions are perhaps best put: that of intimating a horizon to literacy's prowess, one not coterminous with human existence itself. I agree with Brian Stock that the "strong thesis" of literacy and orality holds best to explain changes in societies where "there has been no writing before" (5), that in its "lateral perspective" on such changes, "it assumes something really is happening" in the encounter with new technologies and texts (9). The perspective's value is less predictive than heuristic, generating vantages not only on language but on technological change. We in this society have cause to contemplate the implications of technologies and mentalities of many sorts, upon terms both local and categorical, and this "lateral perspective" can help us at this.[24] In this respect, Jack Goody's oft-criticized notion of "restricted literacy" may bear connotations beyond those usually ascribed to it. It is usually understood as literacy prevented from attaining a hypothetical "full" status by obstacles variously physical (lack of paper or books) and ideological (caste, class, or specialist control). Those "restricted" may be construed as passive, bounded entities that would burst out gloriously if only they hadn't been stifled so. But E. Verne, for one, points to another dimension to the term: Verne's notion of withdrawal from literacy as a political act meant to *recover* language suggests an active self-restriction or restraint. So, in a quite different way, does Andrea Fishman's account of literacy and schooling among the Amish, who "restrict" themselves in ways that we intellectuals may be loathe to credit but that have evidently conduced to sustained relations with neighbors and place. Why should writing, what Goody calls "the technology of the intellect," be exempt from the critique of technology in general? From the "lateral perspective" of the indigen, we may recognize that, as Kenneth Levine notes, *all* literacy is restricted literacy, however ironical our attempts to comprehend this from our own vantages as people of the book.

It is nature writers, I think, who are most drawn to such attempts in the realm of literary adaptation. When Wendell Berry asks, "Why not write and live at the same time?" he is acknowledging a split that he means to dissolve in practice; yet there seems also the further, faint suggestion that some literate activities may have the same alienating effect that other technologies have. The nature writer's narrative of retreat stands to configure such tensions over writing as technological intervention, as a human artifact foreign to place, or as the residue of a creaturely connection thereto. It raises the issue of literacy in/against nature, in ways discerned in Muir's musings over the metaphor of the Book of Nature and over the relative effectuality of labor or "play" within nature—the latter issue including the "bread problem," the question of material subsistence through or despite economies underwritten by elaborated literate technologies. The nonliterate indigen is the mediating figure in several of these tensions, of course, cropping up in all the authors I have considered above and in many other places in the developing generic canon. Not writing (though not "lacking" writing), the indigen is permitted (not restricted) to dwell exclusively in the realm of "living," the place itself—so the story goes.

NATURE SAVANT AND LITERATE INDIGEN

But this is not the whole story; it remains a lateral perspective. We're not about to stop reading and writing or teaching others to do so. Reaffirming this, I appear to be doing what Finnegan would expect, lamenting a lost world, only to assert that our own destiny lies "upwards and onwards through literacy." I am not that sanguine: far from heading "upwards," we may be fortunate just to back away from what seems to impend. If we admit the force of the literacy thesis, we find writing linked to a host of social, technological, and environmental depradations mostly unknown in its absence. It is only reasonable though far from easy to seek to turn literacy to purposes and ends it has never widely sanctioned and may be ill-equipped to serve. But as Leslie Silko emphasizes near the end of *Ceremony*: "It isn't easy. It never has been easy" (259). Nothing of this sort can be envisioned, I think, without the aid of revised "iconic metaphors" for writing, images of writing that Muir in his ambivalences represents, as does Silko in her syncretic "ceremony" against technological "witchery," and Thoreau in his *Journal*, which purified of readers is also purged of "rhetoric" in the manipulative sense of the word.

A further iconic metaphor of writing I would offer is one that upsets the separation of "living" and "writing" in nature while also subverting the rift between speaking and writing as "natural" and "artificial," respectively. This is the image of the youthful savant of nature who is also precocious with letters. A reverse image of the *enfant sauvage*, the nature savant experiences an upwelling of language in the solitary encounter with a nature she grows to know on intimate terms—an exuberant relation embodied in a preternatural affinity for literacy. A prototype is the remarkable Opal Whiteley, who at age six began a secret diary that she inscribed with crayons on brown bags and other scrap paper and hid in a hollow log in her forest "cathedral" near the Oregon logging camp where she lived, a settlement fortuitously named Walden.[25] In 1920, when Whiteley was twenty-two, her childhood diary was published to immediate acclaim and a gush of publicity, only to be discredited as a fraud shortly thereafter—falsely discredited, on flimsy evidence by slapdash, uncomprehending reporters. Like Muir's, Whiteley's story seems a fable of natural genius and exuberance, her diary a testament to a preternatural concourse with nature, by a child who began reading and writing (or as she put it, "printing") quite on her own by age three, with an intensity her subsequent formal schooling sometimes dampened but could not extinguish. Like Muir, Whiteley was a rhapsode, capable of entrancing audiences with discourses on the animals and plants she had observed, had listened and spoken to, collected and catalogued in profusion. Again like Muir, Whiteley's talents turned out to include a practical bent, a thoroughly literate penchant for organizing both textual and human resources, demonstrated in her phenomenal success at managing the statewide youth organization she took over at age seventeen. But unlike Muir's, her tale ends in neglect and unwarranted ignominy, the charges of fraud having stopped cold her book's sales and derailed the prodigy's prospects as writer and nature educator, after which she gravitated toward poverty and madness.

I take Whiteley as a fable for a life in which writing manifests contact with the land, infused with awareness but devoid of self-consciousness, as if Wordsworth had written the *Prelude* not in tranquil recollection but at the time, at a hollow log on site—no Romantic projection but an established fact. Hers is a cautionary tale, too, a litany of the suspicion and incomprehension as well as the morbid curiosity such writing-as-nature may arouse. More successful though still often thwarted was a kindred figure, the naturalist Carrie Dormon.[26] Dormon too began to read and write independently at age three; she too spent hours outdoors in nature study from just as early an age. Among the first women employed in forestry in her home state of Louisiana, she struggled for preservation of wildlands just as tirelessly as she traversed them in her botanical searches. Yet at age fifty-four, she could sound this Opal-like note in her prose:

> I was born with something—I call it the gift of the wild things—and because I am simple myself, and have a sympathetic heart, I can understand animals and simple people to an unusual degree. I see, too, so much that others miss. When I know so many lovely things, I feel greedy keeping them all to myself. (Bonta 250)

This self-characterization comes in a grant application, of all things, a request for a Guggenheim Fellowship. Of course her application was refused; we can imagine the response this confession of simplicity aroused. Yet Dormon's simplicity, if that's what it was, did not prevent her from completing four books, mostly on wildflowers, or impede sundry other achievements culminating in an honorary doctorate and recognition of other sorts. There may be other ways to entitle the capacity she describes: empathic resonance, care and awareness, resistance to "preconception," facility at entering "the naturalist's trance."

The nature savant is an iconic metaphor of both immersion and evasion, of literacy impressed to the rhapsode's capacities and stripped of its distancing effects, though not of its social efficacy. Is is a fable of contact with place through, not despite writing. No less important, though, are fables for contact of another sort, the sort that Stock says the literacy thesis is best fitted to explore: contact of indigens with people of the book. A further iconic metaphor, then, comes in the writing of recently nonwriting peoples: indigen literacy. Examples are found in images and attitudes toward both print and story depicted in some Native American writing. In *Ceremony*, there is Silko's syncretic medicine man Betonie, for instance, who recognizes that the healing ceremonies cannot remain static but must change and grow with circumstances, and so collects bundles of old newspapers, phone books, and calendars in addition to dried plants, shrunken pouches, and a trunk of his own sloughed-off hair and nails—all objects to conjure with (120–22). Or there is Louise Erdrich's tribal elder and raconteur Nanapush in *Tracks*, who though educated by Jesuits will not sign his name to government papers, believing the name loses power with such reproduction, but knowing as well what those papers entail. These characters are engaged in cultural and environmental regeneration through story, yet literacy for them is not story's own vehicle but an instrument for rearguard actions, bureaucratic and/or magical adaptations, the enemy's weapons picked up and trained on them. For the authors creating these characters, the same is presumably not true in the same degree. But these authors still perform in writing their acknowledgement of both literacy's powers and its boundedness, its subordination to story and place. The protagonists of these novels, at any rate, are not themselves writers or readers, except of signs, portents, confluences registered (not written) on the land.

The figure of the literate indigen has special potency but offers special problems both for literacy learning and for nature writing's generic identity. For literacy education, it resurrects the inescapable "violence of literacy" visited upon nonwriting peoples in the name of ideals that have often named themselves "progresssive"; it chastens those of us who would regard our own present ministrations in similarly sanguine manner. For nature writing, it vexes with the recognition that the genre so entitled depends on categories foreign to indigenous peoples, those of "nature" and "culture" as discrete entities posed in tacit opposition. Commentators have remarked on this repeatedly. Patrick Murphy notes how both Thomas Lyon in introducing his anthology, and Finch and Elder introducing Norton's massive nature writing volume, posit a split or sense of alienation from nature as a founding condition of the genre, thus as the reason its expositors have so overwhemingly been male and white (31–32, 125). Murphy, in turn, challenges this formulation, which he views less as describing than prescribing a generic nature-culture opposition favoring white males. To redress this, he pleads for inclusion of more Native American voices, especially women's, in the developing nature writing canon. One effect of his stance is to drag Murphy back into the generic quagmire I described at the start, as he embroils his students and himself in discussions as to which of this or that poem or novel, by Indian or white, might best qualify as "nature writing" (130). He holds a particular antipathy toward the nonfiction essay, nature writing's mainstay, which he regards in dichotomous terms as a fixed form perpetuating a rationalistic mentality (33). Yet for all his disparagement of "alienated white guys escaping into the woods" (129), Murphy thematizes his own volume through retreat scenarios of the most patent sort: recollections of "how the world changed" when as a child he would cross from housing development to open land and spend time "alone in the woods walking and climbing"; present musings on how "the noise of the rest of our lives recedes" as he and his family traverse their two-acre parcel at the fringes of town (xi–xii). These scenarios of "engagement with the nonhuman"—presumably true as told and thus testaments in "nonfiction"—constitute the seeds of nature writing of exactly the sort Murphy disparages.

I don't blame Murphy for treasuring his "white guy" recollections; I have my own of similar cast. It is likely that his work, which he terms "ecofeminist," depends on these sensations in deeply rooted ways, as my own work does. My points, rather, concern the relations between "white guy" voices and those of indigen others as generically constituted. It will not do, I believe, to dismiss the likes of Thoreau with charges of rationalistic "autonomy" (5), not when Thoreau, like Murphy himself, was a white guy smitten with the "anotherness" (35) of indigens. We might better face up to such conditions of "nature writing" as affect its relations to Native peoples. One is the prospect I've already cited: that the character of writing itself is in part what's at issue in relations of white-male "contact" with indigen and place alike. Second, in producing "nature writing" in English at this point in time for readers who seek out such work, even Native authors participate in a dynamic that incorporates Thoreau and partakes of a cultural logic inscribed in this language, one informing the generic inheritance. This hardly means that these authors need do so slavishly or prescriptively.

A third point extends from this. Not all writing about or from "nature" need take form or be designated as "nature writing." I hold for an understanding of "nature writing" that regards it as entitled not loosely but exactly, as writing consumed by those who seek depictions of a "nature" distinguished by difference or distance from human culture. The genre is a study of conditions that give rise to it. If much Native

American writing does not enact such generic conditions, this needn't surprise or trouble us, nor should it cause us to malign either that writing or its generic "other," or to construe either as environmentally less pertinent. More relevant a category to question might be that of "literature" itself, which is suspect on all sorts of grounds.[27] Its utility is especially questionable for comprehending the oral expressions of indigenous cultures. An example that John Hay cites and Murphy denounces—that of an Eskimo woman's spontaneously recited sea song—is surely as evocative yet irrecoverable as Hay makes it out to be, in print and translation only faintly hinting at the socio-environmental context in which it emerges, one so different from our own (Murphy 125–26). To enter it as a "poem" in an anthology is not wrong, exactly, but it does beg as many questions as it addresses. Once "transcribed" and entered in a printed volume of *any* sort, let alone an anthology of nature writing, the song becomes in crucial respects more kindred to Western, white-male, "energy-consuming" *literary* modes than to the cultural situation it arises in; for as Karl Kroeber notes, "so far as the Indian song transfers energy rather than absorbing it, it is not part of any purely literary tradition at all." No longer subject to socially empowering literal repetition but rather to "rereading," it becomes "a *text*, that is, the source for non-repetitive reiterations" that call for criticism, in the process not emitting but gathering cultural energy unto itself ("Poem, Dream" 332, emphasis in the original). As Benjamin's meditation on the storyteller also suggests, the category of "literature" is as troubled and alienated as "nature," for many of the same reasons; and all who practice it, white, Native, or other, are subject to its complications.[28]

Finally, the alternative Murphy proposes to nature writing's typical generic formation may be no alternative at all but rather a prospective *outcome* of retreat. "What if instead of alienation we posited *relation* as the primary mode of human-human and human-nature interaction without conflating difference, particularity and other specificities?" Murphy asks (35, emphasis in original). The answer is that, in some of its valences, this is exactly what retreat seeks to accomplish. But to "posit relation" presupposes that there are entities to relate, in this case some "human" and "nature" to "interact." And the upshot of this relation cannot be assumed or "posited" alone. It must be enacted, in bodies and words, the two levels of "conversion," as retreat enacts it. This does not argue against canon-reconstituting or in favor of excluding "others" of any sort. On the contrary, we needn't construe relations of enmity where affinity and resistance are more productive.[29] The same principles and sensations that lead Hay to climb out on Katahdin's "wing of the universe" surely underlie his interest in the Eskimo woman's song. So it is with Murphy's own scenarios of retreat as they inform his ecofeminist predilections. We *all* live in a "post-contact" world; we needn't suppress difference or evade generic skeletons in the closet to acknowledge this state. The nature-culture split, like oral-literate distinctions, may serve best not as a dichotomy nor as a border to be patrolled, but rather as a speculative instrument—something we have to work with, in the double sense of "have" as what is available to and what is incumbent upon us. Retreat is a way of beginning where we are.

This is further a credo of teaching, one Ann Berthoff offers, that of "beginning where they are":[30] where students are, that is, though in this respect we're in the same boat. The figures I have exhibited here—the literate indigen, the nature savant, and above all Muir in his mingled public and private aspects—are emblems of education, alike in dramatizing issues of "contact" with place and society and in intimating both prospects and horizons to literacy's sway, consonant with its status as expression and technology. The identity of the writer, these figures show, is irremediably both empowering and problematic. They demonstrate, for instance, that it's only natural for students to evade the role of writer. Most people have no difficulty so doing and are no more to be maligned than commended on this score. If you were to take these figures as iconic metaphors, then, as models for the "product" of a writing class, what would you have? Not people who assumed the role cheerfully, that's for sure, pulling the blinds and scalding their eyeballs at a cathode ray tube for hours each day as I'm doing. But you would have people who had learned what it was like to act this way on behalf of something valuable. You'd have people who knew how to write *without* acting this way, who could grab whatever pad or brown bag came to hand without imposing upon themselves the notion that by writing they need behave as a writer. You'd have people for whom writing was an emblem of living, of participation in a world that does not begin and end in writing. You'd have people whose writing had improved, but for whom the most important outcome of a class in writing was *not* that their writing had improved. In short, you'd have a better world, which is to say, you'd have a fable—one no less enabling in its way than those to which I've counterposed it.

CHAPTER SEVEN

Keeping It Simple

Reinvention and Recovery of Nature in General Education

> . . . a sense of place complex
> enough to represent reality
> and simple enough
> to be profoundly clear.
> —A. R. Ammons,
> *Lake Effect Country*

Thoreau's statement of his intent "to front the essential facts" has served as a touchstone to this study, a shorthand for the mission and form of retreat in nature. The project of "fronting" authorizes the more radical of the two "relinquishments" that Buell finds in nature writing: the relinquishing of one's own human self. This is confirmed later in *Walden*, with Thoreau craving the "fact" that like a scimitar will slice him in two and "conclude his mortal career" (98). Intimating such radical facts entails endless complexities, linguistic resourcefulness of sorts Richard Poirier notes in reflecting upon the difficulty of "writing off the self."[1] And indeed *Walden* involves difficulties of the first order, as the critical industry devoted to its exegesis demonstrates.

Yet in the paragraph following Thoreau's mission statement, there appears an even more celebrated dictum: "Simplify, simplify." This exhortation summarizes the method Thoreau employs in undertaking the first, more fabled form of "relinquishment" Buell cites: the relinquishing of artifactual encumbrances, a divesting that culminates in

the "epic of voluntary simplicity" of which *Walden* is a primary
instance. An ascetic equation is at work here: as material accoutrements are stripped away, spiritual and aesthetic elaborations accrue.
Material and experiential complexities exist in inverse proportions.
Intoning "Simplicity, simplicity, simplicity," Thoreau does not exhort
his auditors to simple-mindedness: quite the reverse. It may even seem
as if the injunction to "simplify" is a front for complexities that cannot
present themselves directly. Yet surely some aspects of material *and*
linguistic existence can be simplified to good effect—or at least,
Thoreau's continuing relevance would seem to confirm this as a possibility or faith.

My thesis about the narrative logic of retreat is simplified in the
extreme. It can be reduced, as I have said, to the paired terms of the
expression "nature writing," figured as opposing entities to be reconciled
through conversion in narrative. The genre thus constituted in a sense
projects its own dissolution, to be brought about either through merging
its paired categories, erasing the separate category of "nature," or re-
dressing the separations suggested in "writing." In narrative terms, this
prospect is figured in the human recognition of the nonhuman, a recognition in one sense necessarily impossible or partial, in another continually reachieved in ways that expose the inadequacies of the informing
opposition.

As is true of any more-or-less formalist approach, the interest and
value of the logic of retreat lies in what can be done with it. I have tried
to show what I think can be done, but I do not pretend my demonstra-
tions are exhaustive, any more than is the informing logic. To further
exhibit its applicability, I considered examining any number of other
published works, other nature narratives from Abbey to Zwinger. Leaving these analyses unwritten, though, I will turn instead to some retreat
narratives by students in a first-year writing class. I want to raise issues
relevant to my thesis in the realm of general education, where knowledge and attitudes transcending specialization are presumably formed. A
key issue concerns the significance of generically constituted personal
experience of nature for writing and literature instruction, environmental education, and the cultivation of an "ecological literacy" that would
comprehend both.[2] Part of what's at issue, I imagine, are the virtues and
pitfalls of the generic "simplicity" that developing writers enact in narrative, and the propriety of excavating social complexities to be discerned
therein.

RETREAT SCENARIOS IN STUDENT WRITING

The class in question, an introductory course in writing and literature fulfilling a first-year college composition requirement, mainly involved critical reading of texts but also invited students to emulate the generic formations discussed, particularly prose nonfiction on nature.[3] Not all students opted to pursue this option but a significant number did, in both journals and essays. I will look at essays by four students, two women and two men, none of whom planned to major in English or aspired especially to the status of "writer." These essays are expressive of questions of various sorts, which I will synopsize after I have discussed them.

I'll look first at an essay entitled "A Realization in Nature," by a student named Jaime (pronounced "Jamie"). Of all the students in this class, Jaime seemed most impelled to recount her impressions of outdoors experiences, with two of the four essays in her final portfolio categorizable as narratives of retreat and a third employing outdoors reminiscence as a backdrop to an analysis of Abbey's attitude toward progress. Her essay partakes of nature writing's generic character, including those aspects that Joyce Carol Oates disparages as "MYSTICAL ONENESS." To a practiced literary sensibility, her essay seems less than expert, at points veering toward overearnestness and cliché. Yet what appear to be clichés sometimes border upon other, more compelling notes. Here are the essay's opening paragraphs:

> The sun trickled through the trees and dripped off the bough as the snow disappeared. It fell onto my cheek and off to be absorbed by everything around me. My eyes squinted from the shower of nature falling upon me. It was a magical and mystical scene, seen so many times, but never really observed. The simple things are always overlooked and just accepted. Microscopically, though, it really isn't that simple. Simple things are made up of complex mini-systems that each contribute some meaning to life.
>
> Soon that thought was carried off on the wind and nothing was left but a whisper. The key to the answers for the questions of life seemed to be found on the lips of nature. On a clear day you can see forever and hear the voices that call to you from the Earth.

This is student writing, to be sure—rough-edged, incognizant of such breaches of literary decorum as the personification of "nature" or nostrums about "the questions of life" and how far one can see "on a clear day." Yet there are transformations here that fascinate me: how sunlight and melting snow are conflated; the way the perception of "simple things" gets introduced, then rendered complex through science, then dispersed in the flow of temporal experience; the way the resultant "whisper" gets parlayed into earthly "voices" that at once translate, supersede, and surpass science's remnant breath. Jaime proceeds to situate these "voices" in the tangible chattering of squirrels. She falls well into the grip of the pathetic fallacy at points, yet imparts nicely what the "fallacy" can best impart, a sense of a creature's own agency, in this remark: "So heartily they eat in the winter, from their intelligence they gain weight." The Earth's voicing is taken up next in a cardinal's call, and then by the writer herself, who assumes the bird's "air of happiness" and disseminates it in a "whisper" of her own, one that "is passed along and heard by all."

By now the writer is seated on the forest floor, within "the maze of sunlight and shadows" playing across last season's matted leaves:

> The maze itself enchants me and I find myself staring at the ground. It has that brown green color and is firmly matted to the Earth. The winter is harsh on this summer vegetation. The ground has the feel of uncertainty to it, constantly changing. The countless flaws: the impressions of human footsteps, the rise and fall of the land, the blades of grass that seem to be swept around randomly. These all come together to form one flowing continuum. This coincides with life and its ups and downs, it never stops, but marches on until the end of time. It grows, bends and winds, but never ceases to exist. The blanket of Earth is a collection of memories of lives which keeps all under it warm.

Here is the "realization" Jaime speaks of in her title. It is extended in a further episode in which a butterfly materializes next to her, the "maze" of its wing pattern reproducing the light-maze on the ground. Though this transcendent "continuum" could be read as sentimental, Jaime enacts her realization in a manner that lends a double valence to the "impressions" that others' footsteps have left. She establishes the resemblance of her human memories to those the place itself both evokes and incarnates, without effacing the facticity of her situation or leaping too precipitously above "the rise and fall of the land" itself. Her essay has grown in my understanding over several readings, in ways that make me wonder if I sufficiently credited it when I read it first, though I liked it well enough at the time. I am better disposed than I was to accept Jaime's concluding sentiment, which diffuse as it is can be read as an affirmation of the narrativizing process itself, the repetitions that Harpham figures as conversion: "The whispers I leave in nature come back to me on that spring breeze. I find many anwers in nature and within myself."

Another essay, Beth's "How Shall I Exist?," concerns conversion of a sort closer to the term's core sense. At one point during the semester, shortly after we'd read Dillard's *Pilgrim at Tinker Creek*, which profoundly affected her, Beth underwent what can be fairly described as a conversion experience, an epiphany. As Beth describes it in her journal and subsequently in the essay I'm quoting, the experience occurred during a car trip back to campus after a weekend at home. Her fiancé, who was driving, exhorted her to look at the sunset, an attractive yet fairly ordinary one. She did so "reluctantly," with these results:

> I was observing it, rather bored really, when suddenly, something happened—I got sucked in—I saw through the trees, the bare black tree outlines, the symmetrical-down-to-the-very-last-twig trees. What I saw through those dormant trees was the color of the earth's atmosphere behind them, around them, through them, surrounding them, embracing their very tips, and I was a part of it. I was not just an observer; I was being embraced by the earth itself.
>
> I was not actively thinking, per se, but I did have random thoughts: "This is what Annie Dillard meant"; "I want to run and feel the wind rip at my hair"; "I want to race across the forest floor and feel the branches, sticks, and leaves break under my weight. I want to hear them snap and crack beneath my feet"; "I am a wild being."

In this heightened state, Beth is struck dumb, stripped of self-consciousness, "in awe of all Nature's intricacies." Note that in reporting her on-site response, she evokes not only her "wild" impulses but also the generic exemplar of Dillard, who has helped prepare her to narratively "convert," perhaps even to undergo this experience. She also endures a trial by artifact in her resentment of the scattered electric lights that "disturb" her "True vision." Yet it is the experience and not these conventions that grips her: Beth acknowledges the dual necessity and inadequacy of generic expression to accommodate what she has lived through. Her fiancé, having witnessed her trance state, tells her glowingly that she has "just experienced Nature"; assessing this, Beth remarks that "at the time, it sounded all right, but now it isn't correct." What has transpired surpasses this nostrum; it resists articulation.

In the rest of her essay, Beth mulls over the import of her experience: whether the likes of it will ever happen to her again; how its life-affecting force might lead her to change what she now perceives to be the "trivial" character of her life. Some of these musings were prompted by my teacherly exhortations; in the journal version, only the episode itself is recounted. I am not sure how well served Beth was by my encouraging her to thematize her experience. Understandably, her reflections are rather inchoate: she quotes Samuel Johnson on how a person "who has experienced the inexpressible . . . is under no obligation to attempt to express it" (Oates 236), and seems herself a bit over-matched at being tacitly placed under such an obligation. Yet while her essay does not entirely succeed upon formal terms, Beth is still led to rehearse some generative uncertainties, especially as to the propriety of trying to bring about instead of deferring projected life changes in light of so striking a present exigency:

> So, at this level in my life, where I am already swimming in quicksand and unsure of everyone and everything that I have come to know, I cannot stop and ponder life and its myster-ies—but if not now, when? When will I be able to afford this change? When will I say, "OK, now, let it be now"? How can I push it away? How can I not? I shall just have to hold it in the back of my mind and the bottom of my heart until the answer fills them both and I will act upon it. There is nothing more I can do now, but hear them whisper secrets to each other until I finally choose to listen to them.

Coming from someone so ordinarily vocal and self-assured as Beth, this paean to suspended judgment and incubation is stirring to me, raising a caution to my own proclaimed certainties. I would like to think that the internalized dialogue she imagines will not grow inaudible and subside, but will issue in actions that dissolve the conundrum of having to "stop" life to "ponder life."

A student who has requested I call him "Jobu"—a sobriquet more exotic than the ordinary name he goes by, belying his middle-class upbringing and quiet, unassuming character—wrote an essay on similarly elemental sensations, but one that concerns developments unfolding not in a moment but over the better part of his nineteen years. His essay's subject is fire, but he broaches it by evoking the experience of solitude. Solitude, in his definition, "doesn't necessarily mean by myself, alone, solo; rather, it means with a few good friends who share common interests"—certain "solitude companions" who, like him, "were not always, or ever, looked up to by our 'peers.'" The experience of peer group rejection has been formative for Jobu: "The ability to find comfort where others have turned me away has made me the person I am today." Like him, I appreciate from my own school and neighborhood experiences the force of Harpham's realization that an integral aspect of cultural existence is the longing for something pre- or noncultural—or as John Burroughs puts it, "We run to Nature because we are afraid of man" (Bergon 103). Jobu bears this out in associating solitude both with a small, similarly outcast peer group (a pack of fellow high school track team members) and with a treasured setting divorced from scenes of social discomfort: what in the urbanized environs of southern Michigan is known as "up north." Each summer for many years, Jobu and his family had vacationed at the same rustic lakeside resort, where he had experienced both opportunities for solitary retreat in nature and a level of peer-group acceptance mostly unknown to him at his home in Detroit. A series of journal entries preceding this essay had recounted at length a raucous, soda-pop swilling trip taken with his track-team pals to this same resort in the off-season—a trip punctuated with his need to evade even his "solitude companions" and find moments alone outdoors. In beginning his essay, Jobu again evokes this accepting peer group, then relates the origins of his "fascination with fire" in the bonfires held nightly at the resort, which he'd attended since age five. Thus what is mainly a reflection on fire as a means of solitary renewal is situated in a social complex, depicted in a way that does not wholly affirm or deny social existence but rather "raises the issue" toward the end of contemplating its absence.

The essay as it develops is primarily a meditation on control: his early presumption to control this element; his subsequent "learning to submit to fire, submit to that which I can't control." The control he once thought he exercised by moving sticks of wood around in a fire he later comes to regard as negligible, and he develops instead into fire's advocate, one who "hate[s] to let a fire die, let alone be the one to kill it." This progression could be read as a fable of socialization, this learning to "stop and pay homage" to a force larger than oneself spelling acquiescence to a social dispensation one feels powerless to affect. Except there are inklings of an Abbey or Jeffers-like "Inhumanism" at work here as well, in Jobu's enthusiasm for the prospect of a fire that "lives on" despite all human efforts, "burning, destroying, killing" but also rejuvenating. Jobu's stance further recalls Berry's refigurations of control and prediction: "I only think that I know what the fire is going to do." Such incipiently biocentric sentiments are not easily extricated from the impulses both to submit to and to visit destruction upon a pain-dispensing social order. Jobu's attitude teeters on a cusp between an ecological recognition of human limitation on one hand, and quietism, evasion, flight into the self-obliterating recesses of fire on the other. I cannot tell to which side he may ultimately lean, if he ever does; but I know him too well to presume he may be pushed.

The very idea of teacherly pushing raises issues of gender in a patriarchal culture, issues more evident yet in an essay by a young man named Dave. We can better appreciate the posture from which Dave writes by attending first to an associational logic played out in some journal entries of his. Responding to Annie Dillard, Dave remarks on how, like a sponge, she fills up with experience yet through writing is wrung out, in order to "start fresh every day." He proceeds to contrast this capacity for renewal with the way in which, in today's society, "even children are beginning to form chips on their shoulders at a young age." This in turn reminds him of a friend's problems with gang violence, so that in the space of a few sentences, Dave has gone from contemplating Dillard's fresh perception to enumerating the victims of drive-by shootings. This associational sequence is reiterated in an entry a week later, in which an observation on nature writers' "reverence of nature" segues into a scenario of male adolescent insurgency, the recollection of a park across from his high school occupied not by devotees of scenery but by teenage smokers of tobacco and other drugs—a "tainted" memory of a once-attractive place. During the course of our writing class, in contrast to such memories, Dave like many students began to experience renewed appreciation for natural phenomena. Soon after a hike I took with students through the sprawling campus arboretum, Dave returned there alone, remarking in his journal on "all the activity . . . which had eluded [him] before," reporting on observing a dove and being deeply "touched" by the episode. Yet like many students, especially but not exclusively male, Dave formed a real antipathy to Susan Griffin's ecofeminist *Woman and Nature*: for all his dismay over instances of masculinist despoliation and his renewed sensitivity to natural surroundings, he rejected a vision that comprehends both attitudes as correlated in masculinist ideology.

These developments in his journal cast an interesting light upon the way Dave thematizes his narrative of a nature walk. He devises a conceit for his essay that ironizes the masculine character of outdoor "stalking": a trope of military engagement. He is recounting an experience of creeping up upon and observing fledgling birds in a nest, but in a wryly ludicrous manner he refers to the young birds as the "new troops," to their nest as a "base" constructed through "engineering," to the mother bird as a "guardian" off "to procure supplies for the hungry troops," to a flock of geese overhead as a "squadron," and so on. His own stealth in stalking the nest he construes in mock-paranoiac terms as motivated by the suspicion that he might "be walking into an elaborate trap" on his "reconnaissance mission" into contested terrain. Upon his climactic encounter with the mother, though, he compromises this quasimilitaristic posture, insisting that he has come "not on a trip of destruction" but rather as "a curious onlooker"; and through this attitude of openness and trust he becomes privileged to "witness such an awesome thing as the creation of life." The entire account, then, is couched ironically as an *adventure* of a prototypically masculine sort. Dave's strategem intrigues me for the way it satirizes the relative absence of conflict and risk in the solitary outdoor ramble, while still honoring the sensations of vigilance, motion, concealment, recognition, and adrenalin-stoked surprise that render so peaceful a venture an adventure nonetheless. One might think of adventure thus construed as sublimating the masculine aggressiveness that impels gang violence; but it might be more helpful to take a reverse tack, to regard gang stalkings as a postindustrial perversion of the ancient impulse to stalk wild creatures outdoors. I would like through my teaching not to push but to encourage Dave and young men like him to develop masculine identities in such relatively more life-affirming manners, even as I acknowledge how unlikely they are to accept the more comprehensive perspectives of ecofeminism and biocentrism in any but partial, grudging ways.

Here, then, are some issues I derive from the work of these students. In Jaime, I find issues of generic expectations, "literary" or otherwise. What are the consequences for a developing writer of recapitulating generic formulae or clichés (which may themselves be genres writ small)? In privileging originality, teachers may overlook how generic forms may enable, motivate, and conduce to commitment of certain orders, not least to the act of writing itself. Admitting a generative power to cliché is not tantamount to suspending one's critical faculties: if I read Jaime's essay without balking at its formulaic aspects while still bringing such critical faculties to bear upon it as I would with published texts, I discern virtues I might otherwise neglect. I recognize how both levels of conversion, the experience and its expression, materialize not despite but through the generic forms she adopts.

With Beth, I find issues of the relation of writing to an "inexpressible" located in both the moment of conversion and the inestimable durations that writing and commitment may take to grow. I am reminded of how arbitrary are the academic "terms" within which we operate, how unreasonable the expectation that the orders of conversion we project for students, as well as those they project for themselves, should be accommodated within these rigid temporal schemes. Given the injunction that they be so contained, I see other issues arising: the propriety of exhorting students to seek formal closure to realizations that must unfold in a rhythm of their own; the problem of evaluating what is of necessity half-formed; the virtue of welcoming suspension of closure in matters that seem legitimately to resist it. And there is the problem of how to credit experience that seems peripheral or antithetical to the precepts of a course, as a conversion experience must seem in the context of a course stressing argument or critical analysis. This relates to an issue central to ecological education: how to accommodate or even cultivate experiences of pleasure and joy in the exercise of human faculties that are not exclusively linguistic.

Compounding these issues, which inform Jobu's essay as well, are others extending from his prizing of solitude and his trials with social experience. There's a sense in which some individuals who've had difficulties in social milieus may be relatively well positioned to escape "preconception," to detect vagaries of social existence that better-"adjusted" people may overlook. Thoreau, as usual, is the prime exhibit: while it would be wrong to reduce his proto-ecological recognitions to a question of his relations with his neighbors, it does appear as if his relative alienation was a necessary though hardly sufficient condition of his attaining such insights.[4] I am not suggesting that Jobu is another Thoreau, poised on the brink of recognitions so momentous. He is a shy young guy, and nature writing's tenor of solitary retreat may do no more than help confirm him in a habit of withdrawal. Yet he is strong-minded and his solitude is sharply qualified, allied with human relations that are close and fulfilling. Perhaps larger commitments will come to attract him, authorized by the biocentric predilections for which his pleasure in solitude has prepared him. The impulse to quietude and withdrawal is the risk that a privileging of retreat must run. Yet there's a countervailing risk to denigrating solitude in an exclusive focus on the social: namely, that modes of attention crucial to environmental awareness will be neglected, with results corrosive to an order of social commitments as well, not just to the individual psyches concerned.

The question of attention pervades Dave's essay of ironical masculine adventure in nature, too, as indeed it does all these students' essays. Students who value their stories of retreat in nature do so for the ways these stories capture something tangible and important that habitual social contacts do not provide. This does not mean that social experience can never have such effects or that retreat must necessarily be experienced in this way. But our vaunted loss of "contact" with natural phenomena means that for many, social contact neglects the natural and may even exist as its rival. This is manifest most, I suspect, in the modes of attention one cultivates with or without other people. Paul Shepard cites "quality of attention"—"cultural and habitual differences in the style of day-to-day hearing, seeing, smelling, tasting, and touching the surroundings"—as one factor of the sea change in sensibility accompanying the shift from paleolithic to neolithic ways of life. To hunters and gatherers, "all sound is a voice," all vision potentially significant, continuously and finely differentiated; according to Ortega y Gasset, theirs is "an attention which does not consist in riveting itself on the presumed but consists precisely in not presuming anything and in avoiding inattentiveness"—"a 'universal' attention, which does not inscribe itself on any point and tries to be on all points" (Shepard 21–22). Note the resemblance of this attention to Berry's instructive "silence," to the eschewing of "preconception" both Berry and Finch espouse, to Wilson's "naturalist's trance." Such attention, an evolutionary entitlement, has not disappeared, but it is moribund and devalued. It may even be endangered. Cultivating retreat may be a way of helping to preserve an endangered species of attention, its "conversion" in classroom writing a figurative form of captive breeding.

Dave in his essay recounts an episode of heightened attention, one that he ironically yet justly associates with militarized versions of the masculine hunt. We need not essentialize either attention or gender to identify such outdoor activities with shifts in the character of economies and work, as Shepard clearly does. It is a matter of historical moment and a neglected issue in education that organic nature and technological culture should be so thoroughly mapped along a gendered axis of leisure and work. Shepard's reference to hunting and gathering should remind us that, in relation to questions of economy and subsistence, there is always a "bread problem" in retreat scenarios, one not always or perhaps even usually well addressed. Retreat scenarios are the province of literati, those freed to such pursuits, as Leopold notes, once technology has assured their breakfasts. Richard White contrasts their activities to those of loggers, ranchers, and others whose acquaintance with the land is not diffuse and sentimental but sternly embodied in physical work.[5] White is right to insist that environmentalism has a work problem, as education does, too (though I'd rather that he remark as well how the labor of loggers and ranchers is deficit-financed through internal combustion and mediated through the transvaluation of cash, and to this extent as "abstract" as the work of your average academic). Wendell Berry confronts the bread problem in his subsistence farming; as we've seen, his work and leisure in retreat are rhetorically all of a piece. Thus his work points up a much-untapped resource of retreat, its potential to make an issue of domestic economies: where you live, where you can't live, opening vantages on how you do live. Even camping, lampooned though it sometimes is as guys playing house outdoors, has this potential, highlighting what it takes to get by in a place, rendering those arrangements less transparent. We have tended to write *away* from such understandings, writing having so often been the vehicle of flight from bodily labor, since before the Egyptian scribe advised his son to "take writing into his heart" so he wouldn't have to work with his hands and back. If education is charged in part with preparing its wards for the workplaces of the future, it might entertain the notion that any sustainable cultures to come must depend less on the "virtual" and more on the actual work of the light-powered body in the local milieu. It will not perforce turn scholars into farmers, yet it might devise heuristic devices to cultivate attitudes conducive to this shift—an "environmental education" broadly conceived. Education in literacy I would think to be central to this change, with the narrative of retreat an exhibit in its perils and potentialities.

White's discussion of the rift between environmentalists and those who "work for a living" points up the vagaries of educating for work under the present technoliterate dispensation. Even observing his counsel not to denigrate the labor of outdoor workers, we must observe how the livelihoods most available to our students and ourselves do not conduce to a felt sense of connection with the terms of one's subsistance—a recognition of the sort White advises us to cultivate. Under these circumstances, and acknowledging that they will not change overnight, perhaps education should be thought of as preparing its charges for vacation as much as for work. Let's say the stockbroker goes to the woods, on a hike, an ecotourist junket, even an ecotherapy session. Goes on a solo—a solitary stint in the sticks. Gets aesthetic, then ascetic; enters a recognition, provisionally chucks some artifactual impediments—then "reenters" the economic world and continues to trade in stocks. What has changed? Maybe nothing, or very little. He or she is not worse off, I would hope, and neither is the world or community. Or are they? Perhaps so, if the excursion lends a sense of absolution to a way of life that in some ways troubles both the world and those who live in it, as the history of pastoral suggests it is capable of doing.[6] The same could go for professors of English or any technoliterate specialist whose work is not in or of the place visited. But if the work is *not* there in the wild place—if as White suggests, the appeal of the outdoor experience resides largely in how it mimics the lost work that was once our shared estate—is the episode of retreat then to be discounted? Recognizing the rift, we may not have debunked it so much as exposed an enduring need, a touchstone in this dispensation in which work is as it is, in need of reformation it may or may not ever get. Though a scene of "occupation" for him, to John Muir the mountains were prized for leisure, as the place where the modern worker, oppressed by machines and letters, is refreshed: it may be that this refreshment hinges on how the lost elements of work are played at or acted out there. This arrangement is dislocated, certainly, as "nature" itself is,[7] but the alternatives, I think, are neither obvious nor equally forceful. The prospect of such lost work may be "nostalgic"; but this attribution is circular, since nostalgia, regenerated in every epoch as the vision of a simpler time just preceding,[8] may itself be a by-product or effect of modern work. Utopias are projected nostalgias; the regard of past worlds may be indispensible to the contemplation of possible ones.

CYBORGS AND SOLOS

It is this complex of attention and work that I imagine general education might better engage. Imagining this, I undoubtedly project elements of my own psychosocial makeup and history. Rather than follow the lead of commentators on nature writing who establish their credentials by narrating outdoor experiences of their own,[9] I might as readily narrate vagaries of school or suburban neighborhood, many doubtless peculiar to me. Yet some would be generic, common to those of my kind, whatever that is—white and male for starters, though perhaps not only that. The question becomes, at what level of generality or in what tangible aspects such informing experience resembles that of others. What and whom is my nostalgia good for? This is the same question my students face, and that I face again in facing them.

One reading, stressing historical particularity and difference, would hew to the approach of Donna Haraway and others of social constructionist temper; another would follow contours traced by Paul Shepard and practitioners of ecopsychology. I will touch upon both in turn. Haraway we have visited in the chapter on Van Dyke, where her analysis of Progressive Era "organicism" proved integral to an account of that author's racial anxiety. Scholars of the sort she exemplifies—whom we might term the nature "reinventors"—insist that, as William Cronon puts it, "the nature we study must become less natural and more cultural," in order to inform "an environmentalism capable of explaining why people use and abuse the earth as they do" (36).[10] An overarching reason, these scholars agree, is that nature is a human construct posited as a realm wholly separate from humans, and this construct "naturalizes" oppression and despoliation of innumerable sorts. The Romantic dream of resolving the nature-culture split by refiguring culture in the image of nature is seen as itself complicit in the split. "Nature" is an embarrassment of representations, a projection screen, a hall of mirrors in which race, class, and gender are endlessly, resiliently reproduced. The task for Haraway, then, is to devise terministic means by which to baffle distinctions between nature and culture. She attempts this most notably through "the image of the cyborg"—"a cybernetic organism, a hybrid of machine and organism." The cyborg braids together "science fiction and social reality"; it replaces the spurious unity of "nature" with an ironicized unity predicated on "blasphemy" against that faith, conducing to recognition "of oppression, and so of possibility" (*Simians, Cyborgs, and Women* 149).

With respect to industrial civilization, the cyborg enacts this slogan: If you can't beat 'em, conjoin 'em! If we determine that machine and creature are indivisible, then the burden of the distinction drops away. We can proceed to the more productive business of articulating their interpenetration, in "virtual" realms as surely as in the "real" ones from which they cannot be distinguished.[11] The dissolution of these distinctions is presumed to hold promise for both sides of the divide thus redressed—a refreshed natural environment, a healthier relation to technology—as well as for relations among human groups, with race/class/gender splits undermined along with the dichotomies authorizing them. Haraway provides a version of something we need and are always hard pressed to devise: ways to be at once both careful and precipitous in speaking of important things. Her cyborg "blasphemy" offers one avenue for refusing or suspending certain choices that seem prepared for us, principally the choice between allegiance to "nature" or "culture." Though vastly different from Wendell Berry, she develops a similar realization: that freedom and individuation do *not* equal autonomy and individualism, on neither social nor biological terms.

With respect to industrial civilization, of course, Berry could not disagree more: he would rather we all just walk away. His orientation accords with that of Shepard and the ecopsychology movement, which would most likely strike Haraway and the nature "reinventors" as a Romantic atavism. It's not easy to say which stance bodes better, or to hold them both. The choice (if that's what it is) is complicated by the observation that both camps share a point of departure in questioning where the human being ends and "surroundings" begin. Haraway cites "three crucial boundary breakdowns" that her cyborg image configures, between humans and animals, organisms and machines, and the physical and nonphysical—boundaries she insists current knowledge can no longer support (151–53). In her zeal to erase these boundaries, she might well countenance ecopsychology's insistence that the "self" doesn't end where the skin does, and that the skin itself doesn't end at any definite point.[12]

Yet their differences are pronounced enough, with ecopsychology's emphasis falling not on reinvention but on recovery—as from a "madness" per Shepard or an "addiction" as Chellis Glendinning terms our technological fixations (44). A major difference with implications for general education concerns the valence of nature retreat. Ecopsychology embraces immersion in wildness generally and wilderness experiences in particular, regarding them as therapeutic not just in the event but in the aftermath. Parallels between the therapeutic measures ecopsychologists espouse and the generic conditions and forms of retreat I've described are detailed in Steven Harper's "The Way of Wilderness," which describes the "practice" of wilderness travel he conducts for clients. Harper insists on the character of wilderness as not just scene but agent of instruction, its status as "a leaderless teacher" (186). He discusses the drama of the artifactual inherent to the undertaking:

> We must decide what to take with us and what to leave behind. A critical aspect of experiencing wilderness is the willingness to simplify. But, paradoxically, simplicity is not as easy as it sounds. The tools and techniques we choose to take into wilderness can dilute and drastically alter our direct experience with nature. So we begin by questioning each tool we need. Wilderness work starts with a basic ecological question: what do we really need? (188)

He asserts the importance of a quality he calls "attentiveness," through which wilderness travel becomes "itself an awareness continuum," not a succession of discrete focal points or problems (189). Most importantly, he insists that the effects of the experience ought not to be lost at the journey's end: "the real work begins when we return" (196). The experience is all too easily dissipated, objectified, filed away, when it ought to be consolidated, extended, sustained through contact with kindred others and through physical and contemplative practices. Thus cultivated, the experience may grow into a realization that the wilderness trip itself is not essential for the recognition of wildness to enliven one's existence.

Upon this account and others in its vein, the experience of retreat may have tangible benefits for those who engage it in the right spirit. This is no more than literary practitioners have proclaimed all along, of course, yet practitioners in psychology reaffirm this in concrete, even statistical terms, across a range of participants. To substantiate his conclusion "that the wilderness experience, if conducted as a retreat from cultural dominance, could have a profound impact on the psyche" (123), Robert Greenway, for instance, has compiled questionnaires and interviews from around half of the some 1,400 participants he has conducted through a wilderness excursion program. He has also collected hundreds of "personal responses" in writing and art, and conducted longitudinal studies with dozens of participants (128). The experience of solitude (or "alone time") was almost unanimously pronounced the most important aspect of the trip, yet a preponderance of respondants also cited group fellowship or "community" among its most notable virtues. Three-quarters reported making major life changes upon their return, changes that after five years still "held true" for half of them (129).

Rachel and Stephen Kaplan confirm such trends over a number of outdoor experience studies. Especially interesting are their findings on solitude, as manifested through the "solo," the period (48 hours, in this case) that an individual spends alone during the course of Outward Bound–style wilderness treks (136–40). Among observations on the presence of heightened anxiety or awareness, of boredom or exaltation, difficulty or ease, are recognitions that amplify aspects of the retreat narratives we have examined. For one thing, isolation from other people appeared to be a minimal motivation for solitude, compared to the opportunity to contemplate natural surroundings: "going in" to the wild place seems far more important than "going out" from human others. Yet "traces left by other people were still the most detracting of the visual aspects" for most (139). This was not universally the case, nor was the experience in sum a positive one for all: for some it did not live up to expectations they had developed in advance. Yet even among those who rated it negatively, within a few days the experience had grown in their estimation and begun to enhance their sense of their own capacities. The Kaplans note how unsurprising it is that the solo should occasion discomfort and unease among people so unused to being left alone with their thoughts and senses, without accustomed social and artifactual prompts; these researchers find it "far more surprising that the effects of 48 hours of such solitude are generally so positive" (140). Most important to note is that negative or positive impressions are not single or static, but more generally occur in a progression:

> It is quite characteristic for the low point to come as the first night approaches and for spirits to be raised in the course of the second day. The feelings upon rising after the second day

are particularly positive. The inner sense of peacefulness takes
time to develop. (140)

This is precisely the sequence of events that Wendell Berry narrates in
his "Entrance to the Woods."

If the benefits are this pronounced, why shouldn't experience of
this sort be more widely purveyed under the auspices of a general education? There are obvious logistical problems considering the spatiotemporal attributes of school and the "settled" character of most of our
landscapes, but these are relative, not absolute obstacles to distributing
such experience more widely. The cultural obstacles are deeper-seated.
The most serious, I believe, concerns ethnocentrism. It is mostly white
people who take trips of the sort reported; mostly white people hold
these views, pursue these measures, respond to these generic prompts.
Though practices and depictions of nature retreat emerge in complex
relation to urban life, they remain nonentities to most nonwhite urban-
ites. A concern for wilderness not only is not held by many nonwhites; it
has frequently been used as a weapon against them. This problem goads
Haraway, certainly, as it does ecopsychologists and, however belatedly,
mainstream environmentalists.

If even a portion of what the Kaplans and others report about the
value of nature experience is valid in more than sheerly ethnocentric
terms, then it's evident we are facing a baby-and-bathwater problem of
profound dimensions here. How do we salvage the experience of peacefulness and insight, the cultivation of endangered modes of attention,
the vantage upon cultural dominance that retreat has the potential to
offer, while acknowledging and addressing sociocultural biases so commonly implicated in the practice? There is no one answer, and no
simple one. To Haraway, the cyborg is the figurative strategem that
resolves the dilemma: the "baby" of nature's value is preserved in the
cyborg's organic character, which though not separable can never be
wholly given over to its mechanical attributes. Yet I do not imagine that
the figure of the cyborg is that compatible with the experience of retreat
as most people report it, whether they're white or not, women or not. I
do not see what good it would do if they figured themselves as hybrid
"monsters"[13] under these conditions, or what harm it does if they regard
themselves as creatures in a mostly nonmechanical milieu. It may be
that my assessment is insufficiently complex. But this is exactly where, to
my mind, the ecopsychological approach enacts Thoreau's virtue of

"simplifying." Eschewing totality, it can still insist that relations to non-human nature can be more or less unmediated, the upshot of retreat more or less therapeutic and generative, places and creatures more or less wild, and can enjoin us to act in manners that will maximize these virtues in our own situations, without pretending to rehabilitate a whole universe of terms in the process.

This understanding of nature's value entails risks of essentializing. If the taste for nature on some terms is thought latent and effectually universal, then students who don't care for the idea or experience of "nature" might be dismissed as sidetracked or deprived—even deluded. But what terms are we speaking of—what "nature"? That these are not invariable is part of what's there to be learned. The Kaplans, studying tastes in landscape among various social groups, identify marked differences between the scenic predilections of most whites and those of African Americans from Detroit, the latter preferring an open, managed terrain of lawns, walks and discretely spaced trees to wilder-looking eruptions of brushy cover or deep forest margins—a familiar, graphically safer landscape, where a person can obtain a visual purchase over the whole terrain and no one can lurk unseen (99–103). This rhetorical terrain is itself dangerous, yet it is not far-fetched to wonder how landscape tastes may not be just arbitrary but expressive of socioeconomic dispensations, which in inner Detroit, at least, are less than ideal. This is *not* to imply that any one landscape is normative, nor to advise that inner-city residents don packs and head for the hills or that their children be conscripted into Outward Bound as if into some missionary school. This would make no more sense than to suggest that in contemplating the "violence" of literacy, we must all cease to write. It is true and crucial that landscape tastes, like the literate behaviors they interrelate with, are endlessly varied and historically specific. Yet inevitably we mark those variations and track those histories with reference to *something*, some baseline or default notions of equality, social justice, "symmetry" in power relations to which the most stringent social constructionisms still adhere. Even in disparaging "essentialism" we entertain some enduring notion of the contingent. It is worth considering why relations to place should not register among such tacit baseline notions, as not just extending from but informing how we register these endless particularities. If we cannot essentialize, neither can we neglect the implication that understandings of landscape may have more than scenic import, and that this possibility may be suppressed through some of the very circumstances that also conduce to ethnocentrism and social oppression—the separation of labor and livelihood, the reduction of place to commodity. The relation of types of landscape to the types of lives lived in them is a legitimate object of inquiry, among students as well as scholars, especially when conducted with the understanding that, as the Kaplans assert, a feeling for *some* order of natural setting is common to all. No project of "reinventing nature," I imagine, could proceed far without this.

An education that took up such issues through the medium of nature experience as well as through critical inquiry might address social oppression in other ways, too, less rhetorically direct but arguably more palpable. Again, the virtue of simplicity is at issue. An education that made an issue of simplicity of material sustenance, conducing to altered patterns of consumption, pleasure, and fulfillment, might do more to arrest the subjugation of others than does a multicultural agenda that leaves issues of subsistence in place untouched (not to suggest such an agenda *must* do so), considering our habit of balancing our budgets on the backs of people and places the world over. Yet even if it did *not* do this in any immediately apprehensible way, such an approach would still be warranted. For within the dominant culture itself the province of "nature" is obviously contested terrain. It seems to me unwise to let even affluent young white people's potent needs and desires for something called "nature" get monopolized by Jeep Cherokee peddlers and the like, while we literati outsmart ourselves and everyone else deconstructing that term and casting jaundiced glances at the blandishments of wildness. I'm not saying we are obliged to leave all this alone; clearly we cannot. But situationally, I wonder if we cannot behave more simply than this.

After all, these imperatives are not mutually exclusive. We can have our cyborgs and defeat them too. We do not have to choose between making an issue of "nature" in our representational practices and encouraging a practice of wildness in our lives. We can both hike and write; we can scrutinize trees and magazines alike. Even the idea that our sensations of nature are projections forms no impediment to their exploration in retreat. Harper quotes the Gestalt psychologist Fritz Perls as averring that we need "to take responsibility for our projections, re-identify with these projections, and become what we project" (196). In wilderness retreat, says Harper, "we gradually begin to reclaim whatever it is we have projected onto the natural world" (194). This seems a fair agenda for a general education: not just the critical scrutiny but the reclamation of key projections. But this demands their enactment and recollection: "conversion" on both levels.

Thus my study comes down to the propriety of "keeping it simple" in responses to the lives and writing of students, in order to cultivate complexities that will neither obfuscate and browbeat nor court incredulity and suppressed scorn—that will provoke but also affirm. I state this as an ambition, not a testimonial, since my success is partial and the practice I seek only dimly envisioned and fitfully realized. But this stance informs the way I regard the student essays I surveyed earlier, my belief that however challenging I may be in provoking interpretations of Thoreau, I ought not to gainstay my students' own Thoreauvian productions, in which their chances for converting their lives into ecological literacy so largely inhere. It underwrites my desire to do both, to reaffirm *and* reinvent the generic conditions through which experiences of "nature" are mediated, by modelling how practices of "simplicity" are implicated in our understanding of our language's most complex word. It emphasizes the simple virtue of not vaulting but muddling toward transformation, in a manner incremental yet sustained, in acknowledgement of the simple fact that, as Buell insists, our Western ways will not get traded in on some new model anytime soon but had better be ransacked for what resources they can offer toward needed change. Primary among these resources is the cultural script of retreat, which we are stuck with in any event and need to make work for us as well as we can. The dream of simplicity itself is configured therein, modelled in the critiques and affirmations of nature we enact in both classroom and field.

Notes

INTRODUCTION

1. This expression is taken from Stafford's collection, *Things That Happen Where There Aren't Any People* (1980), as from the title poem therein.

2. Both this punning on "substance" and my use of the expression "casuistic stretching" above are adapted from formulations by Kenneth Burke. Burke's discussion of the "paradox of substance," noting how this word "used to designate what a thing *is*, derives from a word designating something that a thing *is not*" (23), underlies his discussion of "antinomies of definition" in *A Grammar of Motives* (1945). His notion of "casuistic stretching," elaborated in *Attitudes Toward History* (1937), incorporates his "proposed methodology to 'coach' the transference of words from one category of associations to another" (230).

3. It is as much as a ritual gesture to invoke Leo Marx, *The Machine in the Garden* (1964), in this regard. I would mention David Scofield Wilson, *In the Presence of Nature* (1978), too, as most pertinent to the subject. Of course, any of the multitude of studies that dwell upon the meaning of wilderness and landscape in American culture might be found applicable. The list could go on, though I will not.

4. One study especially—*Nature Writing and America* (1990) by Peter A. Fritzell—presses with unusual persistence, even aggressiveness,

the claim "that nature writing, in its preeminently Thoreauvian form, is fundamentally an American phenomenon" (3). Thomas J. Lyon, in the prefacing sections to his anthology *This Incomperable Lande* (1989), adopts a similar if less vehement position. Lawrence Buell, by contrast, in *The Environmental Imagination: Thoreau, Nature Writing, and the Formation of American Culture* (1995), demurs from the claim of American exceptionality, preferring to situate nature writing within the domain of postcolonial literary productions more generally. Even so, as his subtitle indicates, his concern is mostly with "formation of American culture," and his treatment does not factually dispute these earlier studies so much as shift the angle of vision toward a body of work central to *that* cultural "formation" as it is to no other.

5. I would remark particularly on the attention being paid to literary nonfiction by many in composition studies, exemplified most by Chris Anderson's book on the New Journalists, *Style as Argument* (1987), and the collection he's edited, *Literary Nonfiction: Theory, Criticism, Pedagogy* (1989). The distinguished composition scholar J. Ross Winterowd has recently weighed in on the topic as well. The rationale for this trend, broadly speaking, is that compositionists ought to develop a detailed critical understanding of the sorts of writing they so frequently ask students to do. The pitfalls, as I see them, are that belletristic attention to style, imagery, metaphor, and so on, treated of in individual authors, may conduce to simple recapitulation of the model-copy, "go and do likewise" school of writing instruction. I conceive of my own study as contributing to the expanding body of work on this subject, and I hope in my approach to have skirted these pitfalls.

1. NARRATIVE AS NATURE WRITING

1. I allude to Ann E. Berthoff's use of a "journal of observations" in which students write "in response to some natural object": "it shouldn't be a rock or a pebble, since they are not *organic*, and one of the points of this looking/seeing is to learn something about *organization*" (13—emphases in original).

2. As testament to the porousness of discursive borders within nature writing, it bears noting how as a "genre," nature writing is in a sense transgeneric, as is evident when one maps the "spectrum" Lyon

delineates onto more general discourse taxonomies or continuums, such as those of James Britton, Louise Rosenblatt, and James Kinneavy. In each case, the more general scheme's entire range is pretty well represented on Lyon's generic map.

3. "I think we've about said it all—we communicate less in words and more in direct denotation, the glance, the pointing hand, the subtle nuances of pipe smoke, the tilt of a wilted hat brim. Configurations are beginning to fade, distinctions shading off into blended amalgams of man and man, men and water, water and rock" (*Desert Solitaire* 185).

4. To be clear, let me specify that by "retreat narrative" I refer exclusively to the sort of nature writing I am delineating, notwithstanding any other references or reverberations the phrase in itself may motivate, whether in formal religious traditions, military sagas, or what have you. This is not to claim that such other reverberations do not inform the particular sense I am claiming for the term; of course they do.

As to the claims of others for the originary status of *Walden* as nature writing: I will cite, for one, Joseph Wood Krutch's landmark introduction to *Great American Nature Writing* (1950), which advances the claim at length. Another, more recent instance occurs in Peter A. Fritzell's *Nature Writing and America* (1990), an extended generic consideration that while vigorously (to my mind, unjustly) criticizing Krutch's discussion, concurs in its claim for Thoreau as generic progenitor. If further evidence is desired, we need look no further than the blurbs gracing the backs of nature writing books in our own day—the frequent, near-ritual comparisons to Thoreau, which demonstrate that it is his "procedures and subjects and goals" (to echo Cavell) that his successors are seen as reenacting.

5. This is why Rousseau's *Reveries of a Solitary Walker* does not initiate the genre of retreat, though it figures prominently in its lineage or "prehistory"; the writer's face, we might say (recalling Atwood), is not sufficiently cut out. Rousseau attends almost exclusively to his personal reminiscences and mental states in nature; although he reports being immersed in botanizing, details of his activities and findings as a student of nature per se are virtually absent from his accounts, as they never would be in Thoreau or his heirs.

6. For a discussion of Burke's "action-motion" distinction as it bears upon ecological criticism, see my "KB in Green: Ecology, Critical Theory, and Kenneth Burke."

2. GOING OUT, GOING IN

1. Forster's much-repeated distinction (from *Aspects of the Novel*) reads as follows: " 'The king died and then the queen died' is a story. 'The king died, and then the queen died of grief' is a plot" (Martin 81). While Forster is distinguishing between story and plot, I have recast this to distinguish between simple temporal sequence—what Hayden White treats as "annals"—and story, which is to say, narrative. My warrant for this change is, first, that it's hard to imagine a story which is *not* plotted or "narrativized"—this seems the very hallmark—and second, that in drafting these opening passages, this happens to be the way I remembered Forster's story, the moral or upshot I found in it. Appeal to memory is telling, I believe, in matters of narrative.

2. Bakhtin's essay on "Forms of Time and of the Chronotope in the Novel" (*Dialogic* 84–258), for instance, details modes or logics of narrative linkage that are not causal: the logic of random contingency that governs "adventure-time" in the Greek romance, for one.

3. Transformation, a key notion in narrative theory, is defined in classical structuralist fashion by Todorov, in "Narrative Transformations" (*Poetics of Prose*, 218–33), as a shift in conditions or attributes of a common predicate. More fundamentally, it may be viewed as "the tension of two formal categories, difference and resemblance," from which narrative issues (233)—a formulation that has force beyond the structuralist search for a narrative "grammar." As for reversal in narrative, a suggestive discussion is found in Hamlin, to which I refer in note 8.

4. In Russian formalist terms, the order in which events are presented is termed the *syuzhet*; their presumptive temporal order is the *fabula*. Considerations of the difference and relation between them are germinal to narrative theory as it has developed in this century.

5. The fact that what's deferred is the causal explanation of the linkage between events only ratifies, from one point of view, the "model" character of Forster's little story. Peter Brooks, in elaborating upon Jonathan Culler's notion of a "double logic" of events and discourse in narrative, observes that "prior events, causes, are so only retrospectively, in a reading back from the end"—a "contradiction [that] may be in the very nature of narrative, which not only uses but *is* a double logic" (29). Brooks's example, the detective story, thus bears a schematic resemblance to the case of the royal deaths, in which what caused what is similarly revealed at the end.

6. The phrase is Paul Ricouer's, from *Interpretation Theory: Discourse and the Surplus of Meaning* (1976).

7. See the first half of chapter 6 for a detailed discussion of Muir's writerly role and habits.

8. I use "conversion" throughout this essay in the sense Harpham gives it, as summarized in the first section of chapter 1. In this instance, though, I also have in mind Cyrus Hamlin's discussion of reversal in narrative—especially his postscript, in which he cites I. A. Richards on the relations between "converse" and "conversion" in light of the root sense of "-verse," that is, *turning*. "Conversion," says Richards, is the turning of the soul to light in the most efficacious manner: "what education, for Plato, was to be" (73). For Richards, too, remarks Hamlin; for me too, I'd say, if "soul" is construed as Gary Snyder defines it: "Our 'soul' is our dream of the other" (180). Hamlin, at any rate, amends his essay to say that "conversion" is preferable even to "reversal" to describe the turning-back that matters most in comprehension of narrative—an afterthought that further aligns his essay with Harpham's formulations.

9. It is found on the penultimate page (439) of *John of the Mountains: The Unpublished Journals of John Muir*, edited by Linnie Marsh Wolfe, and appears to date circa 1913, the year before Muir's death.

10. Oates's statement, from her essay "Against Nature" in the collection *On Nature* (1987, Daniel Halpern, ed.), is acquiring much iterability among nature writing circles, though its status there is far from "exemplary." Drawn from an essay-opening list headed *"The writer's resistance to Nature,"* the particular item I am citing reads: "It [nature] inspires a painfully limited set of responses in 'naturewriters'—REVERENCE, AWE, PIETY, MYSTICAL ONENESS" (236).

11. A clear parallel is the yet more explicit treatment, in Thoreau's *A Week on the Concord and Merrimack Rivers*, of a backvalley farmer named Rice whose surly and standoffish behavior Thoreau redeems by esteeming it a natural manifestation of the rugged character of the place: "He was, indeed, as rude as a fabled satyr. But I suffered him to pass for what he was, for why should I quarrel with nature? and was even pleased at the discovery of such a singular natural phenomenon" (255).

12. Evidently it never was, in Thoreau's estimation. In the story's first draft, the names of his companions are appended only at the very end, as an afterthought, along with a chunk of a poem (by Thomas Heywood) that could be read as a sort of apology for as much as omitting them. The gist of the poem is that anyone the poet cites by first name

alone should not feel slighted on that account, for the poet himself would as soon be thus familiarly addressed (*Journal 2*, 349).

13. I am not claiming that Thoreau's intent to climb a mountain is unprecedented or unrecognizable to his readers. At the time Thoreau writes, in fact, there is increasingly a taste, though not yet a rage, for mountain excursions and tales thereof—though Thoreau's destination remains unusually difficult and remote. A far more popular destination, Mount Washington, had a carriage road running to its summit with an inn at the terminus. Nash (chapters 3 and 4) recounts the trend and the ambivalences attending it; and Fink details the relations of Thoreau's narrative to other mountaineering tales of the time, especially those on Katahdin in particular (see note 23). Instead, my claims amount to these: that Thoreau himself depicts his motives in tacit contrast to those of most people frequenting the terrain, including his own companions; that in some measure he is justified in so doing; and that since the activity itself and the tastes attending it were of recent vintage, the discourses informing it, too, were in a process of development, not settled, inscribed largely within an imported rhetoric of the Romantic sublime, which to the likes of Thoreau was formative but to some extent found wanting—of which more later.

14. I do not wish to enter the contention over whether *Walden* or the *Journal* ought to be regarded as Thoreau's preeminent project or achievement, though I think it is fascinating. For my purposes, it's sufficient to note that if *Walden*, whatever its fissures and compromises, had not somehow come to acclaim, the *Journal* would be languishing in its wooden box.

15. In his survey of the criticism and history of nature writing, Peter Fritzell asserts: "On the whole, the contributions of social, intellectual, and even political historians to the understanding of nature writing have been far more sustained . . . than have the offerings of literary historians and critics, particularly in the United States" (39). See also the voluminous, sometimes contentious notes Fritzell appends on the subject.

16. I mean nothing more complex by this than the fairly obvious fact that we don't create stories about how Huckleberry Finn went about writing *Huckleberry Finn*, whereas numerous stories of Mark Twain's composing circulate: how he launched the story, reached an impasse, put it aside, returned to it, how the later parts differ from the earlier, and so on.

17. These are found in the Berg Journal of April–December 1846, published in the *Journal*, Vol. 2, by Princeton University Press.

18. In his "Historical Introduction" to *Journal 2*, Sattelmeyer states that this "detailed preliminary outline" was "compiled no doubt from field notes" (462). I think it possible they are a near transcription and filling out of such notes, made on site as an aid to recollecting itinerary and highlights, and not much fleshed out. But of course this is sheerest speculation. There seems no evidence that any portion of the draft that follows relied upon or drew from any but these preliminary notes.

19. I draw this phrase from Andrew Plaks's work on Chinese narrative. Yin and Yang are the preeminent instance of a dualism the terms of which are alternated between but not reconcilable or convertable to each other. It might be interesting, I will note in passing, to develop a view of Thoreau's shifts and extremes that resonates with what Plaks describes of Chinese narrative conventions. An example: upon Plaks's account, Chinese notions of character value not continuity and progressive development but rather variability and aptness to the situation at hand. This corresponds interestingly with McIntosh's depiction of a Thoreau intent upon representing each of his "shifting stances" in as extreme, "extra-vagant" a way as possible, and prizing this above any imperatives of attitudinal consistency or reconciliation.

20. Peter Brooks, in elaborating upon Jonathan Culler's notion of a "double logic" of events and discourse in narrative, observes that "prior events, causes, are so only retrospectively, in a reading back from the end"—a "contradiction [that] may be in the very nature of narrative, which not only uses but *is* a double logic" (29).

21. Steven Fink notes of the climactic "Contact! Contact" passage, that "as controversial as this passage is for modern Thoreau scholars, [Horace] Greeley [Thoreau's booster and unpaid literary agent] knew this was exactly the kind of dramatic encounter with the sublime wilderness that readers were seeking." (187).

In calling the passage "extra-vagant," of course, I am echoing this punning pronouncement of Thoreau's: "I fear chiefly lest my expression may not be *extra-vagant* enough, may not wander far enough beyond the narrow limits of my daily experience" (*Walden* 324).

22. This story, as I say, follows Oelschlaeger in stressing Thoreau's status as a rhetorical innovator and the relative inadequacy for his purposes of the prior texts available to him—especially those of Emersonian transcendentalism and its Romantic progenitors. Another story can be told, more like Nash's (and more subtly, Fink's), which would stress Thoreau's continuity with those predecessors and his reliance on prior

texts, especially those of the Romantic sublime. Oelschlaeger's grounds—
mine, too—for emphasizing difference rather than continuity concern
the essential anthropocentrism of Emersonian transcendentalism and its
Romantic antecedents. The plot of the Romantic sublime, as Julie
Ellison notes in her book about Emerson, "enacts a scene of reversal, an
antithetical conversion that turns the mind from God or nature to the
self"—a self which in its "exhilaration" finds "evidence of [its] power
over the things that cause these sensations" of "disorientation and meaninglessness" (6–7). While the terms of this scene accord perfectly with
those of Thoreau's encounter, the outcome—the sense of the self's
power, the turning away from nature—does not. Where Thoreau parts
company is in taking exception to the sense of imaginative mastery and
essentially human splendor that, in the plot of the sublime, succeeds the
perception of inadequacy and threat in the face of the limitless. As his
career develops, Thoreau becomes *less* convinced about or interested in
such subjective all-inclusiveness, such Emersonian world-swallowing.
"Ktaadn" shows Thoreau in the throes of this development: his episode
of "disorientation and meaninglessness"—not just pathetic but literal, as
I have shown—is succeeded by but can hardly be said to culminate in
his "recovery." And that recovery, when it comes, does not take the
shape of celebration of human imaginative mastery, though it does
affirm human prowess in negotiating the physical terrain—that is, in
running rapids.

23. Steven Fink's *Prophet in the Marketplace* (1992) provides a
detailed account of Thoreau's activities as a professional writer in the
context of the popular literary marketplace of his time. His chapter on
"Ktaadn" (150–87) situates that piece within conventions of travel
accounts of the time, especially those about excursions to Katahdin. It
also offers a reading of the essay more consonant with my own than any
of the others I have surveyed, in the way it attends to the narrative's early
preoccupation with human artifacts and disputes the exclusivity and
kind of attention paid to the Burnt Lands passage. Of other works that
discuss how Thoreau moved to accomodate the perceived desires of a
reading public, most notable is Sharon Cameron's *Writing Nature*
(1985), which finds the compromises attending such accomodation to
be a distorting, fragmenting influence on *Walden,* though not on the
Journal, by and large.

3. THE SUBJECT OF *THE DESERT*

1. The conceit of my opening, obviously, is to approach *The Desert* as if it were a book one happened across on a shelf and were looking over to determine its generic type and potential appeal. This is much the way Peter Reyner Banham reports having encountered it—in a linen closet packed with antiquated volumes in a lodge in Pasadena, the book's title alone having lured him to survey its contents (153–54). I will offer a similar account of my own introduction to the book below. For readers unfamiliar with *The Desert* or unconvinced that it warrants and has attracted the sort of attention I mean to pay to it, I offer in this note a precis of reasons for and evidence of interest in it. Those satisfied with my approach of playing dumb and inching up on the book may feel free to skip the remainder of this note, or return to it later.

I will cite three categories of interest in and attention to *The Desert*. The first concerns ethos, so to speak: the fact that the book's proponents in print include figures of some reputation. Edward Abbey's brief mention of it as "an unjustly forgotten book" in his notes on desert writers in *Desert Solitaire* (239) has no doubt done much to jog collective memory of the volume. The book rates a chapter in Patricia Limerick's well-circulated study *Desert Passages* (1985), where it keeps company with the likes of Mark Twain, Joseph Wood Krutch, and Abbey himself. Banham cites a "stern critic" of his acquaintance referring to the book as a "flawed masterpiece," a phrase that Banham prefers to read with emphasis on the second word (155).

A second category involves historical interest, the status of *The Desert* as a predecessor to later, better-known texts. Limerick considers the book in this light; and Peter Wild, whose views I will discuss in detail, asserts its historical importance in very strong terms, deeming it epochal in changing attitudes toward the desert and in paving the way for other writing on the desert. A further historical dimension is found in Richard Shelton's assertion that the book documents a place as it once was and no longer is. Shelton's views, too, I will discuss at further length.

Yet these are not the most important categories of interest in *The Desert*: Limerick hints at this in identifying "a remarkable degree of agreement," a sort of "consensus" of sensibility among Van Dyke and his successors Krutch and Abbey. The implication is that Van Dyke's book exercises a continuing, effectively contemporary appeal. This is an appeal of the sort I've called "participatory," founded upon the text's relations to people's reiterated presence in a place. What held Banham in the linen closet was the sense he derived, while turning to random spots in the volume, that this writer had seen the desert as he (Banham) himself had. It was Van Dyke's gift for seeing and for orchestrating sights that struck him and that primarily accounts for the volume's continuing, albeit underground status among desert afficionados, among whom the book apparently never was quite forgotten. The writer's facility with landscape description combines mellifluous phrasing with observational exactitude and an immense, luscious color vocabulary, as in this sunset view from a peak:

> Plain upon plain leads up and out to the horizon—far as the eye can see—in undulations of gray and gold; ridge upon ridge melts into the blue of the distant sky in lines of lilac and purple; fold upon fold over the mesas the hot air drops its veilings of opal and topaz. (43)

The impassioned attention to visual sensation in this passage is echoed in the character of this writer's attention generally, the participatory sense that "day by day the interest grows in the long overlooked commonplace things of nature!" (95). Nor does Van Dyke's propensity for exclamation detract from this sense.

Finally, there is a contemporary appeal in Van Dyke's frequent expressions of attitudes opposing what we would now call anthropocentrism. He frequently questions the exclusivity of human claims and prerogatives, whether in economics ("Nature has other animals beside man to look after, other uses for her products than supporting human life"—143) or aesthetics ("the opalescent mirage will waver skyward on wings of light . . . though no human eye sees nor human tongue speaks its loveliness"—62). Such views make him attractive to environmentalism in its stronger versions, as do his infrequent, more particular pronouncements, such as this oft-quoted one: "The deserts should never be reclaimed. They are the breathing-spaces of the west and should be preserved forever" (59).

2. The 1980 reprint of the original edition of 1901, introduced by Shelton, was preceded by a 1976 reprint of the second edition of 1903, introduced by Lawrence Clark Powell and published by the Arizona Historical Society. I presume this edition did not circulate widely, at

least not outside the Southwest. The most recent edition prior to this had been one of 1930. Though the book has evidently enjoyed a continuing currency among some desert enthusiasts and afficionados of Southwest letters (see Powell, *Southwest*), its 1980 reappearance as a trade paperback in a series that also features titles by Thoreau and Muir (Peregrine Smith's "Literature of the American Wilderness") certainly marks its effective rebirth.

3. In his foreword to the 1991 reissue of Van Dyke's *The Open Spaces* (1922)—a book in which Van Dyke is considerably more forthcoming about autobiographical particulars—Wild explains the author's neglect of his own personal history in his earlier work:

> As an aristocrat, Van Dyke had an inbred abhorrence of writers who curry favor with the public by flinging their personal lives "abroad in the morning's newspaper." Perhaps overcorrecting, Van Dyke "kept the door barred" against such revelations. Noble as such a position may be, it has left us with a dearth of information about his life and, more important, about the backgrounds of his books. (xvii)

Here Wild presupposes both the "nobility" of the writer's reticence (a function, he postulates, of the writer's literal nobility, his class standing) and the "importance" of seeing this posture contravened through efforts such as his own.

4. In referring to "actions" I mean to echo Arendt's definition of "action," cited by Harpham, as "a mode of being" oriented toward "its own eventual conversion into narrative," its retelling or representation to others (42). See my discussion of "conversion" in chapter 1, above. Speaking of "configuration" I am alluding to Ricouer's use of the term, drawn from Louis O. Mink, to refer to the timeless "single thought," the theme, lesson, effect or idea, that the temporal sequence of a narrative emplots. I summarize and employ Ricouer's discussion at greater length in my analysis of Wendell Berry, chapter 4. Ricouer's notion of "configuration," incidentally, also draws upon Arendt's definition of "action" as being lived toward story.

5. A note on usage: in the first part of this chapter, which analyzes the text of *The Desert* itself, I refer to the narrating voice and figure as "the writer" and mostly eschew mention of his proper name. When in the second part the focus of my analysis shifts to commentary that narrativizes the historical figure of the person who composed the book, I

refer to this figure alternately as "Van Dyke" and "the author," to reinforce his status as published and publicized.

6. Wild's biographical reconstitutions allow us to infer that the jump-
ing-off place Van Dyke had in mind here was the ranch of his brother, the
writer and outdoorsman Theodore Strong Van Dyke, located in Daggett,
California, near Barstow in the heart of the Mojave Desert.

7. A very particular moment of address occurs when Van Dyke asks
rhetorically, "how often have you and I, and that one we both loved so
much, found beauty in neglected marshes, in wintry forests, and in bar-
ren hill-sides!" (viii). I assume that this departed third party, beloved by
both, was Frank Thomson, president of the Pennsylvania Railroad, who
died in 1899. In his autobiography, Van Dyke remarks that Thomson
and Carnegie "had been young men together on the Pennsylvania Railroad" and that Carnegie had continued to bear "good will and friendli-
ness" toward Thomson, despite differences over business dealings that
had soured Thomson on Carnegie, so that evidently the belovedness did
not run both ways (76). In *The Open Spaces*, Van Dyke identifies
Thomson as "the most expert fisherman (and the best companion) I ever
knew" (198) and mentions Thomson's having fished and hunted in
Scotland, probably at Carnegie's Cluny Castle; he offers paeons to both
friends, as leaders and outdoorsmen, in the autobiography as well.

8. Wild (1990) remarks, "it's a measure of the work that the book
continues to transport readers" (217). The notion of transport remains a
commonplace in the rhetoric of the Romantic sublime.

9. An especially interesting instance of this is found in the opening
chapter of Van Dyke's *The Mountain* (1916, 1–19), which depicts a
Sioux hunting party's advance toward the Rockies from the Plains of
Dacota. Though this seems clearly a reminiscence from Van Dyke's own
past, personal reference is still effected by the use of "you," such that it
seems the author is addressing his younger self. After only a few uses,
though, this pronoun drops away, and the narrating presence becomes
almost entirely spectatorial, something of a transparent eyeball; aspects
of the landscape assume agency. (This is the procedure as well in a narrative of a float down the Colorado, in chapter 4 of *The Desert*, 63–76.)
To top all this off, though the "you" does not resurface, later in the chapter are references to the whole band's movements, attributed to a "we"!
This author goes to nearly any length to eschew personal reference and
effect participatory "transport" through orchestration of pronouns.

10. Burke's discussion of "representative anecdote," explaining how a set or cycle of terms, by the logic of their interrelations, may be developed and in a sense "perfected" in narrative, is found in *A Grammar of Motives*, 59–61. A closely related notion is what Burke calls "the temporizing of essence," which concerns the ways one may "translate back and forth between logical and temporal vocabularies," converting logical to narrative order and vice versa (430). Both notions, like so much in Burke, anticipate recent theory—in this case, the moves made by narrative theory to comprehend the transformations between narrative and those modes of discourse called "expository." Both notions help elaborate what in general is called "narrative logic": the ways theme and closure in story reciprocally derive from and determine events narrated.

11. An example: Both modes of peril and persistence are dramatized in Edward Abbey's "Havasu," a chapter of *Desert Solitaire* (196–205), in which the writer faces crises both of physical survival and of personal identity (i.e., sanity) during a long stretch of solitude in a side branch of the Grand Canyon.

12. "[T]he present day climbing of perpendicular walls of rock, the zigzagging in chimneys, the drag by ropes, the crawl by ledges and niches, the creeping along knife-blade edges are merely Alpine Club stunts in an old game of 'follow my leader.' It is the dare of it that makes up the game, and the beauty of the peaks and skies forms small part of it" (*The Mountain*, 195).

13. "The feeling of fierceness grows upon you as you come to know the desert better. . . . There is no living in concord or brotherhood here. Everything is at war with its neighbor, and the conflict is unceasing" (26–27).

14. One aspect of his likely readers that Van Dyke must come to terms with is a lingering anti-Catholicism. Van Dyke wants his readers to identify with the Padres, not construe them as alien or sinister or in any way not exemplary of the civilized qualities he means them to represent. And so he rejects in passing the sorts of objections he might expect in certain quarters of his Protestant readership, exclaiming, "How idle seem all the specious tales of Jesuitism and priestcraft. The Padres were men of soul, unshrinking faith, and a perserverance almost unparalleled in the annals of history" (20). Soul, faith, and perserverance: these are virtues any Protestant would be ashamed to disparage, especially when they are entered in annals.

15. A most thorough account of the nature craze of the era, tracking its many manifestations, is found in *Back to Nature* (1969), by Peter J. Schmitt.

16. The sales blurbs in the back of the two first-edition works I've been using—*The Money God* (1908) and *The Mountain* (1916)—indicate that the author was invariably billed as "Professor John C. Van Dyke," his persona that of an academic authority.

17. It's my impression that this sense of the integrity of a single place is what distinguishes (to cite two modern "canonical" works of nature writing) *Pilgrim at Tinker Creek* and *Desert Solitaire* from other books by Annie Dillard and Edward Abbey, respectively; it's what makes them apprehendable *as* books and not as "collections."

18. See, for instance, *Language as Symbolic Action*, 44.

19. See Powell's 1976 introduction to the Arizona Historical Society's reprint edition of *The Desert*; see also Powell, *Southwest* 315–28, for an account of his search.

20. An important and well-known elaboration of the metaphor of land as woman is found in Annette Kolodny, *The Lay of the Land*, whose discussion bears upon the points I discuss below.

21. Shelton makes this formulation yet more explicit in an article on Edward Abbey's *Desert Solitaire* in which Van Dyke also figures. Both writers, Shelton says, were obsessively "in love with the same landscape," one which "is a hard mistress and not the mistress of their choice, but neither of them had a choice." These troubadors are different in style, "but their music is the same" ("Creeping" 75). Shelton intends as praise this imagery of enthrallment from a feudal court, and uses the metaphor of courtly romance even to account for the descriptive character of both writers' work, which he likens to "a *blazon*, a catalogue of the beauty of the beloved" (76).

22. I will refer to the following works by Wild, using the abbreviations included in parentheses: *John C. Van Dyke: The Desert* (JCVD); foreword to *The Grand Canyon of the Colorado* (GC); foreword to *The Open Spaces* (OS); "Van Dyke's Shoes: Tracking the Aesthetician Behind the Desert Wanderer" (VDS); "A Western Sun Sets in the East: The Five 'Appearances' Surrounding John C. Van Dyke's *The Desert*" (WS). A third book of Van Dyke's—*The Mountain*—with a foreword by Wild has also been reissued. As for Van Dyke's autobiography—*The Autobiography of John C. Van Dyke: A Personal Narrative of American Life 1861–1931* (1993)—having secured and read it after this chapter

was originally drafted, I find that both the book itself and Wild's introduction thereto more than anything ratify impressions I had already formed. There is one important exception, the matter of Van Dyke's veracity, to which I will return apace.

23. Wild, in fact, wants not just to assert that Van Dyke's other works are good books in their own right; he means to claim that a reading of the author's most celebrated work is incomplete without knowledge of these peripheral ones. Noting that all seven of the author's nature and landscape study books have similar subtitles that give them the impression of a series (most bear some version of the phrase "Studies in Appearances"), Wild speculates that "*The Desert* is but one part of the author's larger plan," and claims that "to catch *The Desert's* richness, the book should be looked on as part of this whole" (WS 219). He offers no satisfactory notion as to what this "plan" may consist in; and considering how Wild himself notes the author's chameleonesque capacity "to adjust his prose to fit the subject" (GC xviii), it seems more likely that Van Dyke planned simply to write on one nature "subject" after another, in whatever manner seemed to work. In any case, the current obscurity of these other works (which sold well enough in their time) Wild attributes rather perversely to the very success of *The Desert*. He remarks on the "irony" of its success "overshadowing" the other books (OS xvi), and believes that readers, cognizant of the author's name being "wedded" to the one title, mostly "overlook his other works" and thus "deny themselves the measure of a larger mind" (VDS 416).

Wild's judgment that in these other works a "larger mind" awaits discovery is one I do not share; I hold with Shelton on this score. Those other books of Van Dyke's that I've read or tried to read range from tolerable to tedious; none coheres as *The Desert* does in its integrated impression of presence in place. As to *The Desert* itself, Wild is expansive in his assessment of its achievement and impact, reasonably if ebulliently so. But his claims on its behalf tend to reinforce what he otherwise has an interest in denying: that *The Desert* is read because its subject is the desert, not John C. Van Dyke.

24. Wild notes that Van Dyke "became the [Brunswick Theological] Seminary's most successful fundraiser, turning its Gardner A. Sage Library into a light-filled museum of art treasures gathered from around the globe" (OS xxi). Lacking any information on the conditions of his tenure as head of the library, still I am led to speculate as to whether Van Dyke's success in raking in cash had anything to do with the privilege he clearly

enjoyed of taking off for long periods to travel through foreign galleries and domestic wild lands—leaves of absence including the three-year span culminating in publication of *The Desert*.

25. Among the claims Van Dyke advances in *The Money God* are that concentration of wealth in the hands of corporate titans places these resources in a trust from which they may be efficiently circulated for the common good; that even the extravagances of these men—their banquets and estates—are useful in that they create employment; that large capital projects like railroads are beneficial in a like sense, perhaps even more so than the same amount of money expended in scattered acts of philanthropy like Carnegie's libraries; and that the class of professionals and domestics— including doctors, clergymen, and of course professors—is in fact more poorly paid and exploited than the working classes.

26. Not only the vanished natives of *The Desert* are silent. The Plains Indians he reminisces about in *The Open Spaces* were, per Van Dyke, "brutal, sullen, unsocial," and silent: "Hour after hour they would ride on without saying a word" (25). And there's the first chapter of *The Mountain*, which as I've mentioned in a note above, describes a journey with the Sioux across the Plains to the Rockies—evidently drawn from personal experience, though characteristically eschewing the first person. It is a marvelous narrative (the high spot of a nearly unreadable book) and oddly more powerful not just for the absence of an "I" but for the fact that the Indians never speak.

27. My thoughts on the "vatic personality" are informed by Weston La Barre, *The Ghost Dance: Origins of Religion* (1972).

28. In his introduction to Van Dyke's *Autobiography*, Wild recounts the author's evident prevarications (xxviii–xxxi); he explores them further in an article co-written with Neil Carmony, a desert naturalist who has exposed taxonomical discrepencies that put the lie to Van Dyke's account (see Wild and Carmony). David Teague discusses the problem of reconciling *The Desert* with evidence both of its author's deceptions and of his unreflective complicity with his patron Carnegie's ecological and social depradations, especially the violent suppression of the Homestead Strike in 1892. Teague further explores this "paradoxical legacy" in an article co-written with Wild, in both articles broaching the question as to whether Van Dyke's desert episode was undertaken not just for the purpose of recovering from respitory ailments but also as a sort of secret mission for Carnegie arising from that strike, with Van Dyke delivering

anonymous largesse to the former mayor of Homestead, Pennsylvania, who had been discredited and drummed out of town as a result of his support of the strikers. Teague and Wild's article is supplemented by a sizable selection of Van Dyke's correspondance bearing out these events.

While I credit their efforts to recover the more problematic dimensions of their subject, I dispute Teague and Wild's take on Van Dyke as a sort of wily, riddling trickster figure rather than the querulous, duplicitous, opportunistic poseur and snob I discern in the evidence they assemble. In stressing what they term the "contradictions," these commentators appear to neglect the continuity between the author's book and his "secret life," failing in particular to read the book itself in light of that life, rather than in contradistinction thereto.

29. I would cite, for instance, the work of Paul Shepard in any number of his books (such as *Nature and Madness*) and of Neil Evernden in *The Natural Alien*.

30. See the 1984 afterword to *Permanence and Change* for comments on "Bodies That Learn Language"—Burke's final version of his evolving definition of humankind (295). Here, from the 1984 Afterword to *Attitudes toward History*, is one elaboration of the resistance Burke often develops between a (relatively) fixed biological inheritance and the essential mobility of its symbolic enactments—this one further echoing Harpham's formulations in that it concerns the character of *narrative*:

> Note first that all human attitudes have an overall double provenience. By the very nature of language, an essential form of duplication arises. And it will be with us, as a determining influence upon our destiny, as long as we continue to be the kind of creature we now are. I refer to a kind of duplication that arose when our primeval ancestors, by learning language, no longer experienced a sensation solely as a sensation. For instance, when they touched something that *felt hot*, their newfound ways with language enabled them to *duplicate* the *sensory* experience in "transcendent" terms of a *nonsensory* medium such that our aforesaid primeval ancestors could say, "*That feels hot.*"
>
> And precisely at that time here on Earth the realm of *Story* entered the world. (382—emphases in original)

See my article, "KB in Green: Ecology, Critical Theory, and Kenneth Burke," for more on Burke's pertinence to ecological thought.

31. An especially useful instance: Evelyn Fox Keller proposes "the concept of order" rather than law in nature, a concept "wider than law and free from its coercive, hierarchical, and centralizing implications," since it provides for self-generation and spontaneity, not just external constraint (cited in Schleifer et al. 40). Schleifer, Davis, and Mergler regard *natural history* as exemplary of a "narrative order" in Keller's sense, of a sort that can "complicate the simplicities of law without descending into chaos or irrationalism or monological assertions of taste and intuition." Narrating "events" in sequence, mixing chance and necessity, natural history "is a local rather than a monumental narrative" (97).

4. FAMILIAR MYSTERIES

1. What I am calling Berry's "narratives of movement in nature" consist, as I say, in the essays of *The Unforeseen Wilderness*; they also include the essays of part III of *The Long-Legged House* ("The Rise," "The Long-Legged House," and "A Native Hill") and one essay from *A Continuous Harmony* ("Notes from an Absence and Return"). These essays belong to a particular period in Berry's work, dating from the late sixties and very early seventies—the time when Berry's own rehabitation of his native spot of Kentucky was most at issue. Whether these essays constitute Berry's only forays into "nature writing" as such will depend, of course, on how you define the term. Upon the broad criteria that Thomas J. Lyon offers, a great deal more of Berry's essay writing—perhaps all of it—qualifies as "nature writing," falling into those categories that Lyon labels "Farm Life" and "Man's Role in Nature," the latter predominantly philosophizing. Finally, while nature writing is generally considered a variety of literary nonfiction, Berry's work in fiction and poetry is also strongly marked by "nature" themes.

2. Of the five essays comprising Berry's contribution to *The Unforeseen Wilderness*, four are reprinted (with some changes, mostly cuts) in his *Recollected Essays* of 1981. It is in this form that the essays have been most widely available and presumably most influential, and so it's to these versions I'll refer. The one essay *not* reprinted in the later volume—chapter 2, "The One-Inch Journey"—is more topical: in its concern with the dam project, floods and their "control," and the character of photography in the understanding of place, it introduces the book's specific polemical purpose and the role of its co-maker. Also not

reprinted is the first half of the book's fifth and final essay, "The Journey's End," which serves a synopsizing function for the book as a whole unnecessary in the context of the later essay compilation. But the topical, summarizing functions that make these omitted works expendable for the later collection make them useful to my purposes; I will draw on them, as well.

All page citations from Berry's essays refer to *Recollected Essays* unless other noted. Sections of *The Unforeseen Wilderness* omitted from that collection are drawn from the 1991 edition of the book, issued by North Point Press (the original version was published by the University Press of Kentucky). Page citations from those sections are prefaced with the initials UW.

3. The title essay in *Standing by Words* (1983) is probably Berry's definitive pronouncement on the subject. Example: "We assume, in short, that language is communal, and that its purpose is to tell the truth" (26).

4. Having flagged the first, I would like to remark on my procedure for selecting these meaning-value terms. My procedure, obviously, is not systematic; it may even seem arbitrary, as if I am intuiting or divining which of the story's multitude of words ought to be highlighted in this way. But while it may appear to, this procedure does not presume that the items it singles out must invariably stand out upon a first reading. My blow-by-blow recapitulation of the narrative I'm analyzing will in some ways mimic a first reading; yet my identifying of central terms is predicated on at least one subsequent reading (several more, in point of fact). Thus my method is a sort of narrativizing itself: I have to know how this story and some others come out in order to model its unfolding in this manner. Yet I deny that the terms I highlight are necessarily found prominent *only* upon rereading, any more than a story must be heard twice in order to be comprehended at all. I believe that such terms are "marked" and recognized in the text in something of the way that Riffaterre describes for instances of a "marked metonymy": that is, "by stylistic overdetermination or simply by repetition" (36; see note 13). My procedure will at times dramatize these modes of "marking"; but a more thorough analysis thereof would be laborious in the extreme and no more conclusive, I think, than the approach I am pursuing.

5. The book's opening chapter, "A Country of Edges," makes this clear: its second sentence evokes as characteristic of the place the sensation of leaving the ridges and coming "into the sound of water falling"

(223); and the disquisition on water that follows identifies the river as "the motive force of a landscape, the formal energy of all the country that drains into it" (225).

6. And Berry *does* write on site, evidently: "Going off to the woods," he reports, "I take a pencil and some paper (*any* paper—a small notebook, an old envelope, a piece of a feed sack), and I am as well equipped for my work as the president of IBM"—this since writing (*hand*writing, at least) "is preeminantly a walker's art," one that "can be done on foot and at large" (*What Are People For?* 194). Presumably he needs to stop moving his feet before moving his pencil, though.

7. The formulation is Thoreauvian, recalling the passage in "Walking" about going "into the woods bodily, without getting there in spirit" ("I am not where my body is,—I am out of my senses. In my walks I would fain return to my senses"—99) as well as sentiments in *Walden* about the accelerated pace of telegraph and railroad.

8. Note again, for instance, the paean to water in the opening to the first chapter: "I like to hunt out a pool among the rocks and drink. The water is clean and cold. It is what water ought to be, for here one gets it 'high and original,' uncorrupted by any scientific miracle. . . . One drinks in the sense of being in a good place" (224).

9. I should note some sources for and the context of this discussion of Ricouer's I am citing. As Ricouer reports, the notion of a "configurational act" is drawn from Louis O. Mink, who describes it as a "grasping together"; and the phrase "reflective judgment" Ricouer means to be taken in Kant's sense. Most important, the concept and functions of "repetition" Ricouer employs originate with Heidegger's *Being and Time*: the purpose of his essay ("Narrative Time") is to connect narrativity and temporality—to establish the "structural reciprocity" between narrative and the lived experience of time—by reference to Heidegger's analysis of the latter, to which the notion of repetition is key.

10. Thoreau's well-known conceit in *Walden*'s "Solitude," of course, is that no companion is as "companionable" as solitude.

11. This, in sum, is Neil Evernden's contention about or analogy for the human species, put forth in *The Natural Alien* (1985).

12. Preparation implies present action to influence external circumstances; planning involves projecting and shaping future events. Whorf makes this distinction in his exploration of time concepts among the Hopi, which he says are cyclical: "One might say that Hopi society

understands our proverb 'Well begun is half done,' but not our 'Tomorrow is another day' " (1956, 148).

13. "Marked metonymy" is Michael Riffaterre's term. Riffaterre holds that "the metaphorization of a marked metonymy" governs choices between "equally possible events" in narrative sequence, and that this is a rule readers employ in decoding narrative from surface features of language. "A metonymy is marked when it is singled out from among other descriptive features by stylistic overdetermination or simply by repetition" (36).

14. The narrative I am referring to is section 2 of the three sections of "A Native Hill"—pages 89–104 of *Recollected Essays* (which I cite), 187–202 of *The Long-Legged House*.

15. In this he departs from the conventions of texts of the sort Annette Kolodny discusses in *The Lay of the Land* (1975), a germinal discussion of the female gendering of landscape in American literature.

16. Even Ann Zwinger, among the most gregarious and in the root sense familiar (family-oriented) of nature writers, emphasizes how "essential" it is to go "as far out as possible, and as alone as possible" (102), in the process of developing what she thinks of after all as "an expanding sense of home" (Lueders, *Writing Natural History* 73).

5. SITES AND SENSES

1. The University of Michigan's New England Literature Program is a program in experiential learning and outdoor life held each spring at a summer camp in New Hampshire. Further description of NELP can be found in an essay by its co-founder, Walter H. Clark Jr. (1985).

2. Trimble takes the quotation from Wilson as an epigraph for the introductory essay proper. The anthology as a whole has two further epigraphs, worth noting for the ways they thematize the collection in ways consonant with the terms of my study. The first is the "going out, going in" passage by John Muir that I discussed in chapter 2 as a paradigm of retreat narrative ("I only went out for a walk, and finally concluded to stay out till sundown . . ."). The second, by Rachel Carson, is just as telling a thematic gesture:

> If there is poetry in my book about the sea, it is not because I
> deliberately put it there, but because no one could write truthfully about the sea and leave out the poetry. (xiii)

Besides evoking the mix of fact and rapture, science and personal response that Trimble, with Lyon and others, finds in nature writing, this passage includes a couple other interesting implications: first that the "poetry" is not the writer's own but rather her subject's, presented to her as if to the amanuensis that Brodkey discusses; and further that the writer, in denying the intent to produce poetry, is disclaiming any particular *literary* intent, effectively vacating the office of "Author" that Brodkey finds integral to "the scene of writing"—a matter discussed further just below.

3. These examples—Hubbell and Zwinger—are older women, and their gender relates, I believe, to this matter of occupational indeterminacy and to their late blooming as nature writers. Trimble puzzles over the question of why more women do not become nature writers (as opposed to novelists or poets), whether because of fear of solitude outdoors and/or socialization against interest in scientific pursuits, and tries to relate these factors to the later age at which some women take to the trade. He admits to frustration on this score, though, exclaiming that he wishes he "knew more about why" there are so few women in the business (21). Though the question is certainly overdetermined, as the expression goes, the scarcity of women nature writers, also the age of some, may extend as much from the related matter of occupational affiliation as from acclimation to solitude. Rachel Carson was the first woman hired in a nonclerical capacity by the U.S. Bureau of Fisheries and Wildlife—one of the very few who could have arrived at the genre through a professional identity as a scientist or "field worker," in the manner of Leopold, Eiseley, and many other men past and present. She was also unmarried. Zwinger, the most Carsonesque of current nature writers, was a housewife and mother, a status that conduced to a certain occupational fluidity. She is married to an Air Force pilot who retired early; her career took off once his, so to speak, had landed. Hubbell too was married, and her status as a nature writer is, in *A Country Year*, pretty well predicated on her divorce, a prominent theme in the book. Of currently prominent nature writers, ones who did *not* arrive at the metier relatively late include Annie Dillard and Terry Tempest Williams—the former arriving with as austere, even denatured view of "writing" as any novelist (I discuss this view below); the latter making a living as a professional naturalist, and in fact asserting, pace Trimble, that she is a naturalist first, a writer second (Lueders, *Writing* 41).

For historical accounts of the once comparatively rare phenomenon of the woman naturalist, see Marcia Myers Bonta, *Women in the Field* (1991). Currently, the definitive treatment of women's relations to nature in American culture is Vera Norwood, *Made from This Earth* (1993).

4. Don Gifford's *The Farther Shore: A Natural History of Perception* (1990) provides a detailed look at many such technologically mediated perceptual filters developed over the past two centuries, from Gilbert White and Thoreau to our own time.

5. A most interesting discussion of Thoreau's relation to audience in his *Journal* is found in chapter 4, "Speaker and Audience," of Sharon Cameron's *Writing Nature* (80–107). According to Cameron, the *Journal* "posits a world from which an audience has been banished," and this banishment is linked to the impersonality of the writing, its refusal to attend to the writer's social circumstances and relations, its exclusive preoccupation with a relation to nonhuman nature. Attending to audience would entail embroilment in "distracting personal characteristics" of readers to some degree, characteristics of the precise sort Thoreau has sought to eradicate in his self-depiction—"a self purified of its own features" (85). In Cameron's view, the *Journal* is a text that not only does not anticipate readers, providing for them, if at all, only in the most vexatious, contradictory, and restricted ways; it is a text that literally cannot appear during its author's lifetime, having "neither automony nor visibility" to any but posthumous readers (81). Thus while it does not suffice to think that Thoreau did not mean the work to be read, it seems to be the case that he can conceive of its reception only in the event that the work had been "purified" of his own exclusive reading presence. He cannot imagine reading it *with* anyone else.

6. The cabin's prestige is such that a writer's ethos may be inextricable from the residence. Leopold's sitedness at "the shack" in the first section of *A Sand County Almanac* subtly and indispensably informs his subsequent, more general ethical observations, in ways John Tallmadge explores. And so linked with his rustic accommodations was John Burroughs, in his own and in the public's mind, that he felt moved to invoke his situation even at the start of a book that has nothing to do with it—his late book on Whitman, in the preface of which he relates rising from his desk and stepping outside to survey the panorama beyond his rustic porch (1–2).

7. Who knows if she actually did? An extended thread on the e-mail listserve for ASLE (the Association for the Study of Literature and the Environment) focused on the report that Dillard had owned up to having fabricated some key episodes of *Pilgrim at Tinker Creek*, including the bloody cat-paw prints in its opening (evidently she has never owned a cat) and the giant frog-sucking waterbug (which she read about in a book). So it's hard to say what warrant we have for crediting this anecdote: it could be a set-up like these others.

8. My warrant for this claim is not definitive but is telling. In Daniel Halpern's *Antaeus* collection of journals, notebooks, and diaries, published as *Our Private Lives* (1990), although Dillard is one of just three writers touted on the front cover, her contribution consists almost exclusively of quotations from others' works, plus assorted odd facts and definitions, entered without comment in a notebook (84–87). There is evidence here of a lively, quirky mind, to be sure, but nothing close to "explaining Whitehead," and no hint of a "private life" except, of course, in its scrupulous absence.

9. From Thoreau's *Journal*, entry of July 23, 1951; cited in Cameron (40).

6. WRITER OR RHAPSODE?

1. An "iconic metaphor," per C. A. Bowers, is one having the character not of an analogy but of an image. Brodkey's "writer-writes-alone" serves well as an example.

2. Hoagland's essay, "In Praise of John Muir," appeared in the collection *On Nature* (1987), Daniel Halpern, ed., and subsequently served as the introduction to the Penguin Nature Library reprint edition of *The Mountains of California*. I cite the version in Halpern. Gretel Ehrlich introduced the Penguin reprint of *My First Summer in the Sierra* (1987); this is the introduction I'm referring to in this paragraph. Ehrlich has also introduced the Sierra Club Books edition of *The Mountains of California* (1988).

3. Later, of course, the urgency of the conservation battles Muir waged would constitute a further prod to his efforts to write for publication. Early in his career, though, no such considerations intruded upon him, and the first flush of his writerly reputation did not hinge upon, though it helped enable, his later stature as a crusading conservationist.

As for Thoreau's thwarted impulse to publish: a widely repeated anecdote in Thoreauviana relates how his first book, *A Week on the Concord and Merrimac Rivers*, published in an edition of 1,000, had sold but 300 through its first few years in print, at which point the remaining copies were returned to the author. Thoreau quipped that he owned a library of some 900 books, 700 of which he wrote himself.

4. The claim that Thoreau's *Journal* is his preeminant accomplishment is pursued in brilliant, influential fashion in Cameron's *Writing Nature* (1985).

5. See, for instance, Fox (19), O'Grady (66–67), and Turner (*Rediscovering* 222).

6. "Like words and text, memory is a child of the alphabet. Only after it had become possible to fix the flow of speech in phonetic transcription did the idea emerge that knowledge—information—could be held in the mind as in a store" (Illich and Sanders 15).

7. Jeanne Carr's relationship to Muir, including her influence on his development as a writer, is well discussed in Frederick Turner's biography of Muir, *Rediscovering America* (1985, 199–209).

8. Engberg and Wesling detail Carr's role as recipient and courier of Muir's early manuscripts, relating her reply to his plea that he did not know how to begin writing: "Use quality paper, coarse and lined, and a broad pen, and begin!" (109).

9. Muir's writing career divides neatly into two stages, before and after the so-called "lost years" following his marriage and subsequent plunge into full-time fruit-farming. The first period extends from 1871, the date of his earliest published work, until 1880; the second commences in 1890, with his pivotal articles on the Yosemite for *Century* magazine, and continues full-force until his death in 1914. His books all date from the later period and, posthumously, beyond.

10. In his letter of March 30, 1873, to Jeanne Carr, Muir states of this piece: "I did not intend that Tenaya ramble for publication, but you know what is better." This letter, which includes other notes on articles pending and produced, culminates in the remarks I have alluded to earlier, on the "infinite shortcomings" of the "dead bone-heaps called articles" (Engberg and Wesling 143).

"A Geologist's Winter Walk" in its original version is reprinted in Engberg and Wesling, pp. 145–51; page citations refer to this text. The essay is also reprinted in *Steep Trails* (1918), a posthumous collection of

Muir's magazine work from this period; but that version omits some epistolary gestures retained in the *Overland Monthly,* to which I will call attention.

11. The passage most cited from this article is one in which Muir reports his one serious spill during his years of mountaineering, a mishap he attributes to the dulling influences of city living. The article recounts his recovery through an ascetic regimen of "earnest exercise" upon the rocks (147). In their prefacing remarks, Engberg and Wesling discuss the piece in terms of Muir's protracted and historically epochal process of identity formation, urging consideration of "the ethical issues behind the images of intense joy" (144–45). Other discussions include O'Grady's reading of the piece in consonance with his broader themes of erotic desire and "pilgrimage" (67–70), and Cohen's account of it as a work of serious thinking about getting in shape, the relation of "soul life and limb life" (46–50).

12. I allude to Berry's well-known essay, "Why I Am Not Going to Buy a Computer," originally published in *The Utne Reader* and reprinted in *Harper's.* It appears in his collection, *What Are People For?,* along with letters of rebuttal it inspired, Berry's response to the letters, and a subsequent essay elaborating that response (170–96). The example of the Sumerian cuneiform and schooling is one Goody discusses in *The Interface between the Written and the Oral* (182–84).

13. The argument is made and enacted throughout Kroeber's *Ecological Literary Criticism* (1994). An example:

> Contemporary biological thinking . . . no longer identifies individuality with autonomy and separation. For leading contemporary biologists, the individuality of an organism is not definable except through its interactions with its environment, through its interdependencies. An organism's uniqueness consists in "intersubjective" connections and is determined not by separation but by "attunement," participation in "communities" (both inside itself and in the external environment) defined by historically individualized mutualities of need and desire. (7)

14. Harvey J. Graff is eminent among those debunking such presumptions; see, for instance, *The Literacy Myth.*

15. Of influential commentators on the subject, the most susceptible to Finnegan's critique would probably be Walter J. Ong, S.J.,

whose *Orality and Literacy* is most pertinent of his several treatments thereof. Also qualifying would be Eric A. Havelock, whose *The Muse Learns to Write* (1986) was the last issue of a career devoted to the topic, with special emphasis on ancient Greece.

16. The anthropologist Jack Goody's work on literacy and orality is especially noteworthy for the way it both delineates the larger patterns I'm evoking and shades the nuances and variations thereof in one sociohistorical context after another. See especially *The Domestication of the Savage Mind* (a title the irony of which has been widely and vapidly misconstrued), *The Logic of Writing and the Organization of Society*, and *The Interface between the Written and the Oral*, as well as the earlier, germinal piece in this vein, "The Consequences of Literacy," written with the literary critic Ian Watt.

17. Examples I've found instructive would include: E. Verne's notion of "literacy" as control of one's tools and his case for a politically willed "illiteracy"; Pierre Clastres's meditation on the purposefully stateless condition of so-called "primitive societies," how they confound the formation of a state associated with "the severity of the law," of which "all writing is an index" (177); and in its own way, Karl Kroeber's comparison of an Amerindian oral "poem" to a work by Keats, as productions with "radically different . . . cultural functions" ("Poem, Dream, and the Consuming of Culture" 323), as discussed below.

18. The phrase, "the violence of literacy," constitutes the title of J. Elspeth Stuckey's book on the subject, a polemic about the ways in which literacy is used to perpetuate oppression.

19. "To understand this aridity of culture [in the archaic near East] we must stand apart from the conventions of history, even while using the record of the past, for the idea of history is itself a Western invention whose central theme is the rejection of habitat. It formulates experience outside of nature and tends to reduce place to location. . . . History conceives the past mainly in terms of biography and nations. It seeks causality in the conscious, spiritual, ambitious character of men and memorializes them in writing" (Shepard 47).

20. Ultimately, according to Michael P. Cohen, Muir abandons the book metaphor as inadequate and gravitates toward a nonlinear, organic metaphor of nature as branching tree. See Cohen's discussion in *The Pathless Way*, 104–11.

21. This notion of writing is developed in *Of Grammatology*, especially part 1. It defies summary, of course.

22. This is Jack Goody's phrase, discussed in his introduction to his collection, *Literacy in Traditional Societies*. He proposes it as a less deterministic alternative to the phrase, "the consequences of literacy," which he had propounded in the earlier essay of that name written with Ian Watt.

23. Other explorations in this vein include Eisenstein (1981), Clanchy (1979), Ong (1982), and Goody (1986).

24. One recent work is the first I've seen that assumes the "lateral perspective" of oral-literate distinctions from avowedly biocentric orientation: *The Spell of the Sensuous* by David Abram. A professional sleight-of-hand magician and student of rural Asian cultures, Abram appropriates phenomenological insights from Merleau-Ponty to argue that, with writing, "the animating interplay of the senses" with a responsive environment gets displaced, acquiring "another locus of participation" in the written text:

> As nonhuman animals, plants, and even "inanimate" rivers once spoke to our tribal ancestors, so the "inert" letters on the page now speak to us! *This is a form of animism that we take for granted, but it is animism nonetheless — as mysterious as a talking stone.* (131)

As his title suggests, Abram finds this situation intimated in the double meaning of the word "spell" — to spell a word and to cast a spell — the two senses originally closely allied but increasingly distinct, even opposed (133).

Abram means to include only alphabetic writing in this characterization, asserting that ideogrammatic scripts like Chinese, with their remnant pictorial elements, retain a vestigial yet perceptible connection to sensory phenomena the represent. This distinction between writing systems, which follows a line of thought traceable through Havelock, Ong, and Illich and Sanders, among others, is a vulnerable point in a mostly intriguing discussion (see Harris, *The Origin of Writing*, for a subtle skewering of the alphabet's presumed exceptionality). Another vulnerability is Abram's overgeneralization of the Lord-Parry thesis on oral-formulaic composition — the practice of rhapsodes, Homeric or otherwise. Abram is hardly alone is extending this thesis to nonliterate peoples across the board, even though, as Finnegan remarks, Parry and Lord's "general theories are now in question as *universal* guides to the nature of oral and literate processes" (13). Dell Hymes, for instance, notes the particular shortcomings of the thesis to Native American oral traditions (129). Still, though it must be qualified, Abram's argument does not founder on these objections. He succeeds in giving writing its due while detailing situational advantages to nonwriting, explaining how (as Stock would say) "something is really happening" in the shift to fixation upon text. The names Abram has compiled in his acknowledgments—a who's who of deep ecology—attest to the appeal of this approach.

25. Opal Whiteley's diary, originally published as *The Story of Opal* (1920), was rescued from obscurity and republished by Benjamin Hoff under the title, *The Singing Creek Where the Willows Grow: The Rediscovered Diary of Opal Whiteley* (1986). My information on Whiteley comes from Hoff's extended introduction, "Magical Opal Whiteley." Hoff sums up Whiteley's story in terms of writerly identity:

> Opal's was the story of a uniquely gifted communicator who told of two still largely unknown realms—that of the natural world, and that of childhood. And from its beginning, it was the story of a *writer*. Far from being a literary fraud, Opal Whiteley was an embodiment of literary expression, who lived her love for writing in everything she did. (62)

26. My information on Carrie Dormon is drawn from Bonta's account of her in *Women in the Field*, 250–61.

27. See Scholes, *Textual Power*, and Todorov, *Genres of Discourse*, for critiques of the category of literature on institutional and formal grounds, respectively.

28. Insisting on the problematical character of "literature" as a category for nonwriting peoples, though, needn't lead us to erect a "great divide" between oral and written expression altogether. While some would regard the very notion of "oral literature" as a contradiction in terms—with Ong, predictably, finding it a "monstrous concept" (11)— others prefer to stress commonalities between print literature and oral performance. Examples (by no means exhaustive) of the latter approach include two works mentioned above: Ruth Finnegan, *Literacy and Orality* (especially chapter 4), and Dell Hymes, "Notes Toward (an Understanding of) Supreme Fictions." Work in ethnopoetics, like Hymes's, is especially concerned with the "literary" character of oral performance. For an account both respectful of oral-literate resemblances and cognizant of the pitfalls of ethnopoetic approaches—particularly the pitfall of imposing

rather than discerning notions of literary structure in oral discourse—see William Bright, "Poetic Structure in Oral Narrative."

29. The habit of discerning relations of affinity and resistance is among the most attractive features of Lawrence Buell's recent tome on environmental literature in the Thoreauvian, "pastoral" vein. Explaining how "nature has been doubly otherized in modern thought"—as subservient to human interests and as reinforcing the subjugation of human others—Buell proposes "three avenues" toward melioration: "to anatomize the pathology"; "to take stock of the resources" Western traditions hold for the purpose; and "to consider alternative models" (21). Of these, Murphy favors the third, in response to the first. Buell uses all three, but stresses especially the second, as I do as well. His reasons: while "exogamous models" such as indigenous worldviews may well bear reflecting upon, it is "less likely that at this point in history they will become paradigmatic than that they will assume a more subordinate place as ingredients of a new eclecticism toward which western thinking may evolve." Considering how westernized the entire world is becoming, "a disproportionately large share in determining world environmental attitudes" is likely to devolve upon western culture in any event; thus it befits us "to imagine how the voices of environmental dissent within western culture might help reinvision it and how they themselves must be critically reinvisioned in order to enlist them to this end" (22). I accept this "double-sided perspective" as my own in discussing the formal integrity and multiple valences of retreat narratives, even as these are qualified by "exogamous models."

30. The character of language as "speculative instruments" is a credo of Berthoff's, too, the expression drawn from I. A. Richards and employed repeatedly throughout her work.

7. KEEPING IT SIMPLE

1. "Writing Off the Self" is the final chapter of Poirier's *The Renewal of Literature* (1987), in which he entertains literary "proposals to do away with the self," seeking "to understand why the idea occurs to so many writers popularly supposed to speak for the preservation of human culture, and why, also, the idea itself is so immensely difficult to substantiate or hold onto." The value of exam-

ining such efforts, in which language's very "limitations as a cultural artifact" are explored, Poirier holds, lies in how this enables us "to measure how much in our present circumstance can be usefully worked upon and how much is perhaps irremediable" (182–83)—a value consonant with ecological criticism's stress on adaptation and limits in literary production.

2. In the phrase "ecological literacy" I echo the title of David W. Orr's indispensible book on the subject (1992). Orr's book is largely (though not exclusively) a rejoinder to a Hirsch-type "cultural literacy"; it focuses upon ecologically essential areas of knowledge and their informing philosophies. My own generic and experiential notions of general education are meant to complement more detailed agendas of the sort Orr offers.

3. I refer to students either by their own first name or by a pseudonym the student has chosen, whichever they prefer.

4. Buell elaborates this point about Thoreau's "high degree of social disaffection," one which I have frequently reflected upon myself in reading and teaching *Walden*:

> Doubtless it was a character flaw that he was so severe on ordinary mortals and so grudging in his acknowledgment of his dependence on them. Yet without that flaw he might not have managed to become a memorable critic of anthropocentrism, and he might not have pursued his self-transformative quest with such energy. He might not have been able to imagine humanity as part of a larger ecological community if he had been altogether at ease within the confines of the human community. (388)

5. In his article in William Cronon's *Uncommon Ground*, entitled " 'Are You an Environmentalist or Do You Work for a Living?': Work and Nature," Richard White asserts that environmentalists' failure to come to terms with work in nature leads us to equate nature with leisure and thus to construe it "as an escape, a place where we are born again" in the absence of work. The result: "We will condemn ourselves to spending most of our lives outside of nature, for there can be no permanent place for us inside" (185).

6. Buell discusses pastoral's "internal contradictions," its capacities either to "direct us toward the realm of physical nature . . . or abstract us from it" (31), in his chapter on "Pastoral Ideology" (31–52).

7. Shane Phelan remarks on the valence of the term "nature" for political theory in his "Intimate Distance: The Dislocation of Nature in Modernity" (1993). "In Ernesto Laclau's terms," Phelan reports, "nature has been 'dislocated' insofar as its identity or meaning 'depends on an outside which both denies that identity and provides its condition of possibility at the same time' " (44). Reflecting upon this "dislocated" character as exemplified in Rousseau and Nietzsche, Phelan holds for an "intimate distance," a posture of "continual reflection and contest," toward a category that is both fraught with the perils of an essentializing that authorizes oppression, and indispensible to resisting social and ecological depradations issuing from "the solipsism of modern Western civilization" (59).

8. I am thinking of Raymond William's *tour de force* on the "escalator" of nostalgia for an earlier, simpler way of life, in *The Country and the City* (1973, 9–12). Williams displays a seemingly endless regress of such expressions, in which English writers of a supposedly more rustic and noble epoch themselves express longing for a yet earlier golden age. This phenomenon is attributable in part to people's perennial attachment to their own childhoods. But he notes that the evident similarity of these episodes is deceptive, that the terms and modes employed change in "successive stages" in accord with conditions in which they originate. As Williams trenchantly remarks: "Nostalgia, it can be said, is universal and persistent; only other men's nostalgias offend" (12).

9. John P. O'Grady's opening to *Pilgrims to the Wild* is indicative: "This preface should have been written on a mountain. I tried" (ix). Further examples abound: Scott Slovic's Afterword account of desert hiking, Peter Fritzell's opening invocation of an outdoor childhood, Michael Cohen's periodic references to climbing and living in Yosemite, Patrick Murphy's childhood recollections reported in the previous chapter — even Steven Trimble's mention of the 16,000 miles he racked up behind the wheel while collecting interviews for his anthology, since auto distances redound to the ethos of the contemporary "rambler." Further, there are the visible cabin-dweller credentials of the critic Sherman Paul (*For Love of the World: Essays on Nature Writers*), the philosopher Erazim Kohak (*The Embers and the Stars*), and the poet–nature writer–metaphysician Edward Lueders (*The Clam Lake Papers*).

10. Cronon's remark comes in his introduction to *Uncommon Ground: Toward Reinventing Nature* (1995), a collection he edited of works generated at a residential seminar held at the University of Cali-

fornia at Irvine, a seminar in which Haraway was a key participant. Haraway's significance to the seminar—and my warrant for terming these scholars "reinventors"—is signalled in the collection's subtitle, a deliberate echo of the subtitle of Haraway's influential *Simians, Cyborgs, and Women: The Reinvention of Nature* (1991).

11. Cronon reports on how Haraway and Katherine Hayles brought to the Irvine seminar the question of "nature as virtual reality" (44). He continues:

> The fascinating thing about virtual reality is that although it initially appears to be the least natural of human creations, the most disembodied and abstracted expression of modernity's alienation from nature, it can in fact serve as a powerful and rather troubling test of whether we really know what we're talking about when we speak of nature. One would think that the virtual would stand in pure opposition to the real, but when you put them next to each other this is not nearly so obvious. Yes, a person using computerized sensory apparatus to move through virtual space could hardly be more isolated from the surrounding environment. And yet the better the simulation, the more difficulty we begin to have distinguishing it from the real. The more engaged we become with experiencing it, the more plausible it begins to seem as an alternative to the world we know—indeed, an alternative with real advantages. (45)

It would be simplistic and unsophisticated, I'm sure, to characterize this emission as purely ridiculous—nothing is *that* pure, least of all this "pure opposition." And so I await the invention of the virtual vegetable, which I'm sure will be delicious and nutritive once contrived.

12. "Since the cut between self and natural world is arbitrary, we can make it at the skin or we can take it as far out as you like—to the deep oceans and distant stars. But the cut is far less important than the recognition of uncertainty about making the cut at all" (xix). So claims James Hillman in his "psychological foreword" to *Ecopsychology: Restoring the Earth, Healing the Mind* (1995), ed. Roszak, Gomes, and Kanner.

13. In her introduction to *Simians, Cyborgs, and Women*, Haraway remarks: "Inhabiting these pages are odd boundary creatures—simians, cyborgs, and women—all of which have had a destabilizing place in the

great Western evolutionary, technological, and biological narratives. These boundary creatures are, literally, *monsters*, a word that shares more than its root with the word, to *demonstrate*. Monsters signify" (2). This is an exuberant terministic innovation, certainly, this recasting of "monsters"; but I suspect Haraway has a different notion than I do as to what constitutes a term's "literal" meaning.

Works Cited

Abbey, Edward. *Desert Solitaire*. 1968. New York: Touchstone-Simon, 1990.

Abram, David. *The Spell of the Sensuous: Perception and Language in a More-Than-Human World*. New York: Pantheon, 1996.

Adams, Stephen, and Donald Ross Jr. *Revising Mythologies: The Composition of Thoreau's Major Works*. Charlottesville: UP of Virginia, 1988.

Ammons, A. R. *Lake Effect Country: Poems*. New York: Norton, 1983.

———. *The Selected Poems: 1951–1977*. New York: Norton, 1977.

Anderson, Chris. *Style as Argument: Contemporary American Nonfiction*. Carbondale: Southern Illinois UP, 1987.

———, ed. *Literary Nonfiction: Theory, Criticism, Pedagogy*. Carbondale: Southern Illinois UP, 1989.

Atwood, Margaret. *Selected Poems*. New York: Simon, 1976.

Austin, Mary. *The Land of Little Rain*. 1903. Introd. Edward Abbey. New York: Penguin, 1988.

Bakhtin, M. M. *The Dialogic Imagination*. Trans. Caryl Emerson and Michael Holquist. Ed. Michael Holquist. Austin: U of Texas P, 1981.

Banham, Peter Reyner. *Scenes in America Deserta*. Salt Lake City: Peregrine Smith, 1982.

Barthes, Roland. "Introduction to the Structural Analysis of Narratives." *Image—Music—Text*. Trans. Stephen Heath. New York: Hill and Wang-Farrar, 1977. 77–124.

Benjamin, Walter. *Illuminations*. 1968. Trans. Harry Zohn. Ed. Hannah Arendt. New York: Shocken, 1969.

Bergon, Frank, ed. *A Sharp Lookout: Selected Nature Essays of John Burroughs*. Washington: Smithsonian, 1987.

Berry, Wendell. *A Continuous Harmony: Essays Cultural and Agricultural*. New York: Harcourt, 1972.

———. *Home Economics*. San Francisco: North Point, 1987.

———. *The Long-Legged House*. New York: Harcourt, 1969.

———. *Recollected Essays, 1965–1980*. San Francisco: North Point, 1981.

———. *Standing By Words*. San Francisco: North Point, 1983.

———. *The Unforeseen Wilderness: Kentucky's Red River Gorge*. 1971. Photographs by Ralph Eugene Meatyard. Revised and expanded ed. San Francisco: North Point, 1991.

———. *What Are People For?* San Francisco: North Point, 1990.

Berthoff, Ann E. *Forming/Thinking/Writing: The Composing Imagination*. Montclair, NJ: Boynton/Cook, 1982.

Beston, Henry. *The Outermost House*. 1928. New York: Penguin, 1988.

Bonta, Marcia Myers. *Women in the Field: America's Pioneering Women Naturalists*. College Station: Texas A&M UP, 1991.

Bowers, C. A. *Critical Essays on Education, Modernity, and the Recovery of the Ecological Imperative*. New York: Teachers College P, 1993.

Brandt, Deborah. *Literacy as Involvement: The Acts of Writers, Readers, and Texts*. Carbondale: Southern Illinois UP, 1990.

Bright, William. "Poetic Structure in Oral Narrative." *Spoken and Written Language: Exploring Orality and Literacy*. Ed. Deborah Tannen. Norwood, NJ: Ablex, 1982. 171–84.

Brodkey, Linda. "Modernism and the Scene(s) of Writing." *College English* 49 (1987): 396–418.

Brooks, Peter. *Reading for the Plot: Design and Intention in Narrative*. Cambridge: Harvard UP, 1992.

Buell, Lawrence. *The Environmental Imagination: Thoreau, Nature Writing, and the Formation of American Culture*. Cambridge: Harvard UP, 1995.

Burke, Kenneth. *Attitudes Toward History*. 1937. 3rd ed. Berkeley: U of California P, 1984.

———. *Counter-Statement*. 1931. Berkeley: U of California P, 1968.

———. *A Grammar of Motives*. 1945. Berkeley: U of California P, 1969.

———. *Language as Symbolic Action: Essays on Life, Literature, and Method*. Berkeley: U of California P, 1966.

———. *Permanence and Change: An Anatomy of Purpose.* 1935. 3rd ed. Berkeley: U of California P, 1984.

———. *The Philosophy of Literary Form: Studies in Symbolic Action.* Rev. ed. New York: Vintage, 1957.

Cameron, Sharon. *Writing Nature: Henry Thoreau's Journal.* New York: Oxford UP, 1985.

Carr, David. "Life and Narrator's Art." *Hermeneutics and Deconstruction.* Ed. Hugh J. Silverman and Don Ihde. Albany: State U of New York P, 1985.

Cavell, Stanley. *Pursuits of Happiness: The Hollywood Comedy of Remarriage.* Cambridge: Harvard UP, 1981.

———. *The Senses of Walden.* San Francisco: North Point, 1981.

Clanchy, M. T. *From Memory to Written Record: England 1066–1307.* Cambridge: Harvard UP, 1979.

Clark, Walter H., Jr. "The New England Literature Program." *Teaching Environmental Literature.* Ed. Frederick O. Waage. New York: MLA, 1985. 158–64.

Clastres, Pierre. *Society Against the State.* Trans. Robert Hunter in collaboration with Abe Stein. New York: Zone Books, 1989.

Cohen, Michael P. *The Pathless Way: John Muir and American Wilderness.* Madison: U of Wisconsin P, 1984.

Cronon, William, ed. *Uncommon Ground: Toward Reinventing Nature.* New York: Norton, 1995.

Derrida, Jacques. *Of Grammatology.* Trans. Gayatri Chakravorty Spivak. Baltimore: Johns Hopkins UP, 1976.

Dickstein, Morris. "Damaged Literacy: The Decay of Reading." *Profession 93.* New York: MLA, 1993. 34–40.

Dillard, Annie. *Pilgrim at Tinker Creek.* 1974. New York: Harper, 1988.

———. *The Writing Life.* New York: Harper, 1989.

Ehrlich, Gretel. Foreword. *The Mountains of California.* By John Muir. San Francisco: Sierra Club Books, 1988. vii–xii.

———. Introduction. *My First Summer in the Sierra.* By John Muir. New York: Penguin, 1987. vii–xvi.

———. *Islands, the Universe, Home.* New York: Viking, 1991.

Eisenstein, Elizabeth L. "Some Conjectures about the Impact of Printing on Western Society and Thought." *Literacy and Social Development in the West: A Reader.* Ed. Harvey J. Graff. Cambridge, Eng.: Cambridge UP, 1981. 53–68.

Ellison, Julie. *Emerson's Romantic Style*. Princeton, NJ: Princeton UP, 1984.

Engberg, Robert, and Donald Wesling, eds. *John Muir: To Yosemite and Beyond*. Madison: U of Wisconsin P, 1980.

Evernden, Neil. *The Natural Alien*. Toronto: U of Toronto P, 1985.

Fabian, Johannes. *Time and the Other*. New York: Columbia UP, 1983.

Finnegan, Ruth. *Literacy and Orality: Studies in the Technology of Communication*. Oxford: Blackwell, 1988.

Fink, Steven. *Prophet in the Marketplace: Thoreau's Development as a Professional Writer*. Princeton, NJ: Princeton UP, 1992.

Fisher, Philip. "American Literary and Cultural Studies since the Civil War." *Redrawing the Boundaries: The Transformation of English and American Literary Studies*. Ed. Stephen Greenblatt and Giles Gunn. New York: MLA, 1992. 232–50.

Fishman, Andrea. *Amish Literacy: What and How It Means*. Portsmouth, NH: Heinemann, 1988.

Fritzell, Peter A. *Nature Writing and America: Essays upon a Cultural Type*. Ames: Iowa State UP, 1990.

Fox, Stephen. *The American Conservation Movement: John Muir and His Legacy*. 1981. Madison: U of Wisconsin P, 1985.

Garber, Frederick. *Thoreau's Redemptive Imagination*. New York: New York UP, 1977.

Gee, James Paul. *Social Linguistics and Literacies: Ideology in Discourse*. London: Falmer P, 1990.

Gere, Anne Ruggles. "Kitchen Tables and Rented Rooms: The Extracurriculum of Composition." CCC 45 (1994): 75–92.

———. *Writing Groups: History, Theory, and Implications*. Carbondale: Southern Illinois UP, 1987.

Gifford, Don. *The Farther Shore: A Natural History of Perception, 1798–1984*. New York: Atlantic Monthly P, 1990.

Glendinning, Chellis. "Technology, Trauma, and the Wild." *Ecopsychology: Restoring the Earth, Healing the Mind*. Ed. Theodore Roszak, Mary E. Gomes, and Allen D. Kanner. San Francisco: Sierra Club, 1995. 41–54.

Goody, Jack. Introduction. *Literacy in Traditional Societies*. Ed. by Goody. Cambridge, Eng.: Cambridge UP, 1968. 1–26.

———. *The Interface Between the Written and the Oral*. Cambridge, Eng.: Cambridge UP, 1968.

———. *The Logic of Writing and the Organization of Society.* Cambridge, Eng.: Cambridge UP, 1986.

Goody, Jack, and Ian Watt. "The Consequences of Literacy." *Literacy in Traditional Societies.* Ed. Jack Goody. Cambridge, Eng.: Cambridge UP, 1968. 27–68.

Graff, Harvey J. *The Literacy Myth: Literacy and Social Structure in the Nineteenth-Century City.* New York: Academic P, 1979.

Greenway, Robert. "The Wilderness Effect and Ecopsychology." *Ecopsychology: Restoring the Earth, Healing the Mind.* Ed. Theodore Roszak, Mary E. Gomes, and Allen D. Kanner. San Francisco: Sierra Club, 1995. 122–35.

Halpern, Daniel, ed. *On Nature: Nature, Landscape, and Natural History.* San Francisco: North Point, 1987.

———, ed. *Our Private Lives: Journals, Notebooks and Diaries.* New York: Vintage-Random, 1990.

Hamlin, Cyrus. "Strategies of Reversal in Literary Narrative." *Interpretation of Narrative.* Ed. Mario J. Valdes and Owen J. Miller. Toronto: U of Toronto P, 1978. 61–77.

Haraway, Donna. *Primate Visions: Gender, Race, and Nature in the World of Modern Science.* New York: Routledge, 1989.

———. *Simians, Cyborgs, and Women: The Reinvention of Nature.* New York: Routledge, 1991.

Harper, Steven. "The Way of Wilderness." *Ecopsychology: Restoring the Earth, Healing the Mind.* Ed. Theodore Roszak, Mary E. Gomes, and Allen D. Kanner. San Francisco: Sierra Club, 1995. 183–200.

Harpham, Geoffrey Galt. *The Ascetic Imperative in Culture and Criticism.* Chicago: U of Chicago P, 1987.

———. "Conversion and the Language of Autobiography." *Studies in Autobiography.* Ed. James Olney. New York: Oxford UP, 1988.

Harris, Roy. *The Origin of Writing.* London: Duckworth, 1986.

Havelock, Eric A. *The Muse Learns to Write: Reflections on Orality and Literacy from Antiquity to the Present.* New Haven: Yale UP, 1986.

Hay, John. *The Immortal Wilderness.* New York: Norton, 1987.

Hearne, Vicki. *Adam's Task: Calling Animals by Name.* 1986. New York: Vintage-Random, 1987.

Higham, John. "The Reorientation of American Culture in the 1890's." *The Origins of Modern Consciousness.* Ed. John Weiss. Detroit: Wayne State UP, 1965.

———. *Strangers in the Land: Patterns of American Nativism, 1860–1925.* 1955. Corrected ed. New York: Atheneum, 1969.

Hillman, James. "A Psyche the Size of Earth: A Psychological Foreword." *Ecopsychology: Restoring the Earth, Healing the Mind.* Ed. Theodore Roszak, Mary E. Gomes, and Allen D. Kanner. San Francisco: Sierra Club, 1995. xvii–xxiii.

Hoagland, Edward. "In Praise of John Muir." *On Nature: Nature, Landscape, and Natural History.* Ed. Daniel Halpern. San Francisco: North Point, 1986. 45–58.

Hubbell, Sue. *A Country Year: Living the Questions.* 1986. New York: Harper, 1987.

Hymes, Dell. "Notes Toward (an Understanding of) Supreme Fictions." *Studies in Historical Change.* Ed. and Introd Ralph Cohen. Charlottesville: U of Virginia P, 1992. 128–78.

Illich, Ivan. *Tools for Conviviality.* Berkeley: Heyday Books, 1973.

Illich, Ivan, and Barry Sanders. *ABC: The Alphabetization of the Popular Mind.* 1988. New York: Vintage-Random, 1989.

Jauss, Hans Robert. "Theses on the Transition from the Aesthetics of Literary Works to a Theory of Aesthetic Experience." *Interpretation of Narrative.* Ed. Mario J. Valdes and Owen J. Miller. Toronto: U of Toronto P, 1978. 137–47.

Kaplan, Rachel, and Stephen Kaplan. *The Experience of Nature: A Psychological Perspective.* Cambridge, Eng.: Cambridge UP, 1989.

Knowles, Joseph. *Alone in the Wilderness.* Boston: Small, Maynard and Co., 1913.

Kohak, Erazim. *The Embers and the Stars.* Chicago: U of Chicago P, 1984.

Kolodny, Annette. *The Lay of the Land: Metaphor as Experience and History in American Life and Letters.* Chapel Hill: U of North Carolina P, 1975.

Kroeber, Karl. *Ecological Litearary Criticism: Romantic Imagining and the Biology of Mind.* New York: Columbia UP, 1994.

———. "Poem, Dream, and the Consuming of Culture." *Smoothing the Ground: Essays on Native American Oral Culture.* Ed. Brian Swann. Berkeley: U of California P, 1983. 323–33.

Krutch, Joseph Wood, ed. *Great American Nature Writing*. New York: William Sloane, 1950.

La Barre, Weston. *The Ghost Dance: Origins of Religion*. New York: Delta-Dell, 1972.

LeFevre, Karen Burke. *Invention as a Social Act*. Carbondale: Southern Illinois UP, 1987.

Leopold, Aldo. *A Sand County Almanac*. New York: Oxford UP, 1949.

Lerner, Lawrence. "After Historicism." *New Literary History* 24 (1993): 273–92.

Levine, Kenneth. *The Social Context of Literacy*. London: Routledge, 1986.

Limerick, Patricia Nelson. *Desert Passages: Encounters with the American Deserts*. Albuquerque: U of New Mexico P, 1985.

Lopez, Barry. *Crossing Open Ground*. New York: Vintage, 1989.

Love, Glen A. "Revaluing Nature: Toward an Ecological Criticism." *Western American Literature* 25 (1990): 201–15.

Lueders, Edward. *The Clam Lake Papers: A Winter in the North Woods*. San Francisco: Harper, 1977.

———, ed. *Writing Natural History: Dialogues with Authors*. Salt Lake City: U of Utah P, 1989.

Lutts, Ralph H. *The Nature Fakers: Wildlife, Science & Sentiment*. Golden, CO: Fulcrum, 1990.

Lyon, Thomas J., ed. *This Incomperable Lande: A Book of American Nature Writing*. Boston: Houghton, 1989.

MacIntyre, Alisdair. *After Virtue*. 2nd ed. Notre Dame, IN: U of Notre Dame P, 1984.

Marx, Leo. *The Machine in the Garden: Technology and the Pastoral Ideal in America*. New York: Oxford UP, 1964.

Martin, Wallace. *Recent Theories of Narrative*. Ithaca, NY: Cornell UP, 1986.

McIntosh, James. *Thoreau as Romantic Naturalist: His Shifting Stance toward Nature*. Ithaca, NY: Cornell UP, 1974.

Meeker, Joseph. *The Comedy of Survival: Studies in Literary Ecology*. New York: Scribners, 1972.

Miller, Susan. *Textual Carnivals: The Politics of Composition*. Carbondale: Southern Illinois UP, 1991.

Mitchell, W.J.T., ed. *On Narrative*. Chicago: U of Chicago P, 1980, 1981.

Monk, Samuel H. *The Sublime: A Study of Critical Theories in XVIII-Century England.* New York: MLA, 1935.

Muir, John. *A Thousand-Mile Walk to the Gulf.* 1916. Foreword Peter Jenkins. Boston: Houghton, 1981.

———. *The Mountains of California.* 1894. Introd. Gretel Ehrlich. San Francisco: Sierra Club Books, 1988.

———. *My First Summer in the Sierra.* 1911. Introd. Gretel Ehrlich. New York: Penguin, 1987.

———. *Steep Trails.* 1918. Foreword Edward Hoagland. San Francisco: Sierra Club Books, 1994.

Murphy, Patrick D. *Literature, Nature, and Other: Ecofeminist Critiques.* Albany: State U of New York P, 1995.

Nash, Roderick F. *Wilderness and the American Mind.* 3rd ed. New Haven: Yale UP, 1982.

Nicolson, Marjorie Hope. *Mountain Gloom and Mountain Glory: The Development of the Aesthetics of the Infinite.* Ithaca, NY: Cornell UP, 1959.

Norwood, Vera. *Made From This Earth: American Women and Nature.* Chapel Hill: U of North Carolina P, 1993.

Oates, Joyce Carol. "Against Nature." *On Nature: Nature, Landscape, and Natural History.* Ed. Daniel Halpern. San Francisco: North Point, 1987. 236–43.

Oelschlaeger, Max. *The Idea of Wilderness.* New Haven: Yale UP, 1991.

O'Grady, John P. *Pilgrims to the Wild: Everett Ruess, Henry David Thoreau, John Muir, Clarence King, Mary Austin.* Salt Lake City: U of Utah P, 1993.

Ong, Walter J. *Orality and Literacy: The Technologizing of the Word.* London: Metheun, 1982.

Orr, David W. *Ecological Literacy: Education and the Transition to a Postmodern World.* Albany: State U of New York P, 1992.

Painter, Nell Irvin. *Standing at Armageddon: The United States 1877–1919.* New York: Norton, 1987.

Paul, Sherman. *For Love of the World: Essays on Nature Writers.* Iowa City: U of Iowa P, 1992.

Perrin, Noel. Introduction, Ernest Thompson Seton, *Wild Animals I Have Known.* 1898. New York: Penguin, 1987.

Phelan, Shane. "Intimate Distance: The Dislocation of Nature in Modernity." *In the Nature of Things: Language, Politics, and the*

Environment. Ed. Jane Bennett and William Chaloupka. Minneapolis: U of Minnesota P, 1993. 44–62.

Plaks, Andrew H. "Towards a Critical Theory of Chinese Narrative." *Chinese Narrative: Critical and Theoretical Essays.* Ed. Andrew H. Plaks. Princeton, NJ: Princeton UP, 1977.

Plato. *Phaedrus and Letters VII and VIII.* Trans. and introd. Walter Hamilton. London: Penguin, 1973.

Poirier, Richard. *The Renewal of Literature: Emersonian Reflections.* 1987. New Haven: Yale UP, 1988.

Powell, Lawrence Clark. Introduction. *The Desert.* By John C. Van Dyke. Tucson: Arizona Historical Society, 1976. Unpaginated.

———. *Southwest Classics: The Creative Literature of the Arid Lands.* Los Angeles: Ward Ritchie Press, 1974.

Ricouer, Paul. *Interpretation Theory: Discourse and the Surplus of Meaning.* Fort Worth: Texas Christian UP, 1976.

———. "Narrative Time." *On Narrative.* Ed. W. J. T. Mitchell. Chicago: U of Chicago P, 1980, 1981. 165–86.

Riffaterre, Michael. "The Reader's Perception of Narrative: Balzac's *Paix du menage.*" *Interpretation of Narrative.* Ed. Mario J. Valdes and Owen J. Miller. Toronto: U of Toronto P, 1978. 28–37.

Roorda, Randall. "KB in Green: Ecology, Critical Theory, and Kenneth Burke.: *ISLE: Interdisciplinary Studies in Literature and the Environment.* (forthcoming).

Rosmarin, Adena. *The Power of Genre.* Minneapolis: U of Minnesota P, 1985.

Rousseau, Jean-Jacques. *Reveries of the Solitary Walker.* New York: Penguin, 1979.

Schleifer, Ronald, Robert Con Davis, and Nancy Mergler. *Culture and Cognition: The Boundaries of Literary and Scientific Inquiry.* Ithaca, NY: Cornell UP, 1992.

Schmitt, Peter J. *Back to Nature: The Arcadian Myth in Urban America.* New York: Oxford UP, 1969.

Shelton, Richard. "Creeping Up on *Desert Solitaire.*" *Resist Much, Obey Little: Some Notes on Edward Abbey.* Salt Lake City: Dream Garden Press: 1985. 66–78.

———. Introduction. *The Desert.* By John C. Van Dyke. Salt Lake City: Peregrine Smith, 1980. xi–xxix.

Shepard, Paul. *Nature and Madness*. San Francisco: Sierra Club Books, 1982.

Siebers, Tobin. *Morals and Stories*. New York: Columbia UP, 1992.

Silko, Leslie Marmon. *Ceremony*. 1977. New York: Penguin, 1986.

Slovic, Scott. *Seeking Awareness in American Nature Writing*. Salt Lake City: U of Utah P, 1992.

Snyder, Gary. *The Practice of the Wild*. San Francisco: North Point, 1990.

Sophocles. *Philoctetes*. Trans. David Grene. *Sophocles II*. Ed. David Grene and Richard Lattimore. Chicago: U of Chicago P, 1957. 189–254.

Stafford, William. *Things That Happen Where There Aren't Any People*. Brockport, NY: BOA Editions, 1980.

Stock, Brian. *Listening for the Text*. Baltimore: Johns Hopkins UP, 1990.

Street, Brian V. *Literacy in Theory and Practice*. Cambridge, Eng.: Cambridge UP, 1984.

Stuckey, J. Elspeth. *The Violence of Literacy*. Portsmouth, NH: Boynton/Cook, 1991.

Tallmadge, John. "Anatomy of a Classic." *Companion to* A Sand County Almanac: *Interpretive and Critical Essays*. Ed. J. Baird Callicott. Madison: U of Wisconsin P, 1987. 110–127.

Teague, David. "A Paradoxical Legacy: Some New Contexts for John C. Van Dyke's *The Desert*." *Western American Literature* 30.2 (1995): 163–78.

Teague, David, and Peter Wild. "The Secret Life of John C. Van Dyke: Decalcomania on the Desert." *Journal of the Southwest* 37.1 (1995): 1–52.

Thoreau, Henry David. *Journal, Volume 2: 1942–1848*. Ed. Robert Sattelmeyer. Princeton, NJ: Princeton UP, 1984.

———. *The Maine Woods*. Ed. Joseph J. Moldenhauer. Princeton, NJ: Princeton UP, 1972.

———. "Walking." *The Natural History Essays*. Salt Lake City: Peregrine Smith, 1980. 93–136.

———. *Walden*. Ed. J. Lyndon Shanley. Princeton: Princeton UP, 1971.

———. *A Week on the Concord and Merrimack Rivers*. New York: Thomas Y. Crowell, 1966.

Todorov, Tzvetan. *The Conquest of America*. Trans. Richard Howard. New York: Harper, 1984.

————. *The Poetics of Prose.* Trans. Richard Howard. Ithaca, NY: Cornell UP, 1977.

Trimble, Stephen. "Introduction: The Naturalist's Trance." *Words from the Land: Encounters with Natural History Writing.* Ed. by Trimble. Salt Lake City: Peregrine Smith: 1988. 1–29.

Turner, Frederick. *Beyond Geography: The Western Spirit Against the Wilderness.* 1980. New Brunswick, NJ: Rutgers UP, 1983.

————. *Rediscovering America: John Muir in His Time and Ours.* San Francisco: Sierra Club Books, 1985.

Valdes, Mario J., and Owen J. Miller, eds. *Interpretation of Narrative.* Toronto: U of Toronto P, 1978.

Van Dyke, John C. *The Desert.* 1901. Introd. Richard Shelton. Salt Lake City: Peregrine Smith, 1980.

————. *The Money God.* New York: Scribner's, 1908.

————. *The Mountain: Renewed Studies in Impressions and Appearances.* New York: Scribner's, 1916.

————. *The Open Spaces: Incidents of Days and Nights Under the Blue Sky.* 1922. Foreword Peter Wild. Salt Lake City: U of Utah Press, 1991.

Verne, E. "Literacy and Industrialization—The Dispossession of Speech." *Literacy and Social Development in the West: A Reader.* Ed. Harvey J. Graff. Cambridge, Eng.: Cambridge UP, 1981. 286–303.

Vygotsky, Lev Semenovich. *Thought and Language.* Trans. Eugenia Haufman and Gertrude Vakar. Cambridge: MIT P, 1962.

White, Hayden. "The Value of Narrativity in the Representation of Reality." *On Narrative.* Ed. W. J. T. Mitchell. Chicago: U of Chicago P, 1980, 1981.

White, James Boyd. *When Words Lose Their Meaning: Constitutions and Reconstitutions of Language, Character, and Community.* Chicago: U of Chicago P, 1984.

White, Richard. " 'Are You an Environmentalist or Do You Work for a Living?': Work and Nature." *Uncommon Ground: Toward Reinventing Nature.* Ed. William Cronon. New York: Norton, 1995. 171–85.

Whiteley, Opal. *The Singing Creek Where the Willows Grow: The Rediscovered Diary of Opal Whiteley.* Presented by Benjamin Hoff. New York: Ticknor and Fields, 1986.

Whorf, Benjamin Lee. *Language, Thought, and Reality.* Cambridge: MIT P, 1956.

Wild, Peter. Editor's Introduction. *The Autobiography of John C. Van Dyke: A Personal Narrative of American Life 1961–1931.* Ed. by Wild. Salt Lake City: U of Utah P, 1993. xv–xxxii.

———. Foreword. *The Grand Canyon of the Colorado: Recurrent Studies in Impressions and Appearances.* By John C. Van Dyke. Salt Lake City: U of Utah P, 1992. vii–xxvii.

———. Foreword. *The Open Spaces: Incidents of Nights and Days Under the Blue Sky.* By John C. Van Dyke. Salt Lake City: U of Utah P, 1991. vii–xxi.

———. *John C. Van Dyke: The Desert.* Boise State University Western Writers Series 82. Boise, ID: Boise State U, 1988.

———. "Van Dyke's Shoes: Tracking the Aesthetician Behind the Desert Wanderer." *Journal of the Southwest* 29 (1987): 401–17.

———. "A Western Sun Sets in the East: The Five 'Appearances' Surrounding John C. Van Dyke's *The Desert.*" *Western American Literature* 25 (1990): 217–31.

Wild, Peter, and Neil Carmony. "The Trip Not Taken: John C. Van Dyke, Heroic Doer or Armchair Seer?" *Journal of Arizona History* 34.1 (1993): 65–80.

Williams, Raymond. *Keywords: A Vocabulary of Culture and Society.* New York: Oxford UP, 1976.

Wilson, David Scofield. *In the Presence of Nature.* Amherst: U of Massachusetts P, 1978.

Wolfe, Linnie Marsh. *John of the Mountains: The Unpublished Journals of John Muir.* 1938. Madison: U of Wisconsin P, 1979.

Wyatt, David. *The Fall into Eden: Landscape and Imagination in California.* Cambridge, Eng.: Cambridge UP, 1986.

Zwinger, Ann H. "What's a Nice Girl Like Me Doing in a Place Like This?" *Western American Literature* 27 (1992): 99–107.

Index

Abbey, Edward, 5, 18, 94, 150–51, 207, 212, 235, 239, 240
Abram, David, 254–55
abstraction, as term in Berry, 126–27, 128, 129, 130, 131, 133, 134, 136
action: and attention, 19; and narrative, 237
Adams, Stephen and Donald Ross, 38, 39, 42, 51
adventure, 10, 24, 35, 213
aesthetic sense, and natives, 77, 99
African Americans, and landscape, 223
airplane, as figure in Berry, 114, 125, 126, 163
alienation, as condition of nature writing, 200–201
American Museum of Natural History, 95
American nature writing, xvii-xviii, 227–28
Ammons, A.R., 10, 205
Anderson, Chris, 23, 59, 228
animals: and narrative, 14–17; presence of, 120; signs of, 41
Anza-Borrego Desert, 94
Arendt, Hannah, 8, 237
artifacts, the artifactual: drama in attention to, 31, 34, 40–41, 43, 62, 70–71, 79, 109–10, 116–17, 121, 131, 132, 136, 141, 153–54, 161, 210; identity as, 55; relinquishment of,

205–06; writing as, xvii, 25, 150, 154, 197
asceticism, 17, 55, 79, 98, 115, 140; and cabins, 161; as competitive, 151; and Muir, 23, 183; and resistance, 73–74; and simplicity, 206
Association for the Study of Literature and the Environment, 250
attention, 215–16
Atwood, Margaret, xiv, 229
Austin, Mary, 57
autobiography, and genre, 8–9

Bakhtin, M. M., 230
Banham, Peter Reyner, 91–92, 235, 236
Beebe, William, 160
Benjamin, Walter, 169, 184, 186–88, 189–90, 202
Bergon, Frank, 16
Berry, Wendell, xvi, 5, 100, Chapter 4 *passim*; on abstraction, 126–27, 128, 129, 130, 131, 133, 134, 136; airplane as figure in, 114, 125, 126, 163; The Camp (residence of), 139–40, 162–63, 166; and community, 123–24, 128; and contact with place, 108, 126, 127, 133, 140–41; on control, 127–28, 130; on creation, 118, 126–27, 129, 131; and desire to moralize, 102–103; didacticism in, 113; enclosure in,

273

sacrifice of, xiv, 55, 79, 84, 115, 256; subjugation to subject, 91; subordination of, 96; writing and written, 39. *See also* writer, self-definition as
self-sufficiency, and nature writing, 155
Seton, Ernest Thompson, 81
Shelton, Richard, 59, 61, 62, 81, 82–85, 86, 91, 94, 95, 96, 97, 235, 236, 240
Shepard, Paul, 193, 215, 218, 219, 220, 243
Siebers, Tobin, 15, 16
silence: as term in Berry, 106, 113, 117, 134–35; and Van Dyke, 91. *See also* noise; quiet
Silko, Leslie Marmon, 198, 200
simplicity, 206, 220, 224–25
sitting, in Berry, 108, 116, 119–21, 123
Slovic, Scott, 9, 39, 115, 159–60, 258
Snyder, Gary, 231
social constructionism, 14, 99, 194, 218, 223
social-historical readings, 36–37, 232
social order, and narrative, 10
social view, of literacy and writing, 146, 168, 172–73, 187, 192–93
Socrates, 179
solitary confinement, as image of writing, 145, 151
solitary writer: image of, 144–47, 184
solitude, 102, 105, 109, 120; and comfort in Berry, 118–19; and community, 124; opposed to loneliness, 128; preparation for, 141; psychological research on, 221–22; and self in Muir, 183; and social experience, 214–15; social uses of, 133; and social view, 188; and spiritual practices, xiv ; in student essay, 211; and writing, 144–47, 163, 167–68, 172, 180
solo, the, 221
specialist, in Berry, 127
speed, in Berry, 110–11, 119, 126
Stafford, William, xiv, 227
storytellers, 184, 187, 189, 202
strangeness, as term in Berry, 108–109, 112, 123, 124, 125–26, 128–30, 141

Street, Brian, 192
Stock, Brian, 196, 199
Stuckey, J. Elspeth, 253
students, 203, 218; writing by, 206–16, 225. *See also* education; teaching
style, as story, 23
Styron, William, 172
subject: senses of, 59–61; Van Dyke as, 61–62, 81, 95
sublime, the: and asceticism, 55; and *The Desert*, 66, 91, 238; and Ktaadn, 44, 53, 232, 234
subsistence, 187, 197, 216–17, 224
summit scenes, 32–33, 41–42, 52, 53–54, 70, 80, 117–18
syuzhet, 22, 230

Tallmadge, John, 249
teaching, of writing, xiv, 145, 171–72, 203, 213
Teague, David, 93, 242–43
Teale, Edwin Way, 160
technology: and cyborgs, 219; and determinism, 191; and literacy, 186–88, 195–97; and scene of writing, 153, 184; and subsistence, 216
terms of meaning and value. *See* meaning-value terms
terministic screens, 81–82
testament, 7, 69, 93, 123, 156–57, 165
Thoreau, Henry David, xv, 16, 19, 26–56, 60, 70–72, 94, 110, 117, 141, 153, 154, 201, 225, 237, 246; cabin at Walden, 161, 162; journals of, 176; life struggles of, 54; and mountain climbing, 232; and nature writing, 5, 6–7, 11, 27, 229; and publication, 175, 251; relation to readers, 234, 249; and relinquishment, 54–55; and reputation, 26; and scenes of writing, 166; on simplifying, 205–06, 222–23; social alienation of, 214–15, 257; and the sublime, 233–34; writerly persona of, 18, 150; and writerly self-definition, 149. Works: *Journal*, 39, 159–60, 232, 249, 250, 251;